DECOLONISATION

DECOLONISATION
Revolution & Evolution

EDITED BY DAVID BOUCHER AND AYESHA OMAR

WITS UNIVERSITY PRESS

Published in South Africa by:
Wits University Press
1 Jan Smuts Avenue
Johannesburg 2001

www.witspress.co.za

First published 2023

http://dx.doi.org.10.18772/22023108448

978-1-77614-844-8 (Paperback)
978-1-77614-845-5 (Hardback)
978-1-77614-846-2 (Web PDF)
978-1-77614-847-9 (EPUB)

This publication is peer reviewed following international best practice standards for academic
and scholarly books.

Project manager: Elaine Williams
Copyeditor: Karen Press
Proofreader: Sally Hines
Indexer: Marlene Burger
Cover design: Hybrid Creative
Typeset in 11 point Minion Pro

CONTENTS

Aids	acquired immunodeficiency syndrome
ANC	African National Congress
AWS	African Writers Series
BCM	Black Consciousness Movement
DRC	Democratic Republic of the Congo
DTA	Democratic Turnhalle Alliance
FNLA	National Front for the Liberation of Angola
Frelimo	Front for the Liberation of Mozambique
HIV	human immunodeficiency virus
KRS	Kat River Settlement
LMS	London Missionary Society
MFA	Master of Fine Arts
MPLA	Popular Movement for the Liberation of Angola
NGO	non-governmental organisation
PAC	Pan Africanist Congress of Azania
RPSCAT	*Report of the Parliamentary Select Committee on Aboriginal Tribes*
RSCA	*Report from the Select Committee on the Aborigines (British Settlements)*
SACA	*South African Commercial Advertiser*
SACP	South African Communist Party
SADC	Southern African Development Community

SAP	structural adjustment programme
SWAPO	South West Africa People's Organisation
TAU SA	Transvaal Agricultural Union of South Africa
UN	United Nations
UNDRIP	United Nations 'Declaration on the Rights of Indigenous Peoples'
US	United States of America
ZANU-PF	Zimbabwe African National Union-Patriotic Front

Decolonisation: Interdisciplinary Perspectives

David Boucher and Ayesha Omar

A global history of the contemporary world is marked by the displacement, dispossession and domination forged by the colonial and imperial encounter. Colonialism and imperialism have been widely accepted as systems of exploitation, dependent upon the devaluation of the languages, cultures and control of colonised subjects systematically cast as ontologically inferior. Colonialism, constitutive of modernity, as Jean-Paul Sartre argues, was not the accumulation of individual undertakings and chance occurrences, but instead an elaborate system that emerged around the mid-nineteenth century, representing moments of rise and decline (2001, 38). As Mahmood Mamdani contends, colonialism forcibly inscribed law, custom, education, language and community, citing the dichotomies of primitive versus civilised and the division of people along tribal, ethnic and racial lines (2020, 2–3). Yet, the second half of the twentieth century is instantiated by powerful acts of resistance, with the challenge to, and decline of, colonialism. During this period, colonial subjects rejected the coloniser, prompting waves of decolonisation in many parts of the world. While modern colonialism and imperialism have been extensively examined in terms of their economic, military and political motivations, decolonisation requires further and more nuanced study.

Decolonisation as a conceptual term relates to more than just a set of historical processes signalling the demise of colonialism. While definitionally it is associated with the historical process of political independence of former colonies – events locatable in time, geography and political praxis – in recent times it has become a floating signifier for a range of contemporary struggles against injustice. Decolonisation can thus at once be construed as a normative idea, a political and economic ideal, or an epistemic project, demonstrating the unsettled nature of its use. The task of this book is to think productively, through various sites and contexts, about the uses and meanings of the term decolonisation, so as to provide complexity to our contemporary understanding. As such, it is interested in exploring the multiplicity of ways in which decolonisation has evolved and the various modes of its articulation. The book proceeds from an interdisciplinary vantage point, drawing together a series of arguments in social and political thought, intellectual and economic history, literary studies, political theory and development studies. These interdisciplinary approaches, as the book demonstrates, conceive of decolonisation from a range of perspectives: as a historical or empirical political process, a problem of political and philosophical theory, and through the lens of epistemic justice. The chapters in the book are thus generative, providing a myriad of lenses on the revolution and evolution of decolonisation in contemporary discourse.

Studies on colonialism and imperialism, coloniality and decoloniality have recently become the 'buzzwords' of the day. They have also been transformed into conceptual categories informed by distinct approaches, evident, for example, in postcolonial theory and the Latin American decolonial school. After having apparently been exiled to esoteric academic ghettoes, they have indiscriminately entered the vocabulary of researchers, policy-makers and political commentators (Saccarelli and Varadarajan 2015, 6). Colonialism and imperialism have become pervasive concepts, often used interchangeably, in modern political analysis, migrating from the relatively specialised fields of study known as postcolonialism and histories of empire, to permeate mainstream political theory, socio-legal studies, social history and public discourse.

The terms colonialism and imperialism are evaluative and descriptive. They describe a relationship or state of affairs that may be open to contestation, but which correlatively evoke an emotion or evaluative response. To designate a state of affairs as imperialistic or colonial today almost invariably implies hostility or moral revulsion towards it, but this evaluative judgement has a relatively unsettled surface (Howe 2002, 9). In the nineteenth and early twentieth centuries, colonialism was almost universally approved by Western powers. Those who opposed it, such as John A. Hobson, opposed only a certain kind of imperialism (Hobson 1988, 246), sometimes referred to as 'insane' imperialism (Boucher, 2018), which is exemplified by Cecil John Rhodes in South Africa (Boucher 2019a, 2020; Brown 2015).

There has been a gradual realisation that the history of the world from ancient times to the present has not been one of states in their relations with each other, but of civilisations. States and their empires, and the peoples who constituted the non-European populations of these empires, had lives integrally, but invisibly, entwined with the social, economic and political lives of their colonisers. Unrest in the colonies was brutally suppressed, and the standards by which the worth of any aspect of indigenous life was judged were European, and on that basis found wanting. In the century up to 1914, when Europe plunged catastrophically into the First World War, the continent had increased its control over global territories from 30 per cent to 85 per cent, and broken the entrenched Asian domination in world trade by securing 65 per cent of the global market, to which the United States of America (US) added another 15 per cent. Through rapid industrialisation and increased productivity, the Western world was able to consolidate its sense of white supremacy. The British Empire alone, at its peak, comprised almost a quarter of the world's landmass, and ruled over 500 million people – almost one-fifth of the world's population (Jackson 2013, 1).

MODERNITY, COLONIALISM AND THE POSTCOLONIAL AND DECOLONIAL APPROACHES

The history of the modern nation state is also deeply entangled in the story of colonialism. Conventional accounts argue that the 1648 Peace of Westphalia was crucial to the creation of the modern nation state. After all, the impetus for this treaty was the need to find a resolution to religious conflict in Europe, and specifically to the Thirty Years' War. These accounts thus perceive the principal role of the modern state as that of an institution designed to safeguard secular peace through religious tolerance. But, as Mamdani powerfully points out, this account neglects the colonial roots of the modern state apparatus (2020, 1). In other words, the Treaty of Westphalia settled intra-European conflicts in a way that facilitated the colonial expansion of European powers abroad. Religious tolerance at home was thus a premise for colonial sovereignty abroad (Mamdani 2020, 3). The process of secularisation and political modernisation was therefore imbricated in the development of the global project of colonisation. Mamdani explicates the relationship between nationalism and colonialism to understand the ongoing colonial violence of the state project today: 'the birth of the modern state amid ethnic cleansing and overseas domination teaches us a different lesson about what political modernity is: less an engine of tolerance than of conquest' (2020, 4).

Recent scholarly interventions by the Latin American decolonial school have similarly emphasised modernity as co-constituted by the colonial project that emerges in 1492. The decolonial school argues that the events of 1492, that is, the conquest of the Americas, are central historical events that have shaped the modern history of coloniality (Mignolo 2011). This American experience of colonialism, they argue, has received scant attention in the analysis of postcolonial theorists. The concept of coloniality advanced by the decolonial school opens up a broader set of questions than the term colonialism implies. Coloniality denotes a political and economic relationship subjecting one nation to another, exemplified in the concept of the 'coloniality of power'. Coloniality uncovers, or unmasks, persistent patterns of power that have been generated by centuries of colonial rule (Maldonado-Torres 2007, 243). The relationships that denote coloniality and decoloniality exhibit different dimensions of power, which reveal deeper and more insidious features of dominance and dependence.

Over 50 years ago, Michel Foucault drew attention to the fact that power does not merely emanate from the top of a social hierarchy and is then imposed on the masses (see Foucault 1980, 2011). He asserts that power permeates laterally throughout society in everyday speech and activity. Extending Foucault's argument into postcolonial theory, Gayatri Spivak is concerned with how power is used to unmask and make visible the international division of labour and its cultural and political consequences, by paying attention to the economic, cultural and political realities of postcolonial contexts. For Spivak, these realities may reveal a level of communication previously buried or hidden, and they are invested with an identity having a moral, aesthetic, or historical significance and value (Spivak 1988, 285). Spivak critiques the essentialism associated with colonised subjects by reclaiming the voice of the subaltern – those marginalised, denied access to power and 'removed from all lines of social mobility' (1988, 275). For Spivak, the marginalised subaltern subject is always defined via his or her difference from the elites (1988, 276). She asserts that the subaltern subject is heterogeneous, and recovering the self-expressed voice of the subaltern is crucial in overcoming the domination and displacement of colonialism.

Similar questions about relations of power have been elaborated by Aníbal Quijano, the Peruvian sociologist, in his theory based on the idea of the subjectivity of knowledge. Quijano's concept of coloniality emphasises the colonial patterns of power and inequality that are not only confined to the spatial and temporal limits of empire (Quijano 2000). He presents us with a matrix of four interrelated spheres of coloniality of power. The first dimension of the matrix is constituted by the economy, including natural resources, appropriation of land and exploitation of labour. The second focuses on the control of authority, including social, governmental and military institutions. Control of sexuality is the third dimension, which means having power over the family, sexual mores and education. Control over the subjectivity of knowledge is the fourth dimension, with a Heideggerian emphasis on *Dasein*, which translates from the German as 'being there'. In English, we would understand this concept as a particular human experience of how we exist in the world, controlling epistemology, ontology and communication.

Argentinian theorist Walter Mignolo elaborates on the Heideggerian aspect of power by emphasising the importance of focusing on the lived experience of colonisation, the coloniality of being. He makes it clear that what is referred to as science, that is, knowledge and wisdom, is inextricably attached to language. Languages, for him, are much more than cultural phenomena in which individuals find their identity. Languages are the repositories in which knowledge is inscribed, and are not something that we have, but are something that human beings are (Mignolo 2003, 29–124).

HISTORICAL DECOLONISATION

Modern decolonisation has been divided into three historical phases, with the first characterised as occurring in the immediate aftermath of the Second World War. It mainly comprised the attainment of independence by Britain's South Asian territories, such as India, Pakistan, Ceylon (Sri Lanka) and Burma (Myanmar). In addition, Britain and France lost control of their territories in the Middle East, such as Palestine, Jordan, Lebanon and Syria. The second phase covered a longer period spanning the 1950s and 1960s, with the demise of European colonial rule over the rest of Asia, North Africa, most of sub-Saharan Africa and the Caribbean. The third phase, including the collapse of the Portuguese empire, had by the end of the 1970s left only a few disparate possessions (Kennedy 2016, 6).

It was evident, however, that formal decolonisation did not mean freedom in any true sense of the word, nor independence, as the colonial powers ensured that their structures of dependency remained intact (Galtung 1973). Numerous African liberation theorists, including Frantz Fanon (1963, 1967), Amílcar Cabral (1973, 1979) and Kwame Nkrumah (1970), warned of the complicity of the black petite bourgeoisie in the newly independent states with their former colonisers in perpetuating the old systems of power and corruption. Nkrumah, for example, brands this relationship 'neo-colonialism'. He argues that 'the essence of neo-colonialism is that the State which is subject to it is, in theory, independent and has all the outward trappings of international sovereignty. In reality its economic system and thus its political policy is directed from outside' (1970, ix).

There is a lingering and sinister legacy of the Europeanisation of the world by imperialist adventurers who had little regard for the lives and livelihoods of those peoples they conquered and oppressed, and by Christian missionaries who paradoxically had regard for their lives but denigrated their cultures and beliefs as primitive and savage. The ongoing commemoration, and even glorification, of imperialists is a constant reminder to the progeny of their victims of the brutal injustices perpetrated by colonialist regimes. In recent years, protesters have brought to the fore historic and continuing injustices and betrayals, ignited by countless instances of racism, including the serial and disproportionate deaths of black people in police custody. Campaigns such as Rhodes Must Fall and Black Lives Matter have turned the spotlight on commemorative statues all over the world, and have led to their toppling in, for example, South Africa, the US and Great Britain. Martinique, the birthplace of two of the most famous liberationists in the modern era of decolonisation, Aimé Césaire (1913–2008) and Frantz Fanon (1925–1961), was also where Empress Joséphine de Beauharnais (1763–1814), the first wife of Napoléon Bonaparte, was born to a wealthy sugar plantation owner. In 1991, her statue was decapitated, and in July 2020 it was permanently demolished by anticolonial protesters, along with a statue of Pierre Bélain d'Esnambuc, a trader who established the French colony on the island in 1635.

The 200th anniversary of the birth of Napoléon was in 2021, which reminds us not only of his imperialistic campaigns but also of his reintroduction of slavery and the slave trade in Martinique and other West Indian colonies (excluding Guadeloupe, Guyana and Saint-Domingue), by decree in 1802.

Throughout the latter part of the nineteenth century, at the height of imperialism, and the early part of the twentieth century, native peoples were infantilised, and indoctrinated with the ideas that they lacked sufficient rationality to rule themselves, possessed no history and culture worthy of the name, spoke primitive languages, and made next to no contribution to the world in neglecting to efficiently exploit the natural resources in the lands where they lived, which constituted a global heritage. The psychological damage, material disadvantage and loss of traditional knowledge and languages that resulted from this underpin the discontent so emotively expressed in the student movement that today calls for decolonisation of the curriculum.

ONE SIZE DOES NOT FIT ALL

In the broadest terms, most liberation theorists agree that imperialism is a consequence of the profit motive and the accumulation of surplus value by a global capitalist system. For some, it is a necessary stage of capitalism, just as national liberation and the advent of socialism necessarily follow. The harsh method of land confiscation, the reduction of the local peasantry to serfdom and the cruel exploitation and extermination, which amounts to a system of pillage, were widespread throughout colonial lands, including African territories under Italian, Spanish, British and Portuguese colonial rule (Hồ 2011, 78). Imperialism, many liberation theorists believe, was a form of piracy migrated to dry land, reorganised and consolidated to plunder the natural and human resources of colonised peoples. In any characterisation of colonialism, however, we have to be sensitive to the unique circumstances that nuance each instance of colonisation, while acknowledging that there are general motivating features.

Hồ Chí Minh, Fanon, Cabral, Ernesto 'Che' Guevara and Fidel Castro, to mention a few, were all sensitive to the uniqueness of circumstances of each colonised people. Hồ Chí Minh, for example, contends that all of the natives living under colonialism were equally oppressed and exploited, but they differed considerably in their intellectual, economic and political development: 'between Annam and the Congo, Martinique and New Caledonia, there is absolutely nothing in common, except poverty' (Hồ 2011, 8–9). Castro contends that every people must adopt the thoughts and theories they consider most appropriate to themselves and which best suit their struggle (2017, 58). The ideas appropriate to Cuba and Vietnam, for instance, were Marxism-Leninism, while for Algeria and Guinea-Bissau they were a considerably modified Marxism, replacing class with race as a significant explanatory factor. In addition, Cabral emphasises the need for detailed knowledge of the circumstances of the colonised in the process of transforming their lived reality. While each revolution may have much to be admired, he argues, 'national liberation and social revolution are not exportable commodities' (2016, 122). There is, nevertheless, a need for a theory or ideology in the struggle against imperialism, without which there are no successful revolutions. In Cabral's view, ideology, or theory, was as essential as financial, military and political support to guide and help to improve the practice of revolutionary movements (2016, 123).

Decolonisation, on the whole and of necessity, has required violence. It is common among revolutionary theorists to legitimate violent insurrection by maintaining its absolute necessity. Fanon, Guevara, Hồ Chí Minh and Cabral, for example, believed that only violent revolutionary insurrection would overthrow colonialism, which used all means in its power to suppress national liberation movements. For Cabral, 'the history of colonial warfare as well as our own experience over ten years of struggle have taught us that the colonial aggressors – and the Portuguese colonial aggressors in particular – only understand the language of force and only measure reality by the number of corpses' (1973, 97). Cabral ended his New Year message in January 1973 with these words: 'Death to the criminal Portuguese colonial aggressors!' (1973, 106). He maintains that against all forms of imperialism, armed struggle is the only way to eliminate foreign domination (1979, 121). But what type of violence to employ in defeating imperial domination was the question (1979, 134). Armed warfare had always been an extension of political warfare, as he expressed most clearly in his addresses to Portuguese settlers, whom he distinguished conceptually from Portuguese colonialism. He offers settlers a choice of supporting the liberation movement, preserving their human dignity by remaining neutral, or backing the colonial regime as mercenaries of a lost cause (1979, 162).

Turning to Cuba, Sartre witnessed first-hand the happiness of the Cuban people whose liberation had been attained by violent insurrection, and he became convinced that it was only by violent means that the oppressed could regain their status as human beings (De Beauvoir 1968, 503–506). Sartre maintains that the objective condition of the colonised must be overcome by confronting the negation to which they are subjected with another negation, that is, confronting violence with violence. He claims that, on the one hand, violence in and of itself is gratuitous, but when deployed on the part of the colonised, it is the act of 'man reconstructing himself' (2001, 166).

HOISTING THE EUROPEANS WITH THEIR OWN PETARD

The period between and including the two world wars accentuated the sense of injustice and hypocrisy among colonised peoples towards their oppressors. The principles enshrined in natural law, and emblazoned in the great freedom charters of the eighteenth century, the 'American Declaration of Independence' of 1776 and the 'French Declaration of the Rights of Man and of the Citizen' of 1791, were clearly inapplicable in relations among civilised peoples and 'inferior races' (Boucher 2019b). As early as 1922, Hồ Chí Minh highlighted the contradiction between the ideals of universalism declared by European liberals and the denial of the very same ideals in relation to their colonial possessions. He argues that in order to 'hide the ugliness of its regime of criminal exploitation, colonial capitalism always decorates its evil banner with the idealist motto: Liberty, Equality and Fraternity, etc' (Hồ 2011, 13). His 'Declaration of Independence of the Democratic Republic of Vietnam' begins with the immortal statements affirming human freedom and dignity from both the American Declaration of Independence and the French Declaration of the Rights of Man and of the Citizen. He condemns the French imperialists for violating their own principles of liberty, equality and fraternity by oppressing their fellow citizens and acting 'contrary to the ideals of humanity and justice' (2011, 51).

Even some of the most enlightened European philosophers, such as Hannah Arendt, looked upon Africa as the 'dark continent' to which the fundamental rights of Europeans, which she equated with citizenship rights, were inapplicable. Africa was one of the many parts of the world, in her view, that fell far below European standards of civilisation, and failed to attain any recognisable civil association with concomitant citizenship rights. Africans lacked civil association on the European model and were 'savages', strangely alien, whose claim to humanity was at best tenuous. Indeed, her sympathies were with the imperialists who had to face 'a horrifying experience of something alien beyond imagination or comprehension: it was tempting indeed to simply declare that these were not human beings' (Arendt 1994, 195; see also Dossa 1980). Just as for Georg Wilhelm Friedrich Hegel and Karl Marx, for Arendt the African past was ahistorical, an exemplification of the worthless activities of natural men who had 'vegetated for thousands of years' (Arendt 1994, 194). Africans were human beings who lacked a specifically human character; human status was a function of a moral community that sustained and endowed it (1994, 300). The Indians and Chinese were for her on an altogether different plane. They had attained human status through the achievements of their civilisations, and therefore their murder by imperialists could not be excused, nor was there any comprehensible reason why they were not treated as human beings (1994, 319). What made the imperialism of the Nazis shocking was its attempt to subdue other European peoples.

What made the Holocaust shocking was the murder of civilised people by civilised people. The right of the Jews to life and citizenship was a juridical fact, extinguished by a systematic stripping away of the entitlement to enjoy citizenship rights; the Jews were reduced from political citizens to rightless natural animals, jettisoned from civilisation. This was not how she viewed Africans (1994, 296–297).

There were, of course, European philosophers, such as Jean-Jacques Rousseau and his compatriot Sartre, who deplored colonialism and neocolonialism. Rousseau argues in his 'Discourse on the Sciences and Arts' (Rousseau 2012) that Europeans were self-appointed exemplars of civilisation and the world's judges. Europeans relegated different peoples to lower levels of civilisation, yet their understanding of them was nothing more than a superficial projection of their own standards. They failed to see, let alone value, the differences between peoples. In his fragment 'Discourse on the Virtue Most Necessary for a Hero' (Rousseau 1994), he denies Aristotle's contention that there are natural slaves born to serve those intellectually superior to them, and he argues the opposite: that the existence of slaves is contrary to nature. To make people slaves is a political achievement that requires systematic brutal reinforcement. In talking specifically of the former Genoan colony, Corsica, Rousseau (1991) emphasises, as Fanon was later to do with regard to African states, that the Corsicans should preserve their new-found independence by refusing to emulate the culture of those who had colonised them.

The racism of the colonists, Sartre maintains, functioned to compensate for the universalism of bourgeois liberalism by, in the case of France for example, demoting their native colonials to the status of subhumans, excluding them from the enjoyment of universal human rights (Sartre 2001, 51). Sartre contends that 'no one is unaware that we have ruined, starved and massacred a nation of poor people [the Algerians] to bring them to their knees' (2001, 148). He argues that 'colonialism denies *human rights* to people it has subjugated by violence, and ... keeps [them] in poverty and ignorance by force ... since the natives are subhuman, the Declaration of Human Rights does not apply to them' (2001, 58–59; see also Memmi 2016, 20).

There was a burgeoning body of anti-imperialist literature emanating from America and the colonies throughout the world. African Americans, for example, drew parallels between European fascism, white racism and imperialism. W.E.B. Du Bois, an African American civil rights activist, argues that fascism was not an aberration, but a logical consequence of Western civilisation, emerging out of slavery and imperialism, and entrenched in a global system driven by capitalist political economy and racist ideologies. He equates the colonialism of France and Great Britain with the use of race prejudice and exploitation by Hitler and Mussolini (Du Bois 1968, 305–306). No atrocity that the Nazis committed in the concentration camps, defiling women and corrupting children, had not already been practised by Christian civilisation on black people in the name of a superior race destined to rule the world (Du Bois 1947, 23). Ralph Bunche, an African American who was to be awarded the Nobel Peace Prize in 1950, argues that fascism, with its exaltation of the state and 'comic-opera glorification of race', gave new and added impetus to imperialism's exploitation of the non-white races of the earth (Bunche 1936, 31).

In Martinique, Césaire maintains that what the European 'cannot forgive Hitler for is not *the humiliation of man as such*, it is the crime against the white man, and the fact that he applied to Europe colonialist procedures that until then had been reserved exclusively for the Arabs of Algeria, the "coolies" of India, and the "niggers" of Africa' (Césaire 2001, 36). In 1955, he argued that the Allies in Europe, before they were the victims of Nazism, had closed their eyes and absolved the Nazis of their sins. A civilisation that colonises is 'already a sick civilisation, a civilisation which is morally diseased' (2001, 21). He maintains that the Europeans had legitimated fascism because, until they themselves were its victims, they were the perpetrators of it (2001, 36). From the point of view of Fanon, a Martinican fighting for Algerian liberation, the immediate and pre-eminent priority and concern for Africans had to be the eradication of genocide perpetrated by the French in Algeria, and of apartheid in South Africa (Fanon 1967, 171–172). Fanon compared the struggle against colonialism with the Allied resistance to Nazism. African peoples, he argued, must emulate the actions of the Allies and fight against the form of Nazism imposed by France, Britain and South Africa, which was a form of physical and spiritual liquidation of African and Caribbean peoples.

Albert Memmi, born under the French Protectorate in Tunisia in 1920, argues that every colonial nation is nascently fascist, because the whole of its administrative and political machinery has no other goal than systematic oppression for the benefit of the few colonisers. The relationships that hold between the coloniser and colonised 'have arisen from the severest exploitation, founded on inequality and contempt, guaranteed by police authoritarianism' (Memmi 2016, 106).

French liberalism, with its emphasis on human rights and democratic institutions, is alien to the colonists, who are compelled to deny such rights and institutions to those they have colonised. Sartre argues that mainland France was ensnared by colonialism in its assertion of sovereignty over Algeria, in that it was compromised by the system that produced colonists who repudiated French institutions. Colonialism compelled France to send democratic Frenchmen to risk their lives to protect the tyranny that the colonial repudiators of democracy had imposed upon the Algerians (Sartre 2001, 52–53).

Cabral similarly invoked 'inalienable rights' in his second address before the United Nations (UN) in 1972, when he referred to his previous address of 1962. In his 1962 address, he had invited the UN to intervene in order to stop the extensive campaign of repression being waged by the Portuguese in Guinea Bissau. Friends of Portugal, he maintained, continued to supply it with large quantities of military equipment and financial aid, despite calling themselves 'champions of freedom and democracy and defenders of the "free world" and the cause of self-determination and independence of peoples' (Cabral 1973, 17). At the foundation of national liberation, Cabral maintains, it is the 'inalienable right of every people to have their own history; and the aim of national liberation is to regain this right usurped by imperialism, that is to free the process of development of the national productive forces' (1979, 130).

From the West Indies to Africa, these sentiments were echoed. The movements for national liberation throughout the world exposed the contradiction inherent in liberal imperialism. While fighting for the very principles of freedom and self-determination they advocated in their fight against the Axis powers, the Allies continued to deny the same freedoms to their colonies.

THE CONTRIBUTION OF THIS VOLUME

From the disciplinary perspectives of history, law, literature, philosophy and practical life, the contributors to this volume strive to enhance our understanding of decolonisation and decoloniality, examining aspects of the process but at the same time contending that it is illusory to believe that these phenomena are a thing of the past. The authors attempt to explain how colonialism, like an insidious virus, mutates into more virulent forms to ensure its survival.

Ndumiso Dladla's contribution in chapter 1 focuses on the invention of blackness in relation to imperial conquest and the making of the 'Other'. The chapter is a philosophical investigation of the question 'what are Blacks?' through the examination of the case of the conqueror in South Africa. Taking the history of that country as its starting point, the chapter defends the hypothesis that Blacks are really creatures of war, invented during the conquest of the indigenous peoples in the unjust wars of colonisation. As a method of establishing sovereignty, conquest is not simply the defeat of the Other in war, but describes instead a relation of domination that can potentially arise following the defeat itself. Making this point, Thomas Hobbes maintained that 'he ... that is slain is overcome, but not conquered; he that is taken, and put into prison or chains is not conquered ... But he that upon promise of obedience hath his life and liberty allowed him is then conquered and a subject and not before'

(Hobbes 1981, 720). Throughout Black history, following this 'promise of obedience', the conqueror has used the fear of death of the conquered through the systemic and systematic deployment of deadly violence to reinscribe the terms of the covenant between them. After a discussion of the evolution of the right of conquest in Western philosophy and its historical application in South Africa, the chapter elaborates on the political ontology of Blackness by focusing on the question of time. It demonstrates that around the world, wherever Blackness exists, it is accompanied by its own horology, which is examined by focusing on three of its components: 'lifetime', 'age' and 'free time'.

Chris Saunders, in chapter 2, argues that scholars in the West who write on the history of decolonisation have tended to argue for the dominance of metropolitan forces in the process, in contrast with activists and historians from former colonised territories who emphasise initiatives from within Africa and Asia, and are more inclined to use the term 'liberation' rather than 'decolonisation' to refer to the process of ending colonial rule. Taken as a whole, the formal decolonisation of Southern Africa that ended white minority rule across the entire region may be viewed as revolutionary, the author argues, though it ended as it began with an emphasis on continuity.

Christopher Allsobrook and Camilla Boisen focus in chapter 3 on a specific iconic moment in the history of colonisation in South Africa to illustrate how legal structures and procedures, particularly the legal determination of trusteeship, were used to dispossess indigenous peoples of their rights and territories. They show how the Kat River Settlement was established by the British in 1829 to create a human barrier consisting of the Khoisan between the Cape Colony to the west and the isiXhosa-speaking territories to the east. It was finally dissolved after a small minority of the Khoisan allied with the amaXhosa in their war against the British Colony. The Kat River Rebellion of 1851, during the Eighth Frontier War, was interpreted by white colonists as evidence that blacks were not yet adequately civilised to understand and be entrusted with rights of citizenship. The perceived betrayal by the minority of Khoisan was seized upon by land-hungry white settlers as a pretext for taking possession of the land.

Allsobrook and Boisen argue that both these interpretations of the rebellion (colonialist and revisionist) underestimate the purchase of imperialist ideals of trusteeship on the justificatory arguments and colonial identities of both factions. They draw out an underlying consistency in the arguments of loyalist and rebel leaders, showing that both sides justified their positions by an appeal to ideals of colonial trusteeship. The idea of the civilising mission was uncontested by both sides in the Khoisan camp, but they strongly defended their rights of citizenship, which they believed they held in virtue of the legal and moral standing of colonial trusteeship. Allsobrook and Boisen contend that their position highlights an ambiguity in the teleology of trusteeship ideology. They contend that the idea of trusteeship both engenders and accommodates nationalist resistance to imperialism.

Ian Spears, in chapter 4, argues that contemporary African states exemplify only partial and incomplete decolonisation. He identifies the formal process of independence as beginning with Sudan in 1956 and concluding with the fall of apartheid in South Africa in 1994. The formality of independence, however, disguises the extent to which Africa has not been fully liberated, because the process of decolonisation remains incomplete. Decolonisation gave rise to new states whose boundaries were faithful to existing colonial territories, rather than to identity groups or precolonial polities within or between territories.

Consistent with many other parts of the world, such as Southeast Asia, the vast majority of African countries are creations of colonialism. African governments resistant to the calls of pan-Africanism insist that the viability of the existence of their states depends on existing boundaries. Decolonisation was, for them, a means to recover sovereignty and regain control, but in a very different manner from the precolonial era. The status quo of colonialist-established borders, Spears argues, is related to power and continuity, and even to complicity. As a consequence, and to the detriment of a pan-African vision for the future, decolonisation effectively ceased at the borders of contemporary African states. Despite a widely shared desire to expunge Africa of its colonial character, decolonisation is bound to be limited given this inheritance.

David Boucher's contribution in chapter 5 examines the arguments of the liberation theorists, with particular emphasis on Fanon, and shows how in their view both colonialism and decolonisation lack legitimacy. Colonialism's lack of legitimacy comes from its hypocritical denial to the colonised of fundamental and universal rights indelibly inscribed in the great Western charters of rights which the colonial powers fought to protect, with the aid of their colonial subjects, against the Axis powers in the Second World War. On the other hand, these theorists denigrate nationalist parties and regimes that were complicit with the social and governmental structures of their former colonisers, effecting an era of neocolonialism. The chapter focuses on the arguments and strategies of liberationists who warned of decoloniality, and of the distortion of black mentalities and ways of being by the insidious penetration and control of knowledge production, language, history and perceptions of inferiority by the former colonial powers. The politics of identity is woven throughout the discussion, and Boucher contends that colonialism is one of the most extreme forms of identity destruction. In introducing Fanon's discussion and critique of Hegel's idea of the struggle for recognition, he enables a better understanding of why the use of violence in the liberation struggle was viewed as an absolute necessity. In an address, 'Why We Use Violence', Fanon argues that colonialism is premised on violence; the colonial regime is always established and sustained by violence, and violence is the only language it understands, and the only claim colonialism has to legitimacy (Fanon 2018).

In chapter 6, Michael Elliott turns our attention to the relationship between anticolonial critique and progress, particularly the role that progressive temporal-historical structures play in attempts to develop anticolonial positions by using the Western critical tradition, despite its potential to undermine their ambitions. The chapter further asks how critical interventions emanating from this source contribute to the (re)tellings or (re)storyings of colonial injustice that reflect culturally specific habits, norms and desires, in ways that contribute to the reproduction or entrenchment of the very injustices they aim to oppose. In essence, the chapter addresses the problem of the potential of Western anticolonialism to be compromised by the temporal-historical forms it assumes. The theme of complicity, as developed from the point of view of African liberation theorists, is examined from the other side of the coin by Elliott. Contemporary critical theory, he argues, is partly the product of and reflects Eurocentric modes of thinking and being, and its normative core needs to be fundamentally re-examined, with a view to rebuilding it on foundations that are uncompromised, thereby avoiding vulnerability to critical failure and closure, refusal or silencing of lines of enquiry and questioning what might be some of the most difficult and important concerns Western anticolonialism has to address.

Paul Patton, in chapter 7, addresses the crucial considerations surrounding the legitimacy of postcolonial regimes directly. The argument he presents raises the question of states that are settler communities with minority indigenous peoples, and by what right they may claim governmental legitimacy. Patton considers two alternative conceptions of legitimacy: the republican conception of Philip Pettit (2012), which separates legitimacy from justice, and argues that they are discrete and involve quite different considerations from each other; and alternatively, John Rawls' principle of political liberalism, which ties justice and legitimacy closely together (Rawls 2005). Rawls acknowledges, however, that legitimacy and justice are independent concepts. A democratically elected regime may have legitimacy because of the process by which it attained authority, yet neither its laws nor its policies may be just. The converse is also true insofar as a regime may be just but not legitimate. Patton argues that legitimacy in a postcolonial state ultimately depends on the degree to which impediments to the capacities of some citizens to participate fully in the rights and benefits available to all under conditions of fair and equal opportunity have been removed. He contends that acceptance of special rights and a distinct constitutional status for indigenous peoples have the potential to heal the wounds of the injustices consequent on colonial non-recognition of indigenous law and culture, and go some way towards legitimising the postcolonial state.

In chapter 8, Steven Friedman takes as his starting point the celebrated study of colonisation by Ashis Nandy, *The Intimate Enemy* (2005), particularly Nandy's observation about Indian responses to British colonisation. Nandy contends that in succumbing to the pressure to be the obverse of the West, the traditional priorities of Indians in regard to their total world view are distorted, and paradoxically bind the Indian even closer to the West. The heart of the problem is the tendency for both the coloniser and the colonised to think in terms of absolute instead of relative differences between cultures.

Friedman's chapter argues that Nandy's observation is an essential element in a South African response to colonisation that does not repeat colonialism's assumptions in the name of replacing them. In particular, he argues against an essentialism in which a reified 'Western culture' is replaced by an equally reified 'African culture' that is just as constraining, and just as likely to be used as a rationale for domination as the colonial ideology it purports to reject. Friedman further argues that we avoid the trap Nandy warns us about if we define intellectual colonisation as an ideology that seeks to suppress or eliminate modes of thought that do not conform to a dominant set of values and its antidote, decolonisation, as the removal of this constraint, not as its replacement by new constraints. This decolonisation does not seek to abolish 'Western culture' but to integrate it into a world view, in which it takes its place alongside African, Asian and Latin American cultures. It therefore recognises the syncretic nature of all cultures and views of the world, and seeks to enhance, rather than obstruct, conversations between them.

From a literary perspective, in chapter 9, Sule Emmanuel Egya addresses the question: who or what determines the ethics and aesthetics of representing Africa in modern written literature, after formal independence and during the decolonisation process? He evaluates the role of the contemporary

African writer in a period of globalisation; the impulse of migration; and what he calls the exogenous mentality of contemporary African writers. Of crucial importance is the fate of African aesthetics, its appropriateness in describing the condition of Africa, and prospectively the need to imagine and construct a discourse that will assist in moving the continent forward on a path of progress. Egya argues that the decolonisation process has not yielded any fruitful revolutionary change in imagining and producing African literature in European languages. The implication is that literature in Africa, especially in sub-Saharan Africa (perhaps with the exception of South Africa) is 'extroverted', still controlled by the protocols invented in Western literary capitals, and may not have benefited from the decolonisation process announced by, among others, Ngũgĩ wa Thiong'o in the 1980s. The role of the African writer in this context, Egya further argues, is not to escape to the 'comfort' of the West, acquire celebrity status and theorise the solutions to problems at home, but pragmatically to engage the continent by imagining alternative instruments of positive development. In other words, African writers, to be more useful to Africa, must resist the lure of Western publishing and publicity capital and harness their efforts, aesthetic and otherwise, towards rescuing Africa, and recuperating the continent's humanity from both home and global agents of underdevelopment.

Amber Murrey, in chapter 10, offers a practical solution and contribution to both the decolonisation of the curriculum and decolonisation of the mind. In particular, it is a contribution to debates within international development and development geographies concerning future trajectories for the discipline that address its neocolonial and colonial constitutions, offering teaching praxis and scholarship in action as a contribution to the decolonisation of development. The author recommends 'pedagogical disobedience', which she describes as 'an anticipatory decolonial development curriculum and praxis that is attentive to the perpetual simultaneity of violence and misappropriation within the colonial matrix of power'. For Murrey, this means embracing decolonial pluriversals, or the numberless decolonial possibilities, that service a *will-to-life* rather than the colonial will-to-conquer or will-to-extract. Employing two useful pedagogical tools and concepts – assassination and appropriation – she outlines a contemporary example of each: the assassination of Thomas Sankara in 1987 and the appropriation of particular indigenous practices by social scientists contracted to work in southern Chad during the construction of the Chad–Cameroon Oil Pipeline. The purpose of these examples is to articulate their practical significance for radical pedagogy consistent with taking seriously student-led demands to 'decolonise the university'.

CONTEMPORARY REFLECTIONS

Finally, it is appropriate to end this introduction with some critical contemporary reflections on decolonisation, with specific reference to South Africa's evolution into a post-apartheid democratic society. As some of the chapters have addressed, problematising the process of the transition to democracy and the neglect of meaningful redistribution and development is critical to the conversation about decolonisation. The maintenance of cheap, black, unskilled labour and high unemployment are, for example, structural features of South African society that have been transferred into contemporary history through the transition's neglect of development and redistribution. These racial, socio-economic inequalities have been intensifying in an extraordinary and insidious way post-1994. The transition process, as some have argued, has therefore served to strengthen a social contract among elite players, delivering so-called political decolonisation in the absence of economic and social justice, or the elite transition from apartheid to neoliberalism.

In acceding to the democratic transition, South Africans forged a vocabulary of tolerance to settle differences through the politics of contestation and nation-building, which further complexified the process of decolonisation. Mamdani (2020) argues that South Africa has succeeded most in breaking out of colonial divisions and forging a new political community through its pursuit of non-racialism, something he describes as a promising, if unfinished, project (2020, 156). The possibility for a new, politically forged community beyond the 'settler/native' division was created, according to Mamdani, through a 'triple shift' (2020, 345). The first shift was from seeking the end of apartheid to offering an alternative to apartheid. The second was to replace anti-apartheid majoritarianism with non-racial democracy representing all South Africans. The third was to redefine the terms for governing South Africa as terms that denied apartheid's logic. 'South Africans sat around the conference table', he states, and while conceding that this national project is an 'incomplete success', he nonetheless argues that South Africans utilised engagement to open the door for dialogue (2020, 144–145).

Mamdani's analysis, while important, falls short of acknowledging why the moment of transition was fundamental in shaping the trajectory of decolonisation in South Africa. It understates the fact that deep economic, social and political cleavages are a consequence of the social contract that was decided upon, and which is viciously exploited by kleptocratic, political elites. Perhaps this point is more powerfully illustrated when we turn to the leading anticolonial thinker Frantz Fanon. In chapter three, 'The Pitfalls of National Consciousness' of Fanon's *The Wretched of the Earth* (1963), he argues that postcolonial states that have gained political independence suffer from a malaise ensconced in political authority. Put simply, leaders of anticolonial and liberation movements fail to genuinely transform the hopes for freedom of millions of colonised people into reality:

> Before independence, the leader generally embodies the aspirations of the people for independence, political liberty, and national dignity. But as soon as independence is declared, far from embodying in concrete form the needs of the people in what touches bread, land, and the restoration of the country to the sacred hands of the people, the leader will reveal his inner purpose: to become the general president of that company of profiteers impatient for their returns. (Fanon 1963, 133)

Fanon's invocation of the questions of bread and land becomes critical to the conversation then, as we attempt to understand the desperation and hunger of millions of Africans in postcolonial Africa, where economic and social marginalisation reveals a skewed economic system, in which power and resources are accessible to only a minority of people.

In South Africa, for example, not thousands but millions remain hopelessly unable to secure a stake in the formal political economy, with staggering levels of unemployment. The transition has remained one of many inflection moments when the redistribution of wealth, questions of economic and social inclusion, labour redress, the development of just and equitable public policy, a rejection of austerity and neoliberalism ought to have resulted in the creation of a decolonised society, or what Fanon describes as a dynamic, transformative project where, ironically, the familiar African National Congress slogans of a 'national democratic revolution' and a 'better life for all' would transcend the scope of ideation. But destitution and high levels of economic despair are deeply and perniciously entangled in the project of political decolonisation, which simply left millions behind. These structural realities serve to remind us that we must interrogate the constitutionally free South Africa that is proudly invoked.

As Fanon powerfully argues,

> the national government ought to govern by the people and for the people, for the outcasts and by the outcasts. No leader, however valuable he may be, can substitute himself for the popular will; and the national government, before concerning itself about international prestige, ought first to give back their dignity to all citizens. (Fanon 1963, 165)

REFERENCES

Arendt, Hannah. 1994 [1951]. *The Origins of Totalitarianism*. London: Penguin.
Boucher, David. 2018. ' "Sane" and "Insane" Imperialism: British Idealism, New Liberalism and Liberal Imperialism'. *History of European Ideas* 44 (8): 1189–1204. https://doi. org/10.1080/01916599.2018.1509226.

Boucher, David. 2019a. 'David George Ritchie: International Relations and the Second Anglo-Boer War (1899–1902)'. *Collingwood and British Idealism Studies* 25 (2): 283–314. https://orca.cardiff.ac.uk/id/eprint/126876.

Boucher, David. 2019b. 'Reclaiming History: Dehumanization and the Failure of Decolonization'. *International Journal of Social Economics* 46 (11): 1250–1263. https://doi.org/10.1108/IJSE-03-2019-0151.

Boucher, David. 2020. 'British Idealism, Imperialism and the Boer War'. *History of Political Thought* 41 (2): 325–348. https://orca.cardiff.ac.uk/id/eprint/124021.

Brown, Robin. 2015. *The Secret Society: Cecil John Rhodes's Plan for a New World Order.* London: Penguin.

Bunche, Ralph. 1936. 'French and British Imperialism in West Africa'. *Journal of Negro History* 21 (1): 31–46. https://www.journals.uchicago.edu/doi/abs/10.2307/2714542?journalCode=jnh.

Cabral, Amílcar. 1973. *Return to the Source: Selected Speeches of Amílcar Cabral.* Edited by Africa Information Service. New York: Monthly Review Press.

Cabral, Amílcar. 1979. *Unity and Struggle: Speeches and Writings of Amílcar Cabral.* Translated by Michael Wolfers. New York: Monthly Review Press.

Cabral, Amílcar. 2016. *Resistance and Decolonization.* Translated by Dan Wood. London: Rowman and Littlefield.

Castro, Fidel. 2017 'Che's Ideas are Absolutely Relevant Today'. In *Socialism and Man in Cuba,* by Che Guevara and Fidel Castro. New York: Pathfinder.

Césaire, Aimé. 2001. *Discourse on Colonialism.* Translated by Joan Pinkham. New York: Monthly Review Press.

De Beauvoir, Simone. 1968. *Force of Circumstance.* Translated by Richard Howard. Harmondsworth: Penguin.

Dossa, Shiraz. 1980. 'Human Status and Politics: Hannah Arendt on the Holocaust'. *Canadian Journal of Political Science,* 13 (2): 309–323. https://doi.org/10.1017/S0008423900033035.

Du Bois W.E.B. [William Edward Burghardt]. 1947. *The World and Africa: An Inquiry into the Part Which Africa Has Played in World History.* New York: International.

Du Bois W.E.B. [William Edward Burghardt]. 1968. *The Autobiography of W.E.B. Du Bois: A Soliloquy on Viewing My Life from the Last Decade of Its First Century.* Edited by Herbert Aptheker. New York: International.

Fanon, Frantz. 1963. *The Wretched of the Earth.* Translated by Constance Farrington. London: Penguin.

Fanon, Frantz. 1967. *Towards the African Revolution.* Translated by Haakon Chavalier. New York: Monthly Review Press.

Fanon, Frantz. 2018. 'Why We Use Violence'. In *Alienation and Freedom,* 653–659. London: Bloomsbury.

Foucault Michel. 1980. *Power/Knowledge: Selected Interviews and Other Writings, 1972–1977.* Edited by Colin Gordon. Translated by Colin Gordon, Leo Marshal, John Mepham and Kate Sober. New York: Pantheon.

Foucault, Michel. 2011. *The Order of Things: An Archaeology of the Human Sciences.* Translated by Alan Sheridan. London: Routledge Classics.

Galtung, Johan.1973. *The European Community: A Superpower in the Making.* London: Harper Collins for the Open University.

Hồ, Chí Minh [Nguyen Tat Thanh]. 2011. *The Selected Works of Hồ Chí Minh.* New York: Prism Key Press.

Hobbes, Thomas. 1981 [1651]. *Leviathan*. London: Penguin.

Hobson, John A. 1988 [1902]. *Imperialism: A Study*. 3rd edition. London: Unwin Hyman.

Howe, Stephen. 2002. *Empire: A Very Short Introduction*. Oxford: Oxford University Press.

Jackson, Ashley. 2013. *The British Empire: A Very Short Introduction*. Oxford: Oxford University Press.

Kennedy, Dane. 2016. *Decolonization: A Very Short Introduction*. Oxford: Oxford University Press.

Maldonado-Torres, Nelson. 2007. 'On the Coloniality of Being: Contributions to the Development of a Concept'. *Cultural Studies* 21 (2–3): 240–270. https://doi.org/10.1080/09502380601162548.

Mamdani, Mahmood. 2020. *Neither Settler Nor Native: The Making and Unmaking of Permanent Minorities*. Cambridge, MA: Harvard University Press and Johannesburg: Wits University Press.

Memmi, Albert. 2016 [1957]. *The Colonizer and the Colonized*. London: Souvenir Press.

Mignolo, Walter. 2003. *The Darker Side of the Renaissance: Literacy, Territoriality, and Colonization*. 2nd edition. Ann Arbor: University of Michigan Press.

Mignolo, Walter D. 2011. *The Darker Side of Western Modernity: Global Futures, Decolonial Options*. Durham, NC: Duke University Press.

Nandy, Ashis. 2005. *The Intimate Enemy: Loss and Recovery of Self under Colonialism*. New Delhi: Oxford University Press.

Nkrumah, Kwame. 1970. *Neo-Colonialism: The Last Stage of Imperialism*. London: Panaf.

Pettit, Philip. 2012. *On The People's Terms: A Republican Theory and Model of Democracy*. Cambridge: Cambridge University Press.

Quijano, Aníbal. 2000. 'Coloniality of Power, Eurocentrism and Latin America'. *Neplanta* 1 (3): 533–580. https://www.muse.jhu.edu/article/23906.

Rawls, John. 2005 [1993]. *Political Liberalism*. Expanded edition. New York: Columbia University Press.

Rousseau, Jean-Jacques. 1991. 'Constitutional Project for Corsica'. In *Rousseau on International Relations*, edited by Stanley Hoffman and David P. Fidler, 139–161. Oxford: Clarendon Press.

Rousseau, Jean-Jacques. 1994. *Social Contract, Discourse on the Virtue Most Necessary for a Hero, Political Fragments, and Geneva Manuscript*. Edited by Roger D. Masters and Christopher Kelly. Translated by Roger D. Masters, Christopher Kelly and Judith R. Bush. Chicago: University of Chicago Press.

Rousseau, Jean-Jacques. 2012 [1750]. 'Discourse on the Sciences and the Arts'. In *Rousseau: The Basic Political Writings*, 1–26. Translated by Donald A. Cress. Indianapolis: Hackett Publishing Company.

Saccarelli, Emanuele and Latha Varadarajan. 2015. *Imperialism Past and Present*. Oxford: Oxford University Press.

Sartre, Jean-Paul. 2001 [1964]. 'Colonialism is a System'. In *Colonialism and Neocolonialism*, 36–55. Translated by Azzedine Haddour, Steve Brewer and Terry McWilliams. London: Routledge.

Spivak, Gayatri C. 1988. 'Can the Subaltern Speak?' In *Marxism and the Interpretation of Culture*, edited by Cary Nelson and Lawrence Grossberg, 271–313. Basingstoke: Palgrave Macmillan.

1

The Invention of Blacks:
Notes on Conquest, Fear and Time

Ndumiso Dladla

Taking South African history as its starting point, this chapter will defend a hypothesis that Blacks are creatures of war, invented during the conquest of the indigenous peoples in the unjust wars of colonisation.[1] As a method of establishing sovereignty, *conquest* is not simply the defeat of the Other in war but describes instead a relation of domination that can potentially arise following the defeat itself. Making this point, Thomas Hobbes maintains that 'he ... that is slain is overcome, but not conquered; he that is taken, and put into prison or chains is not conquered ... But he that upon promise of obedience hath his life and liberty allowed him is then conquered and a subject and not before' (Hobbes 1996, 720). Throughout Black history, following this 'promise of obedience', the conqueror has used the fear of death of the conquered through the systemic and systematic deployment of deadly violence to reinscribe the terms of covenant. After a discussion of the evolution of the right of conquest in Western philosophy and its historical application in South Africa, we will discuss the political ontology of Blackness by focusing upon the question of time.[2] We show that around the world, wherever Blackness exists, it is accompanied by its own horology, which we will examine by focusing on three of its components: 'lifetime', 'age' and 'free time'.

THE HISTORICAL USE OF THE JUST WAR DOCTRINE, WITH SPECIFIC FOCUS ON THE 'RIGHT OF CONQUEST'

In 1542, the Spanish Dominican priest Bartolomé de las Casas published his *Short Account of the Destruction of the Indies* (De las Casas 1992), based on what he had witnessed during his accompaniment of the conquistador Diego Velázquez de Cuéllar on some of the voyages leading to invasion and conquest of Latin America. Political theorist Yves Winter (2012) points out that one of the things that stands out in De las Casas' account of the violence and political struggle involved is that he does not use the term 'conquest'. Winter argues that De las Casas deliberately avoids use of this term to describe the seizure and subjugation of the Americas. Winter argues further that De las Casas' rejection of the term marks the fact that from the sixteenth century onwards in European legal and political discourse, 'the word "conquest" was not merely a label that designated a practice of acquiring territory, of defeating or overthrowing a political order and of subjugating a population' (Winter 2012). Instead, he continues, 'conquest was intimately tied not only to the empirical fact of military defeat and subjection but to a legal and moral claim, to a legal title to rule' (2012). He supports this claim by quoting from Dutch jurist Hugo Grotius, who published his work *De jure belli ac pacis* in 1625 (27 years before the commencement of 'South Africa's' earliest wars of conquest at the hands of the Dutch).[3] According to Grotius, writes Winter, 'the law of nations provides the conqueror with absolute and unlimited rights over the conquered, including the right to kill or enslave any inhabitant or visitor captured in the enemy territory, and to seize and destroy any public or private property' (2012). Conquest, therefore, was a legitimate method of acquiring territory and subjugating populations from the sixteenth through to the twentieth centuries. Because colonising societies were very often themselves a product of intra-European colonisation, colonialism did not as such inaugurate conquest; it did however introduce theoretical problems and a whole discourse concerning conquest (Winter 2012). From the sixteenth and early seventeenth centuries, Winter argues, the 'genealogy of conquest is divided into two separate (though at times intersecting) branches' (2012), one focused on the colonial world and the other related to conquest in Europe. The one related to the colonial world focuses on the normative question of how to legitimise European conquest and colonisation. It focuses also on the 'nature of the subjects that may be conquered' (2012). The other concerns itself with the problem of instituting and transferring sovereignty and political authority.

The latter discourse emerged out of Stuart England, within the context of the English civil war. Here conquest became a political trope through which the foundation of sovereignty and royal authority were debated (Winter 2012). In sum 'the colonial discourse deal[t] with the normative grounds of conquest whereas the European discourse pertain[ed] to its normative implications' (2012).

Returning to the question of De las Casas' discomfort with and rejection of the use of the concept of conquest to describe the savage butcheries of the Amerindians in his *Short Account of the Destruction of the Indies*, Winter points out that De las Casas was not opposed to the idea of conquest itself. He did, for instance, consider it appropriate to describe the war against the 'Moors of Africa and Turks or heretics who hold our lands and persecute Christians and work to destroy our sacred faith' (De las Casas, cited in Winter 2012). It can be inferred from De las Casas' words that conquest 'can only be the result of a war against infidels and not just any infidels but against those who are seen as threats to Christianity' (2012). Winter argues that as a Dominican, De las Casas accepted the Thomist theory of just war 'according to which war is a juridical mechanism that parallels punishment and must therefore rely on a just cause' (2012). It is for this reason that he was not willing to describe as conquest the 'genocidal pillage of the Indies'. This would have been to 'cede the moral distinction between just and unjust war, between the lawful Christian reconquista of the Iberian peninsula and the wrongful Muslim conquests of Christian territories' (2012).

It appears that very soon after the voyages of discovery and the subsequent developments that took place in European discourse, very different approaches arose with regard to the question of conquest in the home of the conqueror in Europe and conquest in the so-called 'New World', which included Africa, Australasia and Latin America. In this chapter, we will make our priority the African experience, though it is comparable in many regards and in different degrees to the Australasian and Latin American situations.

CONQUEST IN EUROPE

Winter (2012) argues that several debates of a political and juridical nature in seventeenth-century England, for example, reveal an unease with the legitimation of the 'right of conquest' with regard to intra-European disputes. Chief among the problems implied by 'the right of conquest' as a legitimate mode of the acquisition of title to territory was that if the claimants of this right 'derived sovereignty from conquest and if conquest [was] seen as a basis for legitimate rule' (2012), they would have a hard time mounting a defence against any other such subsequent claimant/conqueror. He concludes by stating that '[the] concept of usurpation becomes incoherent if conquest is accepted as a source of legal claims' (2012), and suggests that this problem was eventually solved through the introduction of the criteria for just war. This doctrine of 'just conquest', for example, 'allowed the Tories to maintain that monarchy was founded on divine right ... [and] that rebellion against a monarch was both unlawful and unjust (2012).

South African philosopher Mogobe Ramose explains the 'just war' theory according to the philosophy of Thomas Aquinas. He describes 'just war' as having two components:

> the first, *ius ad bellum*, regulates the permissibility of war itself. Whereas the second regulates the conduct of war once it has actually begun. The principles of *ius ad bellum* hold that a war may be said to be just when (1) it is waged at the command of the sovereign; (2) there is a just cause (*iusta causa*); (3) there is the right intention (*intentio recta*). (Ramose 2003, 568)

Ramose adds that these principles apply on the assumption that all other means of peaceful conflict resolution have been exhausted. In addition, all three legal principles must be present and verifiable for any single act of war to be considered just (2003, 568).

Ramose has called into question the principle that only the sovereign may declare war, arguing that while it gives credence to the principle that war is an exclusive matter between sovereign powers, 'the right to self-determination and humanitarian intervention call[s] this exclusivity into question' (2003, 568). He adds that for the second condition of these principles to be met, there must be a 'just cause' for war to be initiated: '(1) to repel an injury (*ad repellendas injurias*); (2) to gain vindication against an offence such as national honour (*ad vindicandas offensiones*); to redress an injury or regain the thing lost; the principle of recoverability (*ad repetendas res*)' (2003, 568).

According to Ramose, the third condition, that is, the principle of right intention 'speaks to the motivation to do good and avoid evil' (2003, 568). This suggests that if war is waged in order to do evil it is immediately impermissible. The ultimate problem with this for Ramose is that it is those who wage war who exclusively determine its reasons or intentions; the likelihood that each side will claim that the other is wrong is rather high.

Now we turn to brief elaboration of the principles governing the conduct of war if it does begin. These determine humane conduct during the war and they are called *ius in bello* (Ramose 2003, 568). Among the laws related to the humane conduct of actual war are that it should stop immediately when the aims for which it was waged have been achieved, and that only soldiers and objects connected to the waging of war may be attacked. This means that it is impermissible to attack the elderly, women and children, or the disabled (2002, 568). In addition, the torturing of the defenceless, as well as rape and the injury to human dignity, are not allowed. Finally, the principle of proportionality, that only necessary force be used to achieve the legitimate aims of war, is also required. Ramose concludes his account by stating that both *ius ad bellum* and *ius in bello* 'are together an attempt to make unavoidable war as human as possible' (2003, 568).

The addition of the condition of justice through Thomist just war theory to the European understanding of the 'right to conquest', however, had little value for the African peoples conquered in subsequent and many unjust wars of colonisation.

CONQUEST IN 'SOUTH AFRICA'

The just war also filtered dramatically into conqueror South Africa. Prior to the 1400s, when Vasco da Gama passed through what he named the 'Cape of Storms', the just war doctrine was already established in Western moral philosophy. By the time the Dutch conqueror Jan van Riebeeck settled in the 'Cape of Good Hope' in 1652, both the just war doctrine and *Romanus Pontifex* were an integral part of the Western philosophical corpus.[4] Thus, even if Van Riebeeck himself might not have known about these two realities, the cultural milieu in which he grew up was alive with knowledge of the just war doctrine and *Romanus Pontifex*. On this basis, Van Riebeeck at best implanted this knowledge in conqueror South Africa, even if this might have been inadvertent, springing from his personal ignorance. Against this background, his dispute with the Khoikhoi treated hereunder contained undertones of at least the just war doctrine (Troup 1975, 53).

The liberal historian Freda Troup, for example, drawing from the writings of Van Riebeeck's men to describe an episode of conflict with a group of indigenous people, writes of an incident in which peoples he described as Khoikhoi sued the Dutch settlers for peace and tried to regain their rights to their land. The concern of their petition was the increasing seizure of land by the Dutch as they acquired more cattle. Van Riebeeck argued that if their land was restored to them it would prejudice the Dutch settlers. According to Troup, the Khoikhoi replied:

'Have we then no cause to prevent you from getting more cattle? The more you have the more land you will occupy ... who should give way, the rightful owner or the invader?' Van Riebeeck made it clear 'that they had now lost the land in war and therefore could only expect to be henceforth deprived of it ... The country had thus fallen to our lot, being justly won in defensive war and ... it was our intention to retain it. (Troup 1975, 53)

Van Riebeeck invoked the just war doctrine indirectly by his claim – in reply to the Khoikhoi people – that the land no longer belonged to them because it had been won 'justly ... in defensive war'. For Van Riebeeck, the invasion of the land of the Khoikhoi was permissible ('justly') in terms of the just war doctrine because its aim was to defend the land Van Riebeeck and his men took possession of by emerging as the victor in war. This claim goes beyond common sense, because none of the three ships that Van Riebeeck commanded on the journey from Holland to the 'Cape of Good Hope' contained land cargo. It is thus preposterous for Van Riebeeck to claim that he was waging a 'defensive war' when he had nothing to defend in the first place. His claim was thus in breach of the just war principles of the *intentio recta* (right intention) and *iusta causa* (just cause).

Van Riebeeck's descendants are the community referred to today as 'Afrikaners' (conventionally represented as broadly conservative) who are usually problematically credited with the sole responsibility for the birth and life of apartheid.[5] I have discussed their historiographical tradition elsewhere (see Dladla 2018). What is important to state here is that the conservative tradition in conqueror South African political history has always asserted its right to conquest quite explicitly on racist grounds, as Bernard Magubane has shown. He writes of the historian George McCall Theal that he justified 'the Dutch and British title and settlement in South Africa on the grounds of the sub-humanity of the original owners' (Magubane 2007, 255), and goes on to examine the writing of Theal himself, who wrote of the killing of the Khoi and San peoples in these terms:

> One may feel pity for the savages such as these, destroyed in their native wilds, though there is little for regretting their disappearance. They were of no benefit to any other section of the human family, they were incapable of improvement, and it was impossible for civilized men to live on the same soil with them, it was for the world's good that they should make room for a higher race. (Theal 1887–1919, cited in Magubane 2007, 255)

Later, Afrikaner historians, however, in their attempts to avoid such justifications, which were predicated on an explicit biological racism leading to genocidal racial war and had become unacceptable after the Second World War, invented some dubious historiographical doctrines. Motsoko Pheko rightly calls these doctrines 'notorious distortions invented by … European settler apologists' (Pheko 1992, 1). He continues to describe these distortions, namely

> [1] that Azania was *terra nullius* (a land belonging to nobody) when the settlers arrived at a small portion of today's Cape Town which they called a 'provision station'. [2] Hence the country was *res nullius* (property belonging to no one). [3] Consequently the settlers, after seizing the African country from its indigenous inhabitants made laws which treated Africans as *filius nullius* (bastards or rightless people). (Pheko 1992, 1).

Pheko goes on to discuss extensive archaeological and anthropological work that subsequently disproved these notorious distortions beyond a reasonable doubt, thereby establishing that Africans had been the original inhabitants of 'South Africa' since time immemorial. Sometimes the conquerors have resorted to an arbitrary method of anthropological differentiation of African people with no scientific basis, conceding that the Khoikhoi people, the majority of whom were conveniently brutally killed in the earliest wars of colonisation, were the indigenous people. According to this version, of notorious distortion, the Khoikhoi are somehow not African; the Africans are the Bantu-speaking people who supposedly arrived simultaneously with the European settlers. In a recent and further bizarre turn of this theory, so-called coloured people are now represented by right-wing Afrikaner nationalist groups like the Freedom Front Plus (Davis 2019) and Afriforum (News24 2012) as the true descendants of the Khoikhoi (Jacobs and Levenson 2018) and thus the only indigenous people of 'South Africa'. We call this development bizarre for two reasons. The first is that it was in fact the ancestors of the Afrikaners who committed the genocides of the Khoikhoi and San peoples, conquered them and seized their lands – this is recorded even in their own historical records. Secondly, the theory by which so-called coloured people are the only descendants of the Khoikhoi is bizarre because what it amounts to is a claim that only those who can trace their heritage to the Khoikhoi as well as their European conquerors are indigenous people.

In fact, it appears in this unexamined theory that partial European heritage is the *conditio sine qua non* for indigeneity. Those who trace the other parts of their heritage to, for example, the Xhosa or Tswana people are not indigenous, despite the inextricable cultural and historical synthetisation of their people and cultures with the Khoikhoi and San peoples. In some versions of this historical fiction, the Bantu-speaking people are even charged with the genocides of their fellow Africans.

This is sometimes used to support the idea that the Africans have no moral and legal basis upon which to reproach the Europeans for invasion, since they themselves are the posterity of genocidal conquerors. This version is also an untenable subterfuge designed to escape ethical and legal responsibility. Shula Marks shows that contrary to much of what she describes as a 'mythology of inveterate hatred between the "Bantu" and the "Bushmen"', much scientific evidence in historical linguistics and archaeology points to a record of sustained and lengthy peaceful interaction and coexistence (Marks 1980, cited in Pheko 1992, 12). She writes:

> the clicks characteristic of the South Eastern Bantu languages, that are unique to this family, also bespeak a long and intimate relationship between the Khoisan and Bantu speakers. Oral tradition in many areas recalls the intermarriage between even some of the Bantu-speaking chiefs with Khoisan women. Chief Mohlebangwe [sic] of the southernmost Tswana people, the Thlaphing – his mother was a Khoikhoi. (Marks 1980, cited in Pheko 1992, 12)

These distortions nevertheless continued to be a part of Afrikaner historiography and have even in the last few years been invoked by Afrikaner parliamentarians in their attempts to rebut African claims for the restitution of stolen land. Another frequently favoured method of denying the invasion and disseizin of land has been the fabrication of treaties between the indigenous conquered peoples and their colonial conquerors. A famous example of this is one of the cardinal tales of Afrikaner history, in terms of which it is claimed that *inkosi* uDingane killed Piet Retief and his company despite having entered into a treaty assigning Retief some land. These claims, which are plentiful in the Afrikaner history, are implausible given that in terms of African culture and philosophy, the ownership of land by a person or group is unheard of. The community are themselves mere custodians of the land, the use and control of which shall fall onto the generation of the unborn as it did upon them. The land belongs to the living-dead (see Mnguni 1952). This representation of history is given despite evidence produced almost 40 years ago settling the scientific debate beyond reasonable doubt (see Chami 2006; Ehret 1998; Eggert 2016; Marks 1980; Vansina 1990). It is still very much current in conservative Afrikaner circles. As recently as February 2016, the farmers' organisation Transvaal Agricultural Union of South Africa (TAU SA) wrote a letter of demand (Bezuidenhout 2016) to President Jacob Zuma in response to a speech he had delivered to the African National Congress (ANC) National Executive Committee on the 104th anniversary of that organisation on 8 January 2016. In that speech Zuma said: 'the challenges of poverty, inequality and the unemployment have their roots in the vast tracts of land that was [sic] stolen from the indigenous people of South Africa' (Bezuidenhout 2016). He also argued that 'South Africa's history of apartheid and colonialism characterised by racial hierarchy and systematic institutionalised conquest and dispossession of the indigenous people of this country, is directly related to our current challenges of unemployment, poverty and inequality' (Bezuidenhout 2016).

This the TAU SA took issue with, citing several of the discredited dogmas of conservative historiography discussed above as their preferred method of defence for the conquest of the indigenous peoples in the unjust wars of colonisation. The legal representatives of the union, Van Dyk Theron, claimed in the letter addressed to Zuma, for instance, that 'allegations about land that had been stolen in South Africa, together with other allegations which you have made referring to Jan van Riebeeck, and similar statements, have led our client to believe that yourself and the ANC are intent upon discriminating against whites, and in particular white land owners' (Bezuidenhout 2016). They also said that while they accepted that colonialism and apartheid had had adverse effects in the history of 'South Africa', their 'client has a serious problem with the allegation that vast tracks of land in South Africa were stolen from the indigenous people of South Africa' (Bezuidenhout 2016). The letter then gave reason for the lawyers' client's 'serious problem', writing:

> That is factually and historically simply incorrect. Firstly, all the current land owners of land in South Africa have not stolen such land, but have lawfully purchased the land that they own. That has been the case in respect of most of the land in South Africa for at least a century.

The myopic limitation of the historical period in question is reminiscent of the 'South African' constitution and coincides with the period after the passing of the notorious Natives Land Act (No. 27 of 1913), in terms of which the state as a whole dispossessed those Africans who still had any land in their control after the early wars of land theft.[6] The state, after seizing the land (as a communal conqueror on behalf of the entire white population), then sold some of this land to whites while making it near impossible for the indigenous people conquered in the unjust wars of colonisation to acquire any. This makes the claim of TAU SA's lawyers thoroughly disingenuous.

Their letter does not stop there. It goes on to state that

> the allegations that were made by [Zuma] and the ANC are made with the intent and innuendo to convey that: [1] white people who own land are thieves; [2] the whites who came to South Africa were thieves, criminals and robbers; [3] whites in South Africa stole land without remuneration or agreement; [4] all black tribes were indigenous to South Africa when whites arrived in 1652. (Bezuidenhout 2016)

The letter concludes with a demand for an unconditional apology from the ANC and President Zuma, failing which, they undertake to institute action for hate speech at the Equality Court in terms of the Promotion of Equality and Prevention of Unfair Discrimination Act (No. 4 of 2000).

The other white political community in conqueror South Africa that has benefited from the conquest of the indigenous people in the unjust wars of colonisation is largely English-speaking, and traces its historical and cultural roots to Britain. This community has since the nineteenth century claimed the liberal political tradition as its own and sought to distinguish its ethical and political record from that of the Afrikaners on the basis of liberalism. The intellectual roots of this community's conception of conquest come from the imperialist liberal tradition. Winter writes that although 'conquest seems incompatible with liberalism because it contradicts the fundamental postulates of individual freedom and representative government ... it is all the more remarkable that the founders of liberalism as a political philosophy – Thomas Hobbes and John Locke – managed to generate a theory of liberal conquest' (Winter 2012). Hobbes' *Leviathan* lists two methods in terms of which sovereignty can be established, either by institution or by acquisition. It is the latter that is of interest to us here, unlike sovereignty by institution, writes Hobbes; it is no covenant among individuals but a covenant between conqueror and conquered. Hobbes' basic idea was that conquest was not the victory itself; rather it was 'the acquisition by victory of a right over the persons of men. He therefore, that is slain is overcome, but not conquered; he that is taken, and put into prison or chains is not conquered ... But he that upon promise of obedience hath his life and liberty allowed him is then conquered and a subject and not before' (Hobbes 1985, cited in Winter 2012).

In this way, it would appear that Hobbes' version of conquest requires consent by the conquered, even if the choice they are given is only between life and death; if the conquered agree to 'choose life', then their conqueror has rights over them.

Locke's own development of Hobbes' theory of conquest was through a tricky rejection of 'the right of conquest' and the adoption of what Winter calls 'conquest by exception' (Winter 2012). According to Winter, Locke denied the idea that the sparing of someone's life whom one had defeated in war or combat gave the victor an automatic dominion over the vanquished. Instead, for Locke, for such a right to come into being, the vanquished must have forfeited their life. Among the ways in which such a forfeiture happens, according to Winter, is through the vanquished having waged an unjust war or having broken the law.[7] Locke's own words specify that the only situation in which conquest gives rise to a right is that of a captive in a just war who forfeits their life 'for having quitted reason', that is, by having violated natural law and having acted in 'the way of beasts' (Locke 1988, cited in Winter 2012). Winter suggests that by limiting the claims that derive from conquest to captives in a just war, Locke 'tightens the conditions of conquest; yet by identifying forfeiture with unreason, he introduces a normative account of reason as a criterion for which bodies may or may not be conquered' (2012). He goes on to make the point that 'reason, it turns out is not an anthropological universal but is differentially distributed, hence the importance of education in the liberal version of empire from Locke through Condorcet to Bentham'.

Winter argues that Lockean restrictions on conquest ultimately contributed to different standards for conquests in Europe to those applied in the colonial world. Locke's discussion of what titles to property could be derived from conquest, for example, distinguishes between damage on the one hand and injury on the other. Injury gives title to a person's life, while damage gives right to a person's property. As such, Locke insists that in a just war the rights over the lives of captives belong to the conqueror but not their property, which continues to belong to their family (or presumably whatever mode of testation was in place before conquest in war) (Winter 2012). Locke, however, leaves a space for reparations for damages arising out of war, in terms of which lands and even provinces may be expropriated to recover such damages. According to Winter, Locke insists that the satisfaction of damages for war will rarely provide title to the conquered land. He adds the critical explanatory proviso, however, that this is because 'damages of war can scarce amount to the value of any considerable tract of land, in any part of the world, where all the land is possessed and none lies waste' (Locke 1988, cited in Winter 2012). Winter argues further that the proviso 'any part of the world where all land is possessed and none lies in waste' is one for the colonial world, a condition of difference from Locke's own Britain or Europe. That is, places such as America or Africa where land is held in common sites of 'waste' and potential occupation and possession, without the need for further justification. Winter does this by discussing other texts by Locke where he expresses his conviction that American land is lying waste because of the absence of private ownership and a 'productivity' (2012). He discusses the influence that Locke's theory had on American juris-prudence, for instance in the 1823 case of Johnson v. M'Intosh at the US Supreme Court, where it required the creative interpretation of the law of conquest with a Lockean twist before it could function as a principle of jurisprudence that could be used to deny Indian land claims. According to the Supreme Court at the time, the international law of conquest granted jurisdiction over territory and no property rights over land; the process could be developed if following 'successful conquest', the conquered popula-tion was incorporated and blended with the conqueror's nation and became its citizens or subjects, through which the conquered would gain rights and privileges including the holding of property rights (Winter 2012).

An exception was also established, however, since 'assimilation had not occurred in the case of the Amerindians owing to their fierce and sav-age nature and their intention to fight the white settler population', as well as their failure to recognise the conquest; this 'meant the law of conquest did not in this instance apply' (Winter 2012). But rather than the law of conquest not applying meaning that people kept their freedom and remained unconquered, the twist was that a more ruinous and dispos-sessive and perfect conquest followed, the judge holding that 'as a result of the incomplete conquest the Amerindians were not subjects or citi-zens but mere occupants of their lands and therefore incapable of trans-ferring title to others' (Winter 2012). He went even further, suggesting that 'the conqueror had a duty to seize the lands because they would otherwise be allowed to lay in common waste' (Winter 2012).

Winter expresses surprise at the fact that arrested conquest through the conqueror's trickery turned out to be more profitable than consummated conquest. He goes on to show that in the eighteenth and nineteenth centuries Enlightenment ideals cast a negative light on conquests. He argues, however, that in the case of the English the turn away from conquest was not a repudiation of empire.

It would appear that the central consideration in international politics from then until now was to be what Ramose has called the 'meridian line that decides truth and defines justice' (Ramose 2003, 548). The line for Ramose is a geopolitical construction differentiating the limits between Being and Nothingness. Between beings and nothings, between the territories occupied by those who, according to themselves, had human value and so were among themselves and between themselves subjects of morality and law, and on the other side of the line, those of the nothings, demarcated zones which it was said were occupied by those without the value of life, the barbarians, the savages, those falling outside the boundaries of morality and law and thereby unworthy of its protection.

The differentiation underlying this construction, this 'drawing of the line', had its basis in the restrictive interpretation of Aristotle's concept of *Homo Rationalis*, which it was said did not apply to the African, Amerindian or Australasian. In that way, the line separated the world into the territories where lay reason and those where there lay unreason; culture versus nature, order versus chaos. It was the burden of those with reason, then, those with order and culture, to introduce it to those without, to conquer, colonise and 'civilise' them. The 'civilised' nations' refusal to recognise the humanity of those inhabitants of the 'new world' became the licence for European to pillage, plunder and settle as they wished without limits, without recourse to morality or law.

CONQUEST OF THE INDIGENOUS PEOPLES IN AN UNJUST WAR

Conquest in the unjust wars of colonisation is the foundational process by which Blacks are invented through the reification and objectification of the indigenous conquered peoples. It may be described properly as the phenomenon of a fictive ontology of social being, since from the point of conquest it founds conditions of unnatural but systemised death for the conquered people.

From a historical point of view and with a basis in Western philosophy, conquest of people may result in either enslavement or the dispossession of property, or a combination of both. In the case of Blacks in the Americas, they themselves were stolen out of Africa and put to use on the land of the Amerindians that was occupied by the Europeans. In conqueror South Africa, depending on the will of the conqueror, those among the indigenous conquered peoples who were not simply killed were dispossessed of their land and then afterwards sometimes enslaved. After the outlawing of slavery, the economic relationship was transformed into that of wage slavery.

The seizure of land and other strategies, such as the malicious imposition of poll and other taxes, were designed precisely to bring an end to the remaining social and economic independence of the indigenous peoples and convert them from free workers into employees (wage slaves) to be used at the will and pleasure of the colonial conqueror.

FEAR: CONQUERED LIVES AND LIVING CONQUEST

There is common talk among the indigenous peoples conquered in the unjust wars of colonisation of *'ukwesaba abelungu'* (fearing whites), which speaks to the strength of the state of conquest. *Ukusaba abelungu*, the fear of whites, describes a widespread phenomenon throughout social and economic life in which Blacks, despite being habitually undermined, humiliated or even beaten violently, 'choose' not to defend themselves or respond to this humiliation out of fear of the consequence for their life and limb. Margaret Mead, in a discussion with James Baldwin, shares a memory with him of a time she spent at a plantation in New Guinea, which she extends to apply to slave plantations in the south of the US. She recounts being all alone (the only white person) on the plantation and having to 'run the labor line': 'I had to give them orders based on absolutely nothing but white supremacy. I was one lone white woman. Anyone of them could have killed me' (Mead and Baldwin 1971, 21). She confesses to knowing instinctively, a variety of historical knowledge she shared with the slaves, that should anyone harm her, 'maybe twenty of them would have been killed' (1971, 21). It is on the basis of this shared historical knowledge that white farmers or teenagers can, for example, slap around a black police officer carrying a gun – a sight fairly common in the rural areas of conqueror South Africa. *Ukusaba abelungu* describes no ordinary fear, but the well-inculcated and historically rational fore-knowledge of the results that have actually come to pass whenever Blacks dare to defend themselves against whites.

Despite the prevalence of *ukusaba abelungu* throughout conqueror South African history after conquest, many among the indigenous peoples have risen against these ongoing injustices. Wars challenging conquest of course continued long after the last of the sovereign nations of the indigenous peoples were conquered in the unjust wars of colonisation. Even after the violent suppression of the Bambatha Rebellion of 1906, the 1960 Sharpeville Massacre and the 1976 Soweto revolt, both non-violent stands taken by proponents of the Azanian tradition, were violent massacres by the state of people challenging the state of conquest.

The Sharpeville Massacre is interesting for a number of reasons, as an episode of the violence reinscribing conquest. For one, the reinscription of conquest is commonplace even in the colloquial speech of young whites in conqueror South Africa. The threat often issued to Blacks during altercations, worded in various ways to express the idea that 'you've forgotten your place' or 'I'll remind you of your place', speaks precisely to situations where whites feel the balance established by conquest of the natural deference of Blacks to their authority and superiority is being threatened and must be restored by violence of one variety or another. In the case of the Sharpeville Massacre, the police applied a thoroughly disproportionate and deadly form of violence against unarmed protesters. The events had the effect of changing conqueror South African history forever, and having apartheid declared 'a crime against humanity' by United Nations General Assembly Resolution 2202 A (XXI) of 16 December 1966 (see Dugard 2008). Ironically, at the dawn of 'the new South Africa' this 'crime against humanity', recognised even by the United Nations, was condoned during the 'negotiations' (Ramose 2003, 542) and crowned with the establishment of the Truth and Reconciliation Commission under the Promotion of National Unity and Reconciliation Act (No. 34 of 1995).

The massacre of countless lives at Sharpeville occurred less than a year after the formation of the Pan Africanist Congress of Azania (PAC), during its first major political campaign that aimed at exposing the defective sovereignty of the South African government and had the effect of causing the state to ban all existing liberation organisations. The ANC had existed for half a century without ever being banned, but within a year of the PAC's formation it was both subject to unprecedented state violence and banned wholesale. According to some accounts by historians like Tom Lodge (2011), the arms employed by the state to put down the protest even included armed aircraft – a seemingly strange show of force against an unarmed group of working people. The point, however, is that the state understood Sharpeville as a precise challenge to conquest. The PAC had resolved that armed resistance was unnecessary, since the indigenous conquered peoples were not only a great majority of the population but were also the very basis of the economic system in conqueror South Africa. PAC leader Robert Sobukwe had observed that without the cooperation of the indigenous peoples conquered in the unjust wars of colonisation, the condition of conquest could not hold. The purpose of people burning their passes and then volunteering for arrest was to demonstrate both to the people themselves and to the state where the power actually sat. It was understood that the administrative and economic chaos created by the imprisonment of these people would force the white supremacist regime to reconsider its position. Understanding this threat, the rulers of the day saw the only way to preserve the state of conquest as a reinscription of it, by recourse to the gratuitous violence that had established the *status quo ante*. What else can explain the presence in Sharpeville of such heavy weapons as the Browning machine gun (Lodge 2011, 7), or the four planes (2011, 9) that were flying over Sharpeville just minutes before the gunfire began? Sobukwe himself was arrested and, in an unprecedented event, imprisoned through an Act of parliament rather than by existing criminal law.

When the opposition member of parliament, Helen Suzman, enquired of the governing National Party precisely why they feared him so much that he needed to be arrested in this way, no clear answers were forthcoming (Ntloedible 1995, 89–91). The point, however, was that Sobukwe was threatening the state of conquest. Even after his release from prison, he was forbidden from addressing crowds, placed under severe surveillance, prevented from leaving the country and prohibited from writing or even being recorded. This was based on the fear that he would lead the process of destruction of the state of conquest.

The desired effect of the Sharpeville Massacre was accomplished, as many historians note. There was a climate of fear and reluctance to challenge the state throughout the country for almost a decade afterwards, until the birth of the Black Consciousness Movement (BCM). Born from the remaining ashes of Sharpeville and nourished by its spilled blood, this new Azanian movement was to grow until it was too threatening to the state of conquest. It was put down during the Soweto revolt in 1976. Six years earlier, the BCM leader, Bantu Stephen Biko, in an article entitled 'Fear – An Important Determinant in South African Politics', had identified both the periodic episodes of state violence on the one hand, and the perpetual harassment of Blacks by an oversized state security apparatus on the other, as having the purpose of maintaining conquest through the cultivation of fear (Biko 1979a). In our own time, the widespread police harassment and brutality directed at Black communities as well as the Marikana Massacre of 2012 serve as living proof of the continuity of the problem in the 'post-apartheid' period, along with the many 'service delivery protests' that produce countless casualties among the ranks of the indigenous conquered peoples.

BLACK HOROLOGY

> Although many structures of Dasein remain in the dark with
> regard to particulars, it nonetheless seems we have reached the req-
> uisite, primordial interpretation of Dasein with the clarification of
> temporality as the primordial condition of the possibility of care.
> (Heidegger 2010, 355)

Time in relation to Blacks, time according to Blacks, or Black time offer
a most concrete example of the ontological implications of race. The
apparently universal notion of 'human life' with its partner, 'lifetime',
are the very parameters and boundaries that provide the framework
within which human constructs such as ethics and politics gain their
meaningfulness. The pursuit of a good life is predicated on an idea of
a given lifetime – presumably human and thus universal. Markers such
as childhood and adulthood are demarcations of cultural points on
the continuum. They correspond to a variety of obligations and rights
that are due to human beings within the ethical universe.

The idea of a good life or of human adulthood is not simply contingent on the content of ethics or biology but is structured most fundamentally by politics. The way in which racism has structured the time
of Blacks ever since their conquest in the unjust wars of colonisation
calls for wonder about whether the time of Blacks can meaningfully be
made sense of within the schema of human life (lifetime). It is because
of the speciational differentiation of time that we speak, for example,
of the lifetimes of animals according to their species. We are able to
speak of *dog years* and *cat years* and translate them into the parameters
of human life expectancy, and do so because of biology and human
domination and its attendant anthropocentric paradigm of interspe-
cies relations (if it were not so perhaps we would know our own dog
and cat years more readily than theirs in relation to our own reality
of lifetime). In the instance of the 'human race', the evidence points
to the disturbing but useful potential of translation between Black

years and white years. We will use this section of the chapter to provide a brief sketch through which the depth of conquest's temporal penetration into the experience of the indigenous peoples conquered in the unjust wars of colonisation might emerge. These notes may be considered a prolegomenon to a Black horology, rather than an exhaustive explication or summary.

Lifetime (life expectancy)

Around the world in all white polities (Mills 1997), the lifetime of Blacks is considerably shorter than that of whites (Burgard and Treiman 2006; Haal et al. 2018; Levine et al. 2016). This is to say, at the biological level, the hearts of Blacks stop beating several years before white hearts. This is not a result of any natural process but of the human-made cruelty of racism (white supremacy), which finds expression in the realms of politics and economics.

Childhood and adulthood

Racist ideas extending to Blacks both at an individual and a communal level have had their basis in an idea of underdevelopment, in which Blacks develop more slowly than white people.[8] Their history is supposed to be in its infancy and behind that of others. Depending on the particular variety of theory, Blacks are also supposed to suffer from an intellectual arrested development, in which, even as their bodies age similarly to those of whites, their mental development is said to stop during the phase of their adolescence (Dubow 1989), leading to an intelligence differential between the intellectually immature Blacks and the intellectually superior whites.

These ideas and practices, far from being artefacts in the history of scientific racism, continue to inform present-day culture. The widespread reference to Blacks who work in the various domestic and hospitality fields as kitchen 'girls', garden 'boys', or bar 'boys' is only one example. This appellation is deeply rooted in the history of slavery in the West.

Kelly Wrenhaven describes the situation in ancient Greece as follows: 'the connection between slaves and the *oikos* is further demonstrated by another word for "slave", *pais*. Its meaning is flexible and may connote descent, age and/or condition' (Wrenhaven 2013, 19).

Later, she elaborates the point in support of our own argument for the connection between white supremacy in South Africa and slavery in ancient Greece, when she argues that the common factor among the competing but related uses of *pais* is the idea of subordination and dependence, not unlike the relation of a child to its parent. Wrenhaven writes:

> When used in the context of slavery, *pais* is particularly demonstrative of the perception of the slave as interminably puerile. This is because the word was applied indiscriminately to slaves of all ages, much as 'boy' was applied to male slaves of any age in the slave-holding American South. The idea that the slave is forever child-like is expressed by the Greek sources, which often depict slaves as lacking the intellectual and moral potential to advance to maturity. (2013, 19)

Wrenhaven goes on to argue that the word also establishes a connection between 'the child's "susceptibility to desire, pleasure, and pain" and the slave's perceived lack of *sophrosyne* ("self-moderation/control") ... The word *pais* also recalls how slaves were subject to physical violence, particularly for disciplinary reasons' (2013, 20).

The nature of Black life ironically is that despite the childhood that white people reserve for Blacks in their interpersonal relations with them, or in international relations with their countries, Blacks in general sometimes do not experience childhood at all. The kinds of deaths caused by HIV and Aids, resulting from the mass incarceration of Black adults, and the many hours Black parents must work to support their families, altogether rob Black children of their childhood. The responsibility is not unlike domestic child labour. This is not to discount the many Black children who must work in order to support their families. Numerous studies of implicit bias have also demonstrated how whites perceive Black children as adults (see APA 2014; Goff et al. 2014). In the US this 'error in judgement' (APA 2014) has been used to justify the brutality of the police towards young Blacks.

Free time

A lifetime read closely does not only describe life expectancy but *free time*. If one woman owns lots of land and has inherited material wealth that makes it unnecessary for her to work, she will over the course of her life be in a position to use her time according to her own will. The case for the poor woman who must work, on the other hand, is that she will have less time to exercise her will freely and instead will have to volunteer her body into employment. In conqueror South Africa, 'volunteer' is a euphemism that runs the risk of deception. The historical tragedy was one of the confiscation of the existing wealth of Blacks precisely in order to force them to become the wage slaves of whites. Added to the necessity of employment for subsistence are the subtractions of time that are created by colonial spatial planning (Biko 1979b, 100–102).

The case of Blacks getting up in the early hours of the morning and travelling from the townships on the city outskirts all over conqueror South Africa in order to arrive at work on time, expending hours per day travelling, still goes on today as it did in Biko's time. The resulting effect on free time is that in the same year, the white person who lives a walking distance from work and spends 10 minutes getting there expends 3 000 minutes, or a little more than 2 days, of the working year travelling to work and back, while their counterpart who spends 3 hours per day travelling to work expends 900 hours, or more than 37 days, in the same period. After a decade, just this fact of travelling to work and back has already cost Blacks a year of free time. The disproportionate number of Blacks in prisons also has an effect on this free time, since the use of time is not according to one's free will.

CONCLUSION

The polysemantic range of meanings revealed by the historical linguistic origins of the word 'invent', which is the root of the first noun of this chapter's title, are befitting for a word that includes among its layers of meaning 'the creation, production or construction of something by original thought' (Brown 1993, 1408). A lesser-known connotation of invention described by the *New Shorter Oxford Dictionary on Historical Principles* (Brown 1993) as 'now rare and obsolete' is derived more directly from its Latin etymology *invenire*, literally 'to come upon or discover'. This connotation, listed as the second, is recorded as '2a devise, contrive, plan and plot'; related to this meaning is the more common one '2b to devise as untruth (a statement or story or an element of one)' (Brown 1993, 1408). The history of the problem of Blackness, enjoyed by its inventors and suffered by its inventions, is certainly a testament to this wide range of meanings of the word 'invention'. This chapter has been an attempt at the disclosure of the roots of the contrivance or plot, in terms of which the untruth that the indigenous conquered people are ontologically defective and natural servants of their European conquerors was devised. We began by dis-covering the evolution and devolution of the 'right of conquest' in Western political and legal thought and its application in the 'new world', culminating in an examination of the history of its application in conqueror South Africa. We then showed precisely how conquest in the unjust wars of colonisation was the foundational process by which Blacks were invented through the reification and objectification of the indigenous conquered peoples. From Hobbes, especially, we dis-covered that conquest properly describes a relation of domination, Blackness in our case being its subservient component, subjected by the threat of death. This chapter then may be understood as an exposition of the phenomenon of a fictive ontology of social and political being, since the moment of conquest founds conditions of unnatural but systemised potential and actual death for the conquered people. The dying itself is no fiction, but a concrete political, social and economic reality sustained by the threat of death. This unnatural and premature death, we argued, may well provide the most tangible expression of the meaning of Blackness; this we did through the examination of human temporality in the final section of the chapter, which explored the analytical value of a Black horology. It would seem that an even more fantastical invention than Blackness and a greater imagination than that of its inventors will be required to disinvent it.

NOTES

1   The use of 'Black' in its capitalised form in this chapter aims to draw the distinction between the racist heritage of biological anthropology, where the classification originated to name people of African descent, and its special status as a contested concept in Black radical thought, in which it is used as part of a liberatory discourse. It is that status which is invoked here.

2   The use of the authorial 'we' is rather crucial for us. The 'we' in our work is a philosophical convention emerging out of Ubu-Ntu philosophy, and means to acknowledge that the individual author whose name appears here is indebted to a tradition and a community of interlocutors both living and passed. The text itself is a collective product of long-standing conversation and mutual study, in which individual acknowledgements are futile, since the individuals are related to the community and tradition in a similar way. The best way in which this can be communicated is through the use of we, our and us.

3   The term 'South Africa' represents a conceptual-historical and ethical and political problem since it reflects the political imagination and will of the conquerors of that so-called territory, rather than those of the indigenous peoples conquered in the unjust wars of colonisation. My preferred choice of name for the territory, reliant on a precolonial liberatory imagination and historiography, is Azania (see Chami [2021], Dladla [2018, 2021], Modiri [2021], or Webster [2021] for an elaboration of the problem and its extent. For purposes of reference, where South Africa appears in the present discussion other than in direct quotations, it will be placed in quotation marks to register my protest, or it will be accompanied by the prefix 'conqueror' to identify it accordingly. This convention is commonly used by theoreticians of the Azanian Philosophical Tradition.

4   *Romanus Pontifex* was a papal bull issued in 1455 by Pope Nicholas V granting Africa to King Alfonso V of Portugal, in total disregard of the consent and knowledge of the indigenous inhabitants of Africa.

5   This characterisation is open to challenge since it may be argued that at least politically, all white South Africans are descendants of Van Riebeeck, being successors of a title earned by him by right of conquest.

6   The convention in terms of which the South African constitution is written with an initial capital letter to signify its status as supreme law is reminiscent of the convention of capitalising the writing of 'god' in the so-called 'world religions'. Following

Wole Soyinka in *The Burden of Memory, the Muse of Forgiveness* (1999, 32), we question the ethical tenability and soundness of maintaining the convention that capitalises the 'world religions' as well as their gods and adherents until it is applied to all religions. We must bear in mind the fact that the displacement of the living gods of various indigenous peoples conquered in the unjust wars of colonisation, often in the very name of these religions, was no voluntary and peaceful process but part and parcel of the same murderous epistemicide. It is the same too with law; we identify the constitution so described as the conqueror's law – the status of its supremacy is by no means unchallenged.

7   Our focus here is on Locke's thinking with regard to *conquest in a just war*. He is clear that no rights can arise from engagement in an unjust war to the unjust warrior. He writes, for example, that 'the Aggressor, who puts himself into a state of war with another, and unjustly invades another man's right, can by such unjust war never come to have a right over the conquered' (Locke 1988: 403 S176). The problem with the just war doctrine that we raised earlier with reference to Ramose is precisely that each party to the war represents itself as just. Van Riebeeck is a case in point here. It is for this reason then that our focus is upon Locke's thought in relation to 'just conquest'.

8   Toby Rollo (2018, 307) offers another perspective, arguing that 'the child/human binary does not present a contingent or merely rhetorical construction but, rather, a central feature of racialization. Where Black peoples are situated as objects of violence it is often precisely because Blackness has been identified with childhood and childhood is historically identified as the archetypal site of naturalized violence and servitude'.

REFERENCES

APA (American Psychological Association). 2014. 'Black Boys Viewed as Older, Less Innocent than Whites, Research Finds'. Press release, American Psychological Association, March 2014. https://www.apa.org/news/press/releases/2014/03/black-boys-older. (accessed 15 February 2023).

Bezuidenhout, Jan. 2016. 'JZ Moet Verduidelik oor "Gesteelde Grond"'. *Landbou*, 4 February 2016. https://www.netwerk24.com/landbou/Nuus/jz-moet-verduidelik-oor-gesteelde-grond-20170914.

Biko, Steve. 1979a. 'Fear – An Important Determinant in South African Politics'. In *I Write What I Like: Steve Biko. A Selection of his Writings*. Edited by Aelred Stubbs C.R., 73–79. Oxford: Heinemann.

Biko, Steve. 1979b. 'What Is Black Consciousness?' In *I Write What I Like: Steve Biko. A Selection of his Writings*. Edited by Aelred Stubbs C.R., 99–119. Oxford: Heinemann.

Brown, Leslie (comp.). 1993. *New Shorter Oxford Dictionary on Historical Principles*. Oxford: Oxford University Press.

Burgard, Sarah A. and Donald J. Treiman. 2006. 'Trends and Racial Differences in Infant Mortality in South Africa'. *Social Science and Medicine* 62 (5): 1126–1137. https://doi.org/10.1016/j.socscimed.2005.07.025.

Chami, Felix A. 2006. *The Unity of African Ancient History: 3000 BC to AD 500*. Dar es Salaam: E&D Limited.

Chami, Felix A. 2021. 'The Geographical Extent of Azania'. *Theoria* 68 (168): 12–29. https://doi.org/10.3167/th.2021.6816802.

Davis, Rebecca. 2019. 'Peter Marais and the Freedom Front Plus: A Match Made in Opportunists' Heaven'. *Daily Maverick*, 22 January 2019. https://www.dailymaverick.co.za/article/2019-01-22-peter-marais-and-the-freedom-front-plus-a-match-made-in-opportunists-heaven/.

De las Casas, Bartolomé. 1992 [1542]. *A Short Account of the Destruction of the Indies*. Edited and translated by Nigel Griffin. London: Penguin.

Dladla, Ndumiso. 2018. 'The Liberation of History and the End of South Africa: Some Notes towards an Azanian Historiography in Africa, South'. *South African Journal on Human Rights* 34 (3): 415–440. https://doi.org/10.1080/02587203.2018.1550940.

Dladla, Ndumiso. 2021. 'The Azananian Philosophical Tradition Today'. *Theoria* 68 (168): 1–11. https://doi.org/10.3167/th.2021.6816801.

Dubow, Saul. 1989. 'The Idea of Race in Early 20th Century South Africa: Some Preliminary Thoughts'. African Studies Seminar Paper presented at the African Studies Institute, University of Witwatersrand, Johannesburg, April 1989. https://core.ac.uk/download/pdf/39667561.pdf.

Dugard, John. 2008. 'Convention on the Suppression and Punishment of the Crime of Apartheid'. United Nations Audiovisual Library of International Law. https://legal.un.org/avl/pdf/ha/cspca/cspca_e.pdf (accessed 15 February 2023).

Eggert, Manfred K.H. 2016. 'Geneticizing Bantu: Historical Insight or Historical Trilemma?' *Medieval Worlds* 4: 79–90. https://doi.org/10.1553/medievalworlds_no4_2016s79.

Ehret, Christopher. 1998. *An African Classical Age: Eastern and Southern Africa in World History, 1000 BC to AD 400*. Charlottesville: University of Virginia Press.

Goff, Phillip Atiba, Matthew Christian Jackson, Brooke Allison Lewis Di Leone, Carmen Marie Culotta and Natalie Ann DiTomasso. 2014. 'The Essence of Innocence: Consequences of Dehumanizing Black Children'. *Journal of Personality and Social Psychology* 106 (4): 526–545. https://doi.org/10.1037/a0035663.

Haal, Karel, Anja Smith and Eddy van Doorslaer. 2018. 'The Rise and Fall of Mortality Inequality in South Africa in the HIV Era'. *SSM – Population Health* 5 (August): 239–248. https://doi.org/10.1016/j.ssmph.2018.06.007.

Heidegger, Martin. 2010 [1927]. *Being and Time: A Revised Edition of the Stambaugh Translation*. Translated by Joan Stambaugh. New York: State University of New York Press.

Hobbes, Thomas. 1996. [1651]. *Leviathan*. Revised student edition. Edited by Richard Tuck. Cambridge: Cambridge University Press.

Jacobs, Sean and Zachary Levenson. 2018. 'The Limits of Coloured Nationalism'. *Mail & Guardian*, 13 June 2018. https://mg.co.za/article/2018-06-13-00-the-limits-of-coloured-nationalism/.

Levine, Robert S., James E. Foster, Robert E. Fullilove, Mindy T. Fullilove, Nathaniel C. Briggs, Pamela C. Hull, Baqar A. Husaini and Charles H. Hennekens. 2016. 'Black-White Inequalities in Mortality and Life Expectancy, 1933–1999: Implications for Healthy People 2010'. *Public Health Reports* 116 (5): 474–483. https://doi.org/10.1093/phr/116.5.474.

Locke, John. 1988 [1689]. *Two Treatises of Government*. Edited by Peter Laslett. Cambridge: Cambridge University Press.

Lodge, Tom. 2011. *Sharpeville: A Massacre and Its Consequences*. Oxford: Oxford University Press.

Magubane, Bernard M. 2007. 'Whose Memory – Whose History? The Illusion of the Radical and Liberal Debates'. In *History Making and Present Day Politics: The Meaning of Collective Memory in South Africa*, edited by Hans Erik J. Stolten, 251–279. Uppsala: Nordic Africa Institute.

Marks, Shula. 1980. 'South Africa – "The Myth of the Empty Land"'. *History Today* 30 (1): n.p. https://www.historytoday.com/archive/south-africa-myth-empty-land.

Mead, Margaret and James Baldwin. 1971. *A Rap on Race*. Philadelphia: J.B. Lippincott.

Mills, Charles. 1999. 'The Racial Polity'. In *Racism and Philosophy*, edited by Susan E. Babbitt and Sue Campbell, 13–31. Ithaca: Cornell University Press.

Mnguni [pseud. Hosea Jaffe]. 1952. *Three Hundred Years: A History of South Africa*. Cumberwood: New Era Fellowship.

Modiri, Joel. 2021. 'Azanian Political Thought and the Undoing of South African Knowledges'. *Theoria* 68 (168): 42–85. https://doi.org/10.3167/th.2021.6816804.

News24. 2012. 'Khoisan Demand Recognition, Land'. *News24*, 21 February 2012. https://www.news24.com/News24/Khoisan-demand-recognition-land-20120221.

Ntloedibe, Elias. 1995. *Here Is a Tree: Political Biography of Robert Mangaliso Sobukwe*. Pretoria: Century Turn Publishers.

Parliament of South Africa. 1913. *Natives Land Act (No. 27 of 1913)*. Cape Town: Parliament of South Africa.

Pheko, Motsoko. 1992. *South Africa: Betrayal of a Colonised People: Issues of International Human Rights Law*. Johannesburg: Skotaville.

Ramose, Mogobe. 2003. 'I Conquer, Therefore I Am the Sovereign: Reflections upon Sovereignty, Constitutionalism and Democracy in Zimbabwe and South Africa'. In *The African Philosophy Reader*, edited by Pieter Coetzee and A.P.J. Roux, 543–589. Cape Town: Oxford University Press.

Republic of South Africa. 2000. *Promotion of Equality and Prevention of Unfair Discrimination Act (No. 4 of 2000)*. Cape Town: Republic of South Africa.

Rollo, Toby. 2018. 'The Color of Childhood: The Role of the Child/Human Binary in the Production of Anti-Black Racism'. *Journal of Black Studies* 49 (4): 307–329. https://doi.org/10.1177/0021934718760769.

Soyinka, Wole. 1999. *The Burden of Memory, the Muse of Forgiveness*. Oxford: Oxford University Press.

Theal, George M. 1887–1919. *History of South Africa since September 1795*, vol. 4. London: George Allen and Co.

Troup, Freda. 1975. *South Africa: An Historical Introduction*. Harmondsworth: Penguin.

Vansina, Jan. 1990. *Paths in the Rainforests: Toward a History of Political Tradition in Equatorial Africa*. Madison: University of Wisconsin Press.

Webster, Anjuli. 2021. 'South African Social Science and the Azanian Philosophical Tradition'. *Theoria* 68 (168): 111–135. https://doi.org/10.3167/th.2021.6816806.

Winter, Yves. 2012. 'Conquest: Yves Winter'. *Political Concepts: A Critical Lexicon*. https://www.politicalconcepts.org/conquest-winter/.

Wrenhaven Kelly L. 2013. *Reconstructing the Slave: The Image of the Slave in Ancient Greece*. London: Bloomsbury.

2

The Decolonisation of Southern Africa: Historical Reflections

Chris Saunders

The word 'decolonisation' is now used in a wide variety of settings, with many different meanings. The reflections that follow concern *political* decolonisation, in the sense of a process that ended colonial rule (of which apartheid can be seen as a form).[1] My interest here is in how and why the different cases of colonial rule came to an end in Southern Africa, the last part of the continent to be decolonised. I define this region as the southern portion of the African continent, including what is now the Democratic Republic of the Congo (DRC), which became a member of the main regional organisation, the Southern African Development Community (SADC), in 1997. Though the process leading to the end of colonial rule happened in many different ways and in widely different environments, from the tropics to the Cape of Good Hope, there was an overall process involved, if a very complex one, that covered the whole region. The way it unfolded was heavily contingent on time and place, but one can draw out certain central themes, and, as with any historical process, raise basic questions: 'what happened?' 'why did it happen?' and 'what was the outcome, and what is its significance?' There is not space here for a comprehensive overview, but an attempt will be made to address these questions.

The large literature on political decolonisation in the late twentieth century includes a number of general studies of the ways such decolonisation took place in West Africa and tropical Africa, but in 2022 there was no major study of the overall process in Southern Africa, nor one that addressed the main questions that need to be asked, or saw the process in context, even though we are now almost 30 years from its end. While there are overviews for individual countries and some brilliant in-depth treatments of particular actors, such as those by Piero Gleijeses on the Cubans in Angola (Gleijeses 2013) and by Roger Southall on liberation movements in power (Southall 2013), no work considers how the whole region was decolonised, bringing in comparative perspectives. At least part of the reason for the lacuna is the multifaceted nature of the decolonisation process.

DECOLONISATION AND LIBERATION

The term 'decolonisation' was first used as a scholarly concept, in the way it will be used here, as the process leading to the end of formal colonial rule, by Moritz Bonn in the 1930s. Then a distinguished academic at the London School of Economics, Bonn had experienced first-hand the particularly brutal form of German colonialism in South West Africa, and he anticipated what he called 'the crumbling of empires', in part as a result of the desire of colonised people to end their subjection to colonial rule (Gordon 2013). When the term 'decolonisation' gained general currency after the Second World War, it usually referred to the wave of transitions in Asia and Africa from colonial rule to independence, which the author of a general work on decolonisation regards as 'perhaps the most important historical process of the twentieth century'

(Rothermund 2006, 1). India in 1947 and the Gold Coast in 1957 are prime examples, and they were followed by other countries in tropical Africa. As autonomous states within the British Empire/Commonwealth, South Africa and India were members of the League of Nations between the World Wars and then of the United Nations (UN), but for other countries the formal end to colonial rule, and the creation of a new nation state, was marked perhaps above all by the running up of a new flag and by gaining membership of the UN.

Western scholars who have tackled the history of decolonisation have, not surprisingly, tended to argue that metropolitan influences were dominant, while Third World scholars and activists have tended to emphasise, sometimes exclusively, initiatives from within Africa and Asia. The latter have often used the term 'liberation' rather than 'decolonisation' for the process leading to the end of colonial rule. The Namibian liberation movement, the South West Africa People's Organisation (SWAPO), propagates a myth of its liberation struggle as having been primarily, if not solely, responsible for Namibian independence. Zimbabwe's ruling Zimbabwe African National Union-Patriotic Front (ZANU-PF) continues to assert that the armed struggle it led was the main reason for Zimbabwe's independence.

EXTERNAL AND LOCAL INFLUENCES

Whereas decolonisation has often been used to suggest a process undertaken by, and in the interests of, the colonial power, the process must, of course, also be seen from the point of view of the colonised, and any understanding of decolonisation must include both external factors, whether metropolitan or global, and local and regional ones. These vary from case to case. No generalisation about how power was transferred, whether by armed struggle or other forms of pressure, is possible for the Southern Africa region as a whole. The relative significance of global, metropolitan and local influences must be weighed in each case. While metropoles in Europe, for a variety of reasons, agreed to devolve power, what is so striking about the decolonisation of Southern Africa is the way in which white regimes in the region tried to resist pressures to decolonise. In effect, apartheid South Africa became a metropole for both the Namibian and South African liberation struggles, as the white supremacist Rhodesian Front regime was for the Zimbabwean struggle for liberation (see Onslow 2009; Sapire and Saunders 2012). From this perspective, decolonisation and liberation are either the same thing or two sides of the same coin.

Some writers have, following Frantz Fanon (Fanon 1963), have seen the term decolonisation as inappropriate because it obscures the transition from a colonial to a neocolonial relationship. But there is no reason why this should be the case. The extent to which the structures and effects of colonialism continued into the postcolonial period is a separate question. The sociologist John S. Saul, who writes of the betrayal of liberation, and sees what has happened in Southern Africa since the end of colonial and apartheid rule as 'recolonization by the empire of capital' (Saul 1993: 35; Saul 2008, 2014), nevertheless accepts that the ending of colonial or apartheid rule was a great victory for the liberation forces, and therefore, despite significant continuities, represented a significant turning point in the history of the region.

EVOLUTION AND REVOLUTION

In Southern Africa the process of achieving what some see as 'national liberation' had both evolutionary and revolutionary aspects and phases. In the case of the decolonisation of the Belgian Congo, the advent of independence in 1960 led almost immediately to conflict, superpower involvement and a series of violent transfers of power (for a recent account, see O'Malley 2018). Elsewhere in the early 1960s, the first phase of decolonisation in Southern Africa was a relatively evolutionary one. In order to understand this, it will be necessary to say something of the unfolding of decolonisation within the British Empire. Then, in the mid-1970s, there was a much more revolutionary stage, involving the independence of Angola and Mozambique in 1975, in each case after protracted armed struggle. The Popular Movement for the Liberation of Angola (MPLA) and the Front for the Liberation of Mozambique (Frelimo) came to power in those countries without elections. Then followed three negotiated settlements, involving democratic elections, leading to the independence first of Zimbabwe in 1980, then Namibia in 1990, and finally to the transfer of power in South Africa in 1994, which represented a form of 'independence' for that country. What happened in South Africa in 1994 completed the decolonisation of Southern Africa, as I define it. At the beginning of 1960, all of Southern Africa was still under either metropolitan (British, Portuguese, Belgian) colonial rule or white minority rule (South Africa, Rhodesia); as of 10 May 1994, when an African National Congress (ANC)-led government took power in South Africa, the entire region was freed of formal colonial or white minority rule. Taking the region as a whole, then, there are both evolutionary and revolutionary processes to explore in its decolonisation.

WAVES OF DECOLONISATION

Southern Africa's political decolonisation needs to be seen in the broader context of decolonisation as a general phenomenon. In *Decolonisation: A Very Short Introduction*, Dane Kennedy identifies four waves in the history of decolonisation, all related in some way to global wars (Kennedy 2016). He suggests that these waves are successive, that in some sense the one leads to the next, but presents little convincing evidence for this, even if phrases from the United States (US) Declaration of Independence were adopted by many subsequent countries when they became independent (Armitage 2007; Kennedy 2016). All empires eventually collapse, but, in his view, the collapse of, say, the Roman empire did not produce decolonisation, for decolonisation involves a transition from colonial rule to sovereign nation states. Transitions of that kind began in the late eighteenth century, he argues, the main example being that of the American colonies, following the Seven Years' War, and then that of, say, the independence of Haiti during the Napoleonic Wars. The second wave that Kennedy identifies follows the First World War, with the break-up of the Hapsburg and Ottoman empires and the emergence of new states in Europe and the Middle East, and perhaps too the creation of the mandate system for the former German colonies, though the end of German colonial rule in South West Africa in 1915 was followed by 75 years of South African rule. Kennedy's third wave is the one we most associate with the term decolonisation, following the Second World War: the emergence of the new nations in Asia, then Africa. His fourth wave comes with the end of the Cold War and the break-up of the Soviet empire, and the creation of the new states that emerged from that empire (Kennedy 2016).

Applying this wave metaphor to the decolonisation of Southern Africa, we can see that that decolonisation belongs primarily to the third and fourth waves. Though Kennedy's schema misses the evolutionary nature of British decolonisation, the key decades in the history of the decolonisation of Southern Africa are coterminous with those of the Cold War, which is therefore a major context within which the Southern African decolonisation process should be viewed (see, for example, Onslow 2009). Zimbabwe's independence was negotiated at Lancaster House in London in late 1979 in a lull in the Cold War, before the Soviet invasion of Afghanistan and the advent of the Cold War warrior Ronald Reagan in the US (Westad 2005). The Cold War context, in which the Soviet Union supported the presence of Cuban troops in Angola, and the US worked to remove those troops from Africa, helped to delay Namibian independence for a decade, until the Namibian settlement of December 1988 provided for the transition to Namibian independence and the withdrawal of the Cuban military from Angola. That settlement was made possible because of the winding down of the Cold War and a new Soviet willingness to accept a US-brokered settlement in south-western Africa (Saunders and Onslow 2010). The then South African president, F.W. de Klerk, often said that his breakthrough speech of 2 February 1990, in which he announced that his government would proceed to a negotiated settlement with the liberation movements he unbanned, was decisively influenced by the fall of the Berlin Wall the previous November (see, for example, De Klerk 1999, 160–161; Saunders 2019). After that, the apartheid government no longer feared Soviet intervention in Southern Africa.

If the Cold War context must be part of any explanation of why the decolonisation of Southern Africa took place when and in the way it did, there are, of course, other contexts to consider. By the 1960s, decolonisation was accepted as necessary and inevitable by the international community: in December 1960 the UN General Assembly passed its famous declaration on 'the granting of independence to colonial countries and peoples' (United Nations 1960). This stated, inter alia, that 'the subjection of peoples to alien subjugation, domination and exploitation constitutes a denial of fundamental human rights, is contrary to the Charter of the United Nations and is an impediment to the promotion of world peace and co-operation'. And the declaration continued: 'all peoples have the right to self-determination; by virtue of that right they freely determine their political status and freely pursue their economic, social and cultural development'. Portugal's authoritarian rulers tried to hold out against this, and they were able to do so until the Carnation Revolution in Lisbon in April 1974, in part because of Exercise Alcora, the secret close working relationship that developed with the white rulers of South Africa and Rhodesia to resist decolonisation in the region. That the full extent of that intercolonial cooperation has only recently been revealed (see especially De Meneses and McNamara 2018) suggests that the opening to scholars of other archival sources may still reveal important new aspects of the history of Southern African decolonisation.

BEGINNINGS

When does the process of decolonisation begin in Southern Africa, and why then? While the decolonisation of Southern Africa took place in the second half of the twentieth century, it nevertheless had a prehistory. A constitutional and evolutionary process took the Union of South

Africa, created in 1910, from dependent status within the British Empire to autonomous status within the Empire/Commonwealth. The Statute of Westminster, passed by the parliament of the United Kingdom in 1931, was adopted into South African law by the Status of the Union Act (No. 69 of 1934), which declared South Africa to be 'a sovereign independent state' and removed any power of the British parliament to legislate for South Africa and of the British monarch to grant assent to South African legislation (see Darwin 1988, 1999; Mansergh 1969). Before that, power had been effectively transferred from the imperial government to the colonies in South Africa by the granting of responsible government to the Cape Colony in 1872, to Natal in 1893, and then to the former Boer Republics after the South African War in the first decade of the twentieth century. Elsewhere in the British Empire, such devolutions of power were to colonists who constituted majority populations, but in South Africa, as in 1910, these grants of responsible government gave power to a white minority.

A further evolutionary process within the British Empire/Commonwealth took place in Southern Africa in the 1960s. After Britain had granted Tanganyika independence in 1961, and Kenya independence in 1963, Nyasaland and Northern Rhodesia became independent as Malawi and Zambia, as the Central African Federation broke up in 1964. A few years later, the British High Commission territories of Basutoland (which became Lesotho), Bechuanaland (renamed Botswana) and Swaziland (now eSwatini) became independent, also by a constitutional evolutionary process.

Though the coup in Lisbon in April 1974 was the proximate cause of the independence of Angola and Mozambique the following year, that coup followed wars in Portugal's territories in Africa that had begun in the early 1960s, wars that played their part in leading the junior officers in Lisbon to stage their coup (Macqueen 1997). And as in Angola and Mozambique, so in the cases where there was a negotiated settlement, the main liberation movements – ZANU-PF in Zimbabwe, SWAPO in Namibia and the ANC in South Africa – came to power, if in different ways and with different results (for details, see McKinley 1998; Southall 2013).

PSEUDO-DECOLONISATIONS

With this emergence of new black-ruled independent states in the region went attempts by the white minority regimes in South Africa and Southern Rhodesia to arrange forms of 'pseudo-decolonisations'. These were designed to help enable those regimes to retain power. One was the declaration of independence by the Rhodesian Front regime of Ian Smith in 1965, another the Bantustan policy of the South African government, which aimed to give so-called independence to relatively small areas, often highly fragmented, ruled by client groups. This policy of what was termed 'grand apartheid' was developed in the late 1950s by Prime Minister Hendrik Verwoerd in response to decolonisation elsewhere in Africa, to deflect international criticism of apartheid in South Africa and to divide internal resistance to it. The Bantustan policy, a form of internal decolonisation, was applied in both South West Africa/Namibia and South Africa itself. When the Transkei became the first Bantustan to be led to nominal 'independence' by the South African government in October 1976, only that government recognised it, because it was so obviously an apartheid creation. Though three other territories in South Africa were subsequently given nominal independence – Bophuthatswana, Ciskei and Venda – these experiments in pseudo-decolonisation were doomed to failure because they were not regarded by the international community as legitimate, since they lacked majority support (see Evans 2012).

The Namibian case is perhaps the most interesting example of how the decolonisation process changed over time. The occupying power, the South African government, decided in the 1960s that the Bantustan policy should be applied in what was then known as South West Africa. By the mid-1970s, however, in the face of an escalating armed struggle in the north of that territory, and after the International Court of Justice had given an advisory judgment in 1971 that South Africa's occupation of the territory was illegal and that South Africa should withdraw from it, the South African government accepted that the former German colony should be steered towards independence, and as one entity. The policy of promoting Bantustans there was dropped, and the South African government from 1975 sought to create conditions that would facilitate a handover of power to a regime that would rule the whole of South West Africa/Namibia in South African interests. This was the so-called Turnhalle option, named after a building of that name in Windhoek, the capital of the territory, where an internal dialogue took place. For a time, South Africa hoped that it could transfer power to the party that emerged from that dialogue, the Democratic Turnhalle Alliance (DTA), but the international community made it clear that it would not recognise the DTA, were it to come to power, for the process of dialogue had not included SWAPO, the leading nationalist party, recognised by the UN General Assembly in 1976 as the 'sole and authentic' representative of the Namibian people. SWAPO made clear that its armed struggle would continue until there was genuine independence (see, for example, Saunders 1992, 2002).

Although today SWAPO lays major emphasis on its armed struggle for liberation from 1966, its armed struggle alone did not produce independence. That came about as a direct result of a process begun with the implementation of UN Security Council Resolution 435 from 1 April 1989, a resolution that had been passed more than a decade earlier, in September 1978 (United Nations 1978). Although the formal metropole was South Africa, the UN saw Namibia as a special responsibility, and there was a lengthy working out of a plan for a transition to independence, via the Western Contact Group and other players (Iji 2011). In the war that took place in southern Angola, South African forces increasingly became bogged down in the face of sophisticated weaponry supplied by the Soviet Union and East Germany to the Angolan army and their Cuban allies.

Similarly in the South African case, it is possible to trace the origins of decolonisation to many different points in time. Although the process that led to the transfer of power in 1994 flowed from the breakthrough speech by President F.W. de Klerk on 2 February 1990, unbanning the ANC and other organisations (see Osaghae 1996, 1997), that speech was made in a context of increased pressure on the regime that had begun with the Soweto Uprising of June 1976, if not with the Sharpeville Massacre of March 1960, which led to the banning of the ANC and PAC and the decision by elements within the ANC leadership, in 1961, to adopt the armed struggle.

ENDINGS

When did the decolonisation of Southern Africa end, and why then? The end of colonial and apartheid rule came about in very different ways (see Holland et al. 2010) in the countries of the region. When Agostinho Neto, the leader of the MPLA, declared Angola's independence in Luanda on 11 November 1975, the Portuguese governor of Angola had already left the country, and the MPLA's forces, with Cuban assistance, were battling the forces of the National Front for the Liberation of Angola (FNLA) of Holden Roberto not far outside the capital.[2] In Zimbabwe, by contrast, the war had ended by the time the ceremony took place in the stadium in Salisbury in 1980, with Britain's Prince of Wales in attendance, marking the end of a very brief period of direct British rule of Rhodesia/Zimbabwe. Ten years later, in another ceremony, this time in the stadium in Windhoek on 21 March 1990, the UN secretary general was master of ceremonies when the South African flag came down before a large crowd, with the South African president present to see it happen, and the new Namibian flag was then run up the flagpole. Namibian independence meant an entirely new government coming to power under Sam Nujoma of SWAPO, which was not the case in South Africa, where there was also a negotiated settlement but of a quite different kind, out of which emerged in 1994 a government of national unity that was to last for five years. So, there was a range of different kinds of endings, some evolutionary, others constituting much more of a break and therefore, one can say, revolutionary.

* * *

Leo Marquard, a South African liberal critic of racial segregation, advanced the idea in 1944 that white minority rule was a form of colonial rule (Marquard 1944, 1958), and the idea was elaborated in the 1950s and 1960s by both liberals and the South African Communist Party (SACP). The latter saw South Africa as a sub-imperial power in the region, doing the bidding of imperial powers elsewhere, an example of what it termed 'colonialism of a special type'. For the SACP, South Africa was 'a junior partner of imperialism seeking to dominate the region on its own behalf and on behalf of imperialism', where there was 'a variant of capitalist rule in which the essential features of colonial domination in the imperialist epoch are maintained and even intensified', but where 'the colonial ruling class with its white support base on the one hand, and the oppressed colonial majority on the other, are located within a single country' (South African Communist Party 1962). The idea of 'colonialism of a special type' was taken up, for example, by the World Conference against Apartheid, Racism and Colonialism in Southern Africa, held in June 1977 in Lisbon in the aftermath of the independence of Mozambique and Angola. That conference endorsed 'the position of the African National Congress which declares that the people of South Africa, like those of Namibia and Zimbabwe, are colonised people'.[3] A declaration of the World Conference for Action against Apartheid held in Lagos, Nigeria, in August 1977 said much the same (South African History Online n.d.). If in South Africa a particular form of settler colonialism existed, despite the absence of a distinct metropole, the country had to undergo a process of decolonisation, in which power was transferred from the white minority to the majority.

Yet, South Africa under minority rule became a member of the League of Nations, then the UN, as a sovereign independent nation. Despite all the international hostility directed at white-ruled South Africa, both because of apartheid and because the international community recognised that South Africa's rule of Namibia was illegal, South Africa continued to be recognised in international law as a sovereign independent country – even if it was one that was, in the eyes of the UN General Assembly, guilty of what the Assembly in 1973 called 'a crime against humanity' (United Nations 1973). Though South Africa was forced to withdraw from the UN General Assembly in 1974, it remained a member of the UN itself and continued to participate in Security Council debates, even though increasingly a pariah in the international community. South Africa's effective decolonisation came in 1994, when power was at last transferred from a minority to the majority through a process generally recognised as legitimate, because the result of a democratic process was accepted by all parties.

Since the transfer of power in South Africa, a body of writing has appeared that sees that transfer as similar to what had taken place in the British and French colonies of tropical Africa, with one elite group taking over from another, ushering in a period of neocolonialism (see, for example, Saul 2014). As in the cases of Zimbabwe and Namibia, so in South Africa the party of liberation, the ANC, did agree to concessions in a negotiated decolonisation process, but the neocolonialism argument fails to recognise the agency of the liberation movements in power.

CONNECTIONS

The various stages of the decolonisation process in Southern Africa were, of course, not isolated from each other. What happened in the Congo in the early 1960s – the breakdown of order and UN intervention – had major repercussions elsewhere in the region, strengthening the set-tler resolve not to allow anything similar to happen in their countries (Passemiers 2016, 2019). There are many other examples of one case of decolonisation affecting another. When Mozambique and Angola moved to independence, the 'Viva Frelimo' rallies held in South Africa, and the appar-ent defeat of the South African Defence Force in Angola after the Cuban intervention there, stimulated resistance in South Africa, and fed into the Soweto Uprising of 1976 (Brown 2016). Robert Mugabe's coming to power in Zimbabwe in 1980 helped set back the independence of Namibia, because it strengthened resistance in the South African government to the idea of allowing an election in Namibia that SWAPO would win.

The way in which Namibia became independent, through an election in November 1989 that was declared free and fair and for a constituent assembly that then accepted a liberal democratic constitution, had an important influence on South Africa's transition of the early 1990s (Saunders 1992, 2010). Many other such interrelationships could be explored.

IN CONCLUSION

Any survey of the decolonisation of Southern Africa in the late twentieth century should consider it in the context of earlier processes of decolonisation and against the backdrop of the rise and decline of the influence of the Cold War on the region. There was great variety in the process, and the outcomes were very different. In the Namibian case, for example, unlike those of Mozambique and Angola, the former colonial power, South Africa, retained vast power over its former colony at independence. In Namibia, not even sovereignty over the new nation's only significant port, Walvis Bay, was transferred when the territory became independent in 1990, and it was not until February 1994 that Walvis Bay was reintegrated into independent Namibia. After that, Namibia remained heavily dependent on South Africa economically.

While in 1960 all of Southern Africa was under colonial or apartheid rule, on 10 May 1994 the decolonisation of Southern Africa may be said to have come to an end with the transfer of power to a majority government in South Africa. In explaining that process of change over more than three decades, we have seen that it is necessary to consider both revolutionary changes, in the form of armed struggles and de facto coups, along with evolutionary change. The decolonisations of the 1960s were mostly consensual, constitutional and relatively peaceful, despite strikes, riots and the imprisonment of some nationalist leaders, and evolutionary change continued in South Africa's decolonisation in 1994. While there was little if any continuity in the events leading to the independence of Angola and Mozambique, F.W. de Klerk and Nelson Mandela agreed that the process of transferring power in South Africa from the white minority to the majority should not involve a constitutional break, and so the new draft constitution that was approved by the multiparty negotiating forum in November 1993 went to the old South African parliament for its approval. So while, viewed as a whole, the decolonisation of Southern Africa in the late twentieth century, bringing about the end of colonial and white minority rule across the entire region, can be seen as a revolutionary process, at the same time there were important elements of continuity. All these need more elaboration than is possible here, and it is to be hoped that the decolonisation of the region, and the questions it throws up, only some of which have been considered here, will continue to attract the interest of historians.

NOTES

1   Some paragraphs in what follows draw upon Saunders (2000) and Saunders (2017). I acknowledge the support of the National Research Foundation for my research.
2   By far the fullest and most detailed work on the Cubans in Angola, based in part on Cuban archives in Havana, to which he had unique access, is Gleijeses (2013).
3   https://omalley.nelsonmandela.org/index.php/site/q/03lv02424/04lv02730/05l v03005/06lv03132/07lv03140/08lv03144.htm (accessed April 2019).

REFERENCES

Armitage, David. 2007. *The Declaration of Independence: A Global History*. Cambridge, MA: Harvard University Press.
Brown, Julian. 2016. *The Road to Soweto: Resistance and the Uprising of 16 June 1976*. Melton, Woodbridge: James Currey.
Darwin, John. 1988. *Britain and Decolonization: The Retreat from Empire in the Post-War World*. Basingstoke: Macmillan Educational.
Darwin, John. 1999. 'Decolonization and the End of Empire'. In *The Oxford History of the British Empire: Volume V: Historiography*, edited by Robin Winks, 541–557. Oxford: Oxford University Press.
De Klerk, F.W. (Frederik Willem). 1999. *The Last Trek: A New Beginning*. London: Pan Books.
De Meneses, Filipe and Robert McNamara. 2018. *The White Redoubt, the Great Powers and the Struggle for Southern Africa, 1960–1980*. London: Palgrave Macmillan.
Evans, Laura. 2012. 'South Africa's Bantustans and the Dynamics of '"Decolonization": Reflections on Writing Histories of the Homelands'. *South African Historical Journal* 64 (1): 117–137. https://doi.org/10.1080/02582473.2012.655941.
Fanon, Frantz. 1963. *The Wretched of the Earth*. Translated by Constance Farrington. New York: Grove Press.

Gleijeses, Piero. 2013. *Visions of Freedom: Havana, Washington, Pretoria and the Struggle for Southern Africa*. Chapel Hill: University of North Carolina Press and Johannesburg: Wits University Press.

Gordon, Robert. 2013. 'Moritz Bonn, Southern Africa and the Critique of Colonialism'. *African Historical Review* 45 (2): 1–30. https://doi.org/10.1080/17532523.2013.857089.

Holland, Robert, Susan Williams and Terry Barringer (eds). 2010. *The Iconography of Independence: 'Freedoms at Midnight'*. London: Routledge.

Iji, Tetsuro. 2011. 'Contact Group Diplomacy: The Strategies of the Western Contact Group in Mediating Namibian Conflict'. *Diplomacy and Statecraft* 22 (4): 634–650. https://doi.org/10.1080/09592296.2011.625819.

Kennedy, Dane. 2016. *Decolonisation: A Very Short Introduction*. Oxford: Oxford University Press.

Macqueen, Norrie. 1997. *The Decolonization of Portuguese Africa: Metropolitan Revolution and the Dissolution of Empire*. London: Longman.

Mansergh, Nicholas. 1969. *The Commonwealth Experience: From British to Multiracial Commonwealth*. Toronto: University of Toronto Press.

Marquard, Leo (pseudonym John Burger). 1944. *The Black Man's Burden*. London: Gollancz.

Marquard, Leo. 1958. *South Africa's Internal Boundaries*. Johannesburg: South African Institute of Race Relations.

McKinley, Dale. 1998. *The ANC and the Liberation Struggle: A Critical Political Biography*. London: Pluto Press.

O'Malley, Alana. 2018. *The Diplomacy of Decolonisation: America, Britain and the United Nations during the Congo Crisis, 1960–1964*. Manchester: Manchester University Press.

Onslow, Sue (ed.). 2009. *Cold War in Southern Africa: White Power, Black Liberation*. London: Routledge.

Osaghae, Eghosa E. 1996. 'The Global and Regional Contexts of South Africa's Democratic Transition'. *Politikon* 23 (2): 36–53. https://doi.org/10.1080/02589349608705035.

Osaghae, Eghosa E. 1997. 'The Missing (African) Link in the Comparative Analysis of South Africa's Transition'. *African Sociological Review* 1 (2): 1–21. https://www.jstor.org/stable/24487362.

Parliament of South Africa. 1934. *Status of the Union Act (No. 69 of 1934)*. Cape Town: Parliament of South Africa.

Passemiers, Lazlo. 2016. 'South Africa and the Congo Crisis, 1960–1965'. PhD dissertation, University of the Free State. https://scholar.ufs.ac.za/bitstream/handle/11660/4792/PassemiersLPC.pdf?sequence=1&isAllowed=y.

Passemiers, Lazlo. 2019. *Decolonisation and Regional Geopolitics: South Africa and the 'Congo Crisis', 1960–1965*. London: Routledge.

Rothermund, Dietmar. 2006. *The Routledge Companion to Decolonization*. London: Routledge.

Sapire, Hilary and Chris Saunders. 2012. 'Liberation Struggles in Southern Africa in Context'. In *Southern African Liberation Struggles: New Local, Regional and Global Perspectives*, edited by Hilary Sapire and Chris Saunders, 1–31. Cape Town: University of Cape Town Press.

Saul, John S. 1993. *Recolonization and Resistance in Southern Africa in the 1990s*. Trenton: Africa World Press.

Saul, John S. 2008. *Decolonisation and Empire*. Monmouth: Merlin Press.

Saul, John S. 2014. *A Flawed Freedom: Rethinking Southern African Liberation*. Cape Town: University of Cape Town Press.

Saunders, Chris. 1992. 'The Transition in Namibia and the South African Case'. In *Peace, Politics and Violence in the New South Africa*, edited by Norman Etherington, 213–230. Oxford: Oxford University Press.

Saunders, Chris. 2000. 'The Transitions from Apartheid to Democracy in Namibia and South Africa in the Context of Decolonization'. *Journal of Colonialism and Colonial History* 1 (1). Project MUSE. https://doi.org/10.1353/cch.2000.0003.

Saunders, Chris. 2002. 'Namibia's Freedom Struggle: The Nujoma Version'. *South African Historical Journal* 47 (1): 203–212. https://doi.org/10.1080/02582470208671441.

Saunders, Chris. 2010. 'The Ending of the Cold War and Southern Africa'. In *The End of the Cold War and the Third World*, edited by Artemy Kalinovsky and Sergey Radchenko, 264–277. London: Routledge.

Saunders, Chris. 2017. 'Decolonization in Southern Africa: Reflections on the Namibian and South African Cases'. *Southern Journal for Contemporary History* 42 (1): 99–114. https://dx.doi.org/10.18820/24150509/JCH42.V1.6.

Saunders, Chris. 2019. 'The Fall of the Berlin Wall and Namibian Independence'. *New Global Studies* 13 (3): 351–356. https://doi.org/10.1515/ngs-2019-0033.

Saunders, Chris and Sue Onslow. 2010. 'The Cold War in Southern Africa, c.1975–1990'. In *Cambridge History of the Cold War*, edited by Melvyn P. Leffler and Odd Arne Westad, 222–243. Cambridge: Cambridge University Press.

South African Communist Party. 1962. *The Road to South African Freedom*. London: Inkululeko Publications. https://www.marxists.org/history/international/comintern/sections/sacp/1962/road-freedom.htm (accessed December 2022).

South African History Online. n.d. 'Lagos Declaration against Apartheid'. https://www.sahistory.org.za/archive/lagos-declaration-against-apartheid (accessed April 2019).

Southall, Roger. 2013. *Liberation Movements in Power*. Pietermaritzburg: University of KwaZulu-Natal Press.

United Nations. 1960. 'Declaration on the Granting of Independence to Colonial Countries and Peoples, Adopted by General Assembly Resolution 1514 (XV) of 14 December'. https://www.ohchr.org/en/instruments-mechanisms/instruments/declaration-granting-independence-colonial-countries-and-peoples (accessed 30 December 2022).

United Nations. 1973. 'International Convention on the Suppression and Punishment of the Crime of Apartheid, Adopted by the General Assembly of the United Nations on 30 November 1973'. https://treaties.un.org/doc/publication/unts/volume%201015/volume-1015-i-14861-english.pdf (accessed 30 December 2022).

United Nations. 1978. 'Security Council Resolution 435 (1978): Namibia', 29 September 1978. https://peacemaker.un.org/namibia-resolution435 (accessed 8 January 2023).

Westad, Odd Arne (2005). *The Global Cold War*. Cambridge: Cambridge University Press.

3

The Border of Trust at Kat River for Coloured Settlers, 1851–1853

Christopher Allsobrook and Camilla Boisen

Decolonisation has proved a productive trope for critique over the past decade of the epistemic injustice of exclusionary Eurocentric hegemony in the Western academy, and for inclusion of alternative, heterogeneous and diverse voices. Whereas this rapid uptake of decolonial research gives the impression that the project began recently, we should remember that the struggle for decolonisation is practically coterminous with colonisation. The legacy of colonialism influences the struggle for decolonisation. In the drive to epistemic decolonisation, we must be careful not to dismiss the contributions of those who left this legacy behind, nor to repeat their errors. The tale presented in this chapter of colonial loyalty, of the coloured missionary settler, James Read Jr (1811–1894), and anti-imperial rebellion, of the coloured colonial settlers of the Kat River Settlement (KRS), reminds us of the complexity of the task.[1] On the one hand, it teaches us to appreciate the value and attraction of colonial ideology for colonised subjects, and how colonial ideology influenced the struggle for decolonisation. On the other hand, we learn not to underestimate the willingness to abandon universalism, and the attraction of decolonisation for imperial powers. The metropole proved suspiciously receptive to decolonisation. Ignorance of such ideological complexity leads to anachronistic misunderstanding of decolonial agency in the history of colonialism. Ignorance of the imperial impetus towards decolonisation may also perpetuate epistemic injustices of colonialism, perversely, through our own efforts to decolonise.

The KRS was established by the British in 1829 as a frontier buffer zone of coloured settlers, between the Cape Colony and the isiXhosa-speaking territories. The Kat River settlers divided sharply over which side to join in the Eighth Frontier War (1850–1853). Only a minority joined the rebellion against the Colony. The local pastor, James Read Jr, who tells the tale we retrieve, was no brave nationalist hero but equally, he was no colonial dupe. Nevertheless, his loyalty to the British during the Kat River Rebellion puts him in a separate category from archetypical liberation leaders. He was a moderate Victorian colonial gentleman who advocated for British sovereignty in the eastern Cape Colony as a basis for Khoisan/coloured rights of citizenship. Had they all followed Read's advice, the Kat River settlers could have remained independent. Instead, greedy white neighbours used the uprising as an excuse to crush the settlement and seize its fertile land.

The Kat River Rebellion was interpreted by white colonists as a rejection of British rule and as proof that the coloured settlers were not yet adequately civilised to be trusted as fellow citizens. More recently, Robert Ross (2003, 2014) interprets the uprising in terms of proto-nationalist Black Consciousness, as an early instance of coloured unity with other oppressed indigenous black peoples against colonial oppression. But these interpretations mistake the rebellion for a rejection of colonialism and colonial legitimacy and neglect the loyalists' position. As such, they underestimate the value and attraction of the ideology of assimilative trusteeship (see Allsobrook and Boisen 2017) for these pioneering, coloured, settler citizens of the far east Cape frontier, and, significantly, the influence of this colonial ideology on the interpretation of decolonisation espoused by those who rebelled. Our account of this uprising against colonial authority shows how colonial ideology can serve the cause of the conquered, and its rejection, the cause of the conqueror. Thus, this case study points to an ambiguity in the teleology of trusteeship ideology, which we draw out to explain how it engenders and accommodates resistance, appealing to rights of self-determination, liberty and law to justify imperial sovereignty. Read Jr was the last native speaker of eastern Cape Khoekhoen (Ross 2014, 20) and the first historian of the Kat River Rebellion. He described himself in 1834 as a liberal who believed in the rights of man, Christianity, civilisation and the rule of law, all of which would save the Khoisan from degradation and injustice (Elbourne 2000, 38). As a scion of racial miscegenation and an employee of the London Missionary Society (LMS), 'he had a personal stake in the idea of racial equality through Christian piety, which the Kat River represented' (Carline 2015, 23). Having failed to quell the rebellion against the British, his foremost impulse was to attend to history, immediately, to keep an assiduous record of these events, to preserve a sympathetic account for the public of the grievances and enduring fealty of respectable Kat River burghers. But, in the end, the white settler narrative of race war and African nationalism dominated, which subsequent revisionist historians, ironically, have valorised (see, for instance, Blackbeard 2018; Carline 2015; Elbourne 2000; Ross 2003, 2014; Trapido 1992).

Departing from this historiographical presentism, we argue that, far from being an instance or expression of nascent Khoisan nationalism, or a rejection of colonial ideology, both sides of the Kat River Rebellion were motivated by the colonial ideology of trusteeship (Allsobrook and Boisen 2017). The colonial ideology of assimilative trusteeship legitimised the social order of empire by clothing it in enlightened aspirational principles of emancipation and salvation. The basic motivation for trusteeship is the expropriation of land from indigenous inhabitants, for the exploitation of its resources. Yet, its moral, political and epistemic authority depends on

its promise of self-determination for conquered, enslaved and then eman-
cipated subjects (Boisen 2017). As we have argued elsewhere, the history
of the Cape colonial administration exemplifies an adaptive fusion of universalism and relativism, where trusteeship evolves from an *assimilationist*
ideal into a justification for *national segregation*, wherein plural ethnic
principalities are encouraged to pursue self-determination under imperial
hegemony (see Allsobrook and Boisen 2017). This study of the ambiguous
legacy of trusteeship ideology follows a decisive, historically significant slip
from assimilationist trusteeship at Kat River.

The 1820 British settlers of Albany (the KRS' white neighbours)
undermined this ambitious project for native upliftment, on the grounds
that it did not promote Khoisan welfare. But Read Jr observes that these
settlers, represented by Robert Godlonton, saw civilisation as an inevitable process that would cause 'the black man' to melt away before
the white (Read Jr 1852, 73).[2] Ultimately, the push towards industrial
development put an end to the ideology of assimilation in South Africa,
with the discovery of diamonds and gold in the interior. Though masked
by the extension of the franchise thereafter, in the so-called golden
age of Cape liberalism, the imperial ideology of equal rights for all
British subjects was already considerably discredited with the destruction of the KRS. This was shortly before a general panic about race
warfare spread out across the Colony and the empire, with uprisings
in India (1857) and in Morant Bay, Jamaica (1865). Trusteeship ideology
takes a decisive, historically significant racist turn at Kat River away from
the colonial ideology of assimilation, under covering law universalism,
towards the more recognisably postcolonial ideology of cultural relativist national segregation and independence.[3] The Kat River Rebellion
confronts the ideology of assimilationist trusteeship with its hypocrisy,
foreboding a turn away from the burden of assimilation and direct rule
towards imperial support for segregated, subordinate principalities.
The remainder of the territory occupied by isiXhosa-speaking inhabitants was not colonised but annexed, like Bechuanaland (Botswana)
and Basotholand (Lesotho). While the rebellion did signify a move away

from imposing a universal ideal of (European) civilisation on diverse races, its proto-nationalist parole was not a rejection of empire but an expression of imperial subjectivity.

COLONIAL SETTLEMENT OF KHOISAN SETTLERS IN THE KAT RIVER VALLEYS

Expropriation of large tracts of land from the amaXhosa on the eastern frontier of the Cape Colony during the eighteenth century by white farmers had forced Khoisan inhabitants of the area to become servants on white farms and in towns of the eastern Cape. By the 1830s, the British authorities, who had replaced the Dutch, found themselves trying to govern a complex mixture of ethnic groupings. These included those who would become known as the 'Cape coloured' population. Second, there were white settlers, comprising two distinct groups: Afrikaner *trekboers* and the 1820 Settlers. Third, there were the amaXhosa, with their numbers steadily increasing as colonial borders were extended by progressive annexation of their land. Finally, there were other Bantu groups, such as the amaMfengu. In the interior, the colonial authorities allowed these groups to settle in the colony as farmers to act as a buffer against the amaXhosa (Swain et al. 2003, 89).

This complex mesh of ethnic and colonial groupings and appropriation of indigenous lands was instrumental both in the founding of the KRS in 1829 as well in its destruction in 1851. It was situated at the frontier of the British Empire's legitimating enterprise of trusteeship, whereby Europeans dutifully held land in trust for indigenous peoples, until they reached a stage of civilisation deemed appropriate by their trustees (Boisen 2017). To this end, Ross argues that 'respectability', by European standards, was a major goal for all the colony's inhabitants (Ross 1999, 341). The Kat River settlers, Read Jr claimed, proved themselves worthy, respectable subjects, products of the civilising mission. He wrote that 'the progress of the settlement in agricultural pursuits, cattle breeding, rearing of horses, the establishment of schools, the spread of civilization, sobriety, and the formation of missionary, bible, temperance and teetotal societies was rapid; and the rights of citizens were conceded to by the Government' (1852, x). Yet, full equality with whites was held off indefinitely by spurious measures. Outside of missionary circles, 'racism trumped any ideas of a common behavioural code' (Ross 1999, 343). Thus, the assimilationist ideology of colonial trusteeship was distrusted by white colonists.

Factors for Khoisan settlement in the Kat River valleys

The gradual introduction of liberalism, during the first decades of British administration at the Cape, included formal measures to recognise aboriginal title. Ordinance No. 50 of 1828 guaranteed equal legal rights to all free persons of colour to acquire land on a par with the European settlers, although in practice most Khoisan were landless and few could afford to buy land (Boisen 2017, 332; Bradlow 1983). Read Jr claimed that Ordinance 50 was considered 'the charter of Hottentot liberty'. It 'placed the natives of the Colony on an equal footing with the whites, in the sight of the law'. They 'became free men, and British subjects, in all respects' (Read Jr 1852, x). The legislation removed pass laws, and permitted property ownership for Khoisan, allowing them to withdraw labour for others. Andries Stockenström, the commissioner general of British Kaffraria (the present-day districts of King William's Town and East London), reported that Khoisan families were allotted land in the KRS, since the governor saw that the granting of equal rights could not work 'without a fair field opened for the exertions of its industry' (*Report of the Parliamentary Select Committee on Aboriginal Tribes* [RPSCAT] 1837, 85). This led many freed Khoisan slaves and other displaced groups of mixed ethnicities, without land or tribal leaders, to settle in the KRS, which entered a period of relative prosperity, at least until 1846.

The granting of the franchise to native Africans owed much to the influence of colonial ideology of assimilative trusteeship preached by humanitarian missionaries in the first half of the nineteenth century. The LMS missionary Dr John Philip and his fellow Cape missionaries promoted a Victorian civilising ideal that aimed at Christian conversion of the

Cape's indigenous population. They gave the expectation that conversion was not only spiritually valuable, but – if the Khoisan obeyed a code of respectability – would also provide for material progress and political benefits, including the granting of civil rights. The first delivery of this promise was Ordinance 50 (Ross 1999, 333). Representative government and the free market were championed by Philip and allies such as his son-in-law, John Fairbairn, a newspaper editor in Cape Town, and his colleague, Thomas Pringle (Trapido 1992, 37). Equal rights were seen by the imperial government as the best way to keep peace, loyalty and common interest (Swain et al. 2003, 93). In establishing the KRS, Stockenström hoped for assimilation of European ideas and law of property, to encourage the development of an educated, hard-working, self-subsistent, churchgoing, tax-paying, temperate community (2003, 95).

Fairbairn's newspaper argued that conversion to Christianity, consumption of British manufactures, and the natural incentive of economic self-interest would transform the Khoisan 'from the state of wandering and mischievous Barbarians to that of fixed and peaceable Citizens' (*South African Commercial Advertiser* [*SACA*], 4 April 1829, 15 August 1829). 'Give [the Khoisan] positive material interest in the soil they cultivate,' wrote one correspondent, to teach them the value of property and self-interest (*SACA*, 18 December 1830). The benefits of the civilising mission were met with considerable scepticism by the settlers themselves. As one Albany farmer responded, 'something more forcible than Religious Instruction, good [living], or good wages, [is necessary to] make an adult Hottentot of the present day faithful and industrious' (*SACA*, 4 April 1829).[4] British imperial humanitarianism professed a demonstrable concern for the condition of the native peoples and hoped that extending 'the benefits of "civilization"' would 'enable them to cope with the disastrous ills of colonization' (Elbourne 2003, n.p.). The Afrikaner political historians André du Toit and Herman Giliomee argue that 'officials at the Cape … regarded the unrestrained domination and complete subordination of their labourers as a major moral and political problem'. They were 'responsive to the paternalistic concerns of British imperial policy with the rights and liberties of its subject peoples ... combined with equality before the law ... [L]abour oppression was not only wrong but not in the interests of state', breeding discontent and resistance, and requiring extraordinary measures, expense and trouble (Du Toit and Giliomee 1983, 81). The colonial ideology of assimilative trusteeship that supported social rights for conquered subjects aligned with the enlightened self-interest of imperial power.

This insight is evident in the warning of the *RPSCAT*:

> The oppression of the natives of barbarous countries ... in point of economy, of security, of commerce, of reputation ... is a short-sighted and disastrous policy ... a burthen on the empire. It has thrown impediments in the way of successful colonisation; it has engendered wars, in which great expenses were necessarily incurred, and no reputation could be won; and it has banished from our confines, or exterminated the natives, who might have been profitable workmen, good customers, and good neighbours. (1837, 104)

At home, in Britain, the missionaries were instrumental in raising the moral issue of administering good empire policies to ensure and to promote the well-being of *all* the queen's subjects. As Alan Lester notes, it was the testimony of missionaries, blaming white settlers for the killing and dispossessing of indigenous people in their search for material gain, that chiefly promoted a common humanitarian narrative in Britain's colonial missions (Lester 2008). The push for such testimonials was spearheaded by the social reformer and leader of the abolitionist movement, Thomas Fowell Buxton, and Philip, who initiated parliament's Select Committee on Aborigines (British Settlements) of 1836–1837. This was the high point of imperial support for the KRS and its missionaries, reflecting the influence of the 'Clapham Sect' in parliament, who took pains to ensure that the morality of British colonisation was at the forefront of debate (Lester 2008, 66; Porter 1985, 601).

Philip saw the promotion of the Protestant work ethic and of liberal economic virtues as central to Christian education. His testimony to the Select Committee on Aborigines on 15 June 1836 shows that he recognised the economic colonial rationale for trusteeship ideology, in that his missionary work was helping to create ready markets for European manufactures (*Report from the Select Committee on the Aborigines (British Settlements)* [*RSCA*] 1836, 549–626). Giving his testimony (on 28 August 1835), Stockenström presented the KRS as an ideal picture of the achievements of which Christianised, educated and civilised indigenous people were capable. He described the Khoisan as having worked hard to cut canals and to grow 'an abundance of pumpkins, Indian corn, peas, beans, etc.'. They had enthusiastically taken to churchgoing, as well as attending schools and restraint societies, they were now costing the government nothing and were paying taxes like the settlers. Furthermore, they were even helping to make the frontier of the colony safe, having 'repulsed the Caffres on every occasion on which they have been attacked' (*RSCA* 1836, 154).

The Reads were received as 'star witnesses' at the committee hearings in London and praised for their successful work in bringing civilisation to the KRS (Ross 2014, 137–138). 'In order to raise the people, James Read treats them as brethren,' enthused Philip (McDonald 2010, 524). 'We are all born savages,' writes Philip, '[i]t is the discipline of education and the circumstances in which we are placed that create the differences between the rude barbarian and the polished citizen' (Philip 1828, 316). Philip and Stockenström enthused at length about the success of the KRS, deeming it an excellent working model of their goals:

> They have cost the government nothing but the salary of their minister … they pay every tax … they have rendered the Kat River decidedly by far the safest part of the frontier … The most prejudiced men who have travelled through the locations admit that the Hottentots have done wonders. (*RSCA* 1836, 154)

By 1834, there were more than 4 000 Khoisan settlers at Kat River and, by 1841, upward of 60 dams, with almost 200 kilometres of irrigation furrows (Ross 2014, 57). The settlers had rapidly satisfied normative standards of colonial 'improvement' to the point where they could expect to assimilate. But such expectations of mutual recognition – not unexpectedly – were disappointed. The colonial effort to set a more 'humanitarian' agenda proved short-lived. By the mid-nineteenth century, most proponents were disillusioned by this sort of 'experiment', which presented a serious 'political challenge to British settler practices' (Lester 2008, 65).

By the mid-nineteenth century, with the families of an increasing proportion of emigrating Britons facing violent resistance abroad, humanitarians became figures of ridicule in Britain. Charles Dickens portrayed the aborted Niger Exploration of 1841 as a 'prime example of philanthropic folly' (Lester 2008, 82).[5] The legitimating ideal of assimilation under trusteeship quickly lost its lustre, set against political-economic challenges of white settler greed, anticolonial resistance, and ideological challenges to covering law universalism from cultural relativism and social Darwinism (see also Allsobrook and Boisen 2017). And so, these self-same ideological standards of normative legitimation soon proved double-edged, laying the basis for a radical Christian critique of colonial hypocrisy, developed in urgent meetings at the LMS church at Philipton. The site of the rebellion at Kat River marks a signpost at this disillusioned crossroad in trusteeship ideology, as imperial relations with colonial subjects crossed over towards cultural segregation.

Factors against a Khoisan Kat River Settlement

Ordinance 50 and emancipation achieved formal legal equality for the Khoisan and for former slaves; yet drastic social displacement limited their likelihood of qualification. Equal opportunities for access to resources did not follow. As Edna Bradlow notes, 'emancipation did not liberalize white opinion substantively' (1989, 403). In fact, following the Legislative Council enquiry of September 1841 into the workings of Ordinance 50, white opinion was largely in agreement on the urgent need for a vagrant law, to better control the flow of labour and prevent 'idle' pastoralists subsisting on Crown land or on the interstices of oversized white farms, and 'stealing' stock.

However, the Khoisan underclass was acutely aware that if the government revived vagrancy legislation it would seriously impede their chances of self-employment as farmers. Such legislation confirmed the allegations of frontier rebels that the interests of the Khoisan population were deemed inferior to those of white colonists (Bradlow 1989, 409). The public campaign for vagrancy legislation – principally by the Albany settlers around Grahamstown, led by the newspaper editor, Robert Godlonton – was interpreted by the Kat River settlers as an aggressive affront to Ordinance 50, the cornerstone of their liberty and their rights as imperial subjects. The Kat River people were aware of what was said of them in the press, and the issue caused considerable distrust on both sides, sharpening racial awareness and fomenting mutual antipathy.

Contacts between the Kat River settlers and the amaXhosa were regular and most often peaceful. Chief Maqoma, leader of the neighbouring Rharhabe Xhosa, who had been expelled from the area, came to hear a sermon by Read Jr, after which he celebrated their good relationship. This provoked suspicion of sedition spreading from the LMS mission when the colonists found out, compounded by KRS settlers' agitation against vagrancy laws and by their involvement in the 1836–1837 Aborigines Committee hearings after the war. Playing into this distrust, Maqoma spread strategic rumours that the Khoisan were ready to join the amaXhosa in their attack, which commenced on Christmas Day, 1834. In the event, however, the amaXhosa destroyed the KRS during the Sixth Frontier War, and the Kat River levies were praised by Governor Benjamin D'Urban and Commander Sir Harry Smith for their outstanding contribution (Ross 2014, 80–88, 103, 111, 143). The Kat River Levy of 500 men was the strongest of all burgher forces in this war (Blackbeard 2018, 75). Ten years later, in the Seventh Frontier War of 1846 (the 'War of the Axe'), approximately 1 000 poorly supplied KRS men, constituting 90 per cent of adult males (in contrast with 3 per cent of men in the rest of the Colony), served for free, and for longer than others, who were better supplied and who were given disproportionate spoil in cattle. The military commander, Henry Somerset, remarked that the Khoisan were much more useful in the war than the Boers and the English (Ross 2014, 156, 158, 160, 164). Read Jr claimed that it was 'the cheapest frontier force', on which victory was 'heavily dependent' (Read Jr 1852, xi). Yet, while they were off fighting, the KRS was destroyed, again, with devastating effect.

During the 1840s, the labour shortage became 'the great question', as Reverend William Thompson of the LMS noted (Bradlow 1989, 419). Legislative proposals such as the Vagrancy Bill, and its successor, the Squatters Bill, demonstrated the white farmers' incessant quest for cheap labour and for commercial agricultural growth. This was enough to provoke Khoisan anxieties about a return to their former legal inequality, prior to the imposition of Ordinance 50 (Read Jr 1852, 419). In a letter to Reverend Thompson, Read Jr noted that the framing of the 'Vagrant Act' 'shocked the moral sense of the KRS ... and indicated a want of proper regards to the rights of men and fellow-subjects' (1852, x). The liberal historian William M. Macmillan forcefully presented the contradiction between emancipation and labour policy. It would seem that 'the policy which triumphed in 1828 seemed to commit the Government to plans which must make it possible for numbers of the Coloured people to rise to be something better than common if not servile, labour[er]s' (Macmillan 1968, 233).

To this end, of self-disciplined autonomy, missionaries had educated the Khoisan well and, in so doing, kept to their end of the colonising bargain, in providing a good education for the Khoisan people at the KRS, which, as Philip notes 'is equal to anything we have in any country in Europe' (Philip testimony, 11 July 1836, *RSCA* 1836, 644). Read Jr's schools made a huge impact in spreading literacy to their converts, and the Khoisan settlers often stated that literacy brought them political benefits. But accompanying aspirations for full equality, upheld by early missionaries and increasingly at odds with white colonists' ambitions, were also the chief cause of the rebellion.

For Philip and his fellow missionaries, the Khoisan of the KRS had proved themselves worthy of political equality by exemplifying the model of Christianised, educated and civilised people. But in the Sixth and Seventh Frontier Wars against the amaXhosa they suffered a considerable loss of land and cattle, and they were increasingly mistreated by colonial authorities. In his letter to Colonial Secretary John Montagu, Stockenström warned:

> The Kat River people – so lately and so justly considered one of the most loyal communities in the Colony – after having been twice mainly instrumental in saving the Colony, and being rewarded by malicious calumny and the denial of justice, have from later events, taken it into their heads that a plot exists somewhere to goad them on to some excess, and furnish the plea for their expulsion from the only nook in the land of their fathers which remains to them, and in which they hoped to rest the last ashes of their expiring race. ('Letter to Montagu', 11 July 1850, cited in Stockenström 1887, 431)

In the War of the Axe of 1846, 5 000 Kat River settlers had been kept in concentration camps (for 'safe keeping') where conditions were harsh, and many died. As Read Jr described the situation, religious feelings were 'very much deteriorated and many of the young were drawn into sinful courses' (Read Jr, cited in Ross 2014, 162).

After Maqoma surrendered in 1847, Kat River settler grievances were compounded by the appointment of a succession of 'vulgar partisan' magistrates at the KRS, T.J. Biddulph and then T.H. Bowker, both of whom were allied with the hostile English settlers in Grahamstown (Read Jr 1852, 169–170; see also Elbourne 2000, 25). 'Smith was most impartial', Read Jr complained, with frustration, despite 'his sympathy for the Kat River people' (1852, xv). He continued, 'all know that Sir H[arry Smith] and

Gen[eral] Somerset are entirely under the influence of the Albany people, whose cry is ever war, war, war' (Read Jr, cited in Carline 2015, 30). This alienated the Kat River settlers and destroyed 'the confidence which good subjects should have in just Government' (Read Jr 1852, xix). Against these observations by Read Jr, Smith claimed, 'it is confidently believed ... that some vile agitators within the Colony have excited these Coloured Classes to engage in a revolution against the White Man which these Radicals had not expected' (Elbourne 2000, 29). In fact, it was, as Ross puts it, 'a very Christian uprising ... although the Reads were rather embarrassed to admit it' (Ross 2014, 260). Elizabeth Elbourne identifies considerable evidence that radical Christian millenarian ideas animated the rebellion (1992, 2000). Significantly for our argument, it was betrayal of colonial ideologies of assimilative trusteeship, in which the KRS was invested, which provoked discontent, and not rejection of the ideology.

The five years between the wars marked a period when British authorities, prompted by colonists, 'demolished the coloureds' claim to equal treatment alongside whites' (Kirk 1973, 419). The British failed to recognise that the Kat River settlers had the same legal rights as white colonists (1973, 422). Pressure for vagrancy legislation and colonial home government spread fear among the Khoisan that their liberties as British subjects were under threat from colonists (Ross 2014, 187). Read Jr feared a state controlled by hostile colonists would not oblige non-whites (Kirk 1973, 423). When it became clear, in late 1850, that the peace settlement was about to break down, the Cape Government ordered levies to be mustered, but this was deeply unpopular in the wake of recent devastation. As Read Jr explained, they 'appealed against conscription in 1850, since wars had impoverished them and they had not been rewarded well for service, and another war would destroy the settlement for good' (Read Jr 1852, 6). They asked, instead, to be given permission to serve in their own district. The Dutch also refused, suspicious of the motives for war, which served the interest of a Grahamstown clique who profited by arming both sides (Ross 2014, 194). When the Eighth Frontier

War broke out in December 1850, the Kat River settlers refused to fight on the colonial side. In 1851, a considerable minority of them (along with some Khoi from other mission stations, the Cape Corps and farm labourers' ranks) went over to the other side, to fight against the British (Swain et al. 2003, 96–97).[6] The war became, wrote Read Jr, 'a war of races' (Read Jr 1852, 102).

Failing to appreciate the significance of strong links between the Kat River settlers and the amaXhosa, and the impact of repeated destruction in war of the KRS, on whose levies the security of the Colony was heavily dependent (Ross 2003, 117), the British government was surprised by the rebellion of a minority of Kat River settlers. A dispatch home to Earl Grey (Henry George), the Secretary of State for War and the Colonies, by Sir Harry Smith, conveys the ideological significance:

> I cannot avoid commenting, while upon the subject of this Hottentot revolution, upon an occurrence of so unaccountable a nature, and one unprecedented, I believe, in the history of the world. A mass of civilized men, the greater part born in the Christian faith, and the remainder converted and improving Christians, for years assembled in societies and villages under excellent clergymen, suddenly, and without any cause whatever, rush back, in nearly one torrent, to barbarism and savage life. This extraordinary proceeding must be ascribed either to the in-born evil propensities of man, and the natural objection inherent in his composition to subject himself to rule and the restraint of civilization, or to an agitation said to have been stirred up among these people, respecting which, however, I have as yet gathered no definite information, although it has been very generally declared that such is the fact.[7]

Unwilling or unable to accord full agency to the Khoisan (Elbourne 2000, 38) or to credit their genuine grievances, the British settlers blamed meddlesome missionaries for stirring up rebellion with their radical ideals (albeit the very ideals that legitimated imperial enterprise!). Earl Grey, in wishing to see a quick resolution of the rebellion, remarked that it was ever the duty of officers 'representing a civilised and Christian power to carry severity no farther than is indispensable for this purpose [in dealing with the rebellion], and to endeavour not to exterminate, but to reclaim and civilise, these fierce barbarians'.[8]

It is important to highlight, as Ross has done, that the rebellion was essentially a Christian movement, moved by the colonial ideology of the civilising mission. The Khoisan rebel leader Willem Uithaalder wrote in a plea to get the Griqua to join the rebellion:

> ... we, the poor and oppressed Hottentot race are objects of the present war ... who have been for a considerable time oppressed by the unrighteous English settler who have so continually petitioned the Government by memorials for consent and execution of irregular and oppressive laws, such as Vagrant Laws, which tend to the oppression and complete ruin of the Coloured and the poor of this land – a land which we as natives may justly claim as our motherland ... (Uithaalder, cited in Ross 1999, 344)

At the heart of Khoisan grievances was the issue that they were denied their rights as imperial subjects, which was part of the emancipatory promise of trusteeship. Read Jr maintained that most Kat River settlers asked for help, which never came. The rebellion, he argued, was stirred up by attacks on loyalists at the start of the war, by soldiers who took no care to distinguish them from the rebels (Read Jr 1852, xx–xxi). When he rode out to the rebel camp on 28 May 1851, to convey Somerset's offer of pardon, 'reminding them of the advantages of British citizenship and subjecthood', Hendrik Noeka complained, reports Read Jr, that 'for twenty years they had been faithful subjects to the Queen of England ... but that they had been most shamefully treated' (1852, 31).

Willem Uithaalder's plea was condemned by other Khoisan, such as Read Jr, who proclaimed loyalty to the British Crown as the only way for the Khoisan to secure civil liberties. The Griqua leader Adam Kok replied lamentably to Uithaalder:

> Instead of regarding you [Uithaalder] and your associates as the brave defenders of the Hottentot race, I cannot but consider you as the enemies of all the coloured people of South Africa, for by your rebellion you will impress a strong prejudice on the minds of all thinking persons against the character, the rights, and the claims of the coloured classes.[9]

Siding with Adam Kok, the Reads saw the rebellion as ruining their life's work and went out to try to dissuade the Kat River Khoisan from joining the rebellion (Ross 2003, 136). In a declaration of January 1851, they wrote: 'let the Hottentots remember the blessings they have enjoyed under the British Government and what is now in jeopardy, viz., the elements which constitute social and political happiness, – Christianity, civilisation, and British Institutions' (Read Jr 1852, 28).

In fact, Read Jr saw the rebellion as unwinnable: 'everyone knew that England would ultimately triumph in the war – insane must have been the man who thought otherwise' (1852, 43). He had fought all his life for Christianity, civilisation and the rule of law, which he believed would save his people from degradation and injustice. Although he would later voice sympathies for the rebels' grievances, he admitted that nothing could justify rebelling against British sovereignty, which granted and protected equal social rights. When the rebellion broke out, Read Jr noted that the 'position which some of the whites are said to have taken up against the Coloured' – including incitements to 'bonds, imprisonments, flagellations, and even murders' – changed the character of rebels' proceedings 'from a rebellion to a war of races, in which the Hottentots and the Kafirs were against the whites' (Elbourne 2000, 27).

Essentially, for Read Jr, the British were deviating from their own standards of civilisation, escalating a mild outbreak into a contrived race war. Disillusioned with the 1852 commission of inquiry into the causes of the rebellion, Read Jr said that of the many material reasons for rebellion, it was above all colonial power that had 'extended insult to enrage men' (Read Jr, cited in Elbourne 2000, 30). Read Jr anticipated the interest of exploitative white colonists in portraying the rebellion as rejection of the ideology of assimilative trusteeship and evidence of its naivety.

The immediate aftermath of the Kat River Rebellion illustrates the dilemma of Read Jr. The missionaries were blamed by colonial society and its officials for the outbreak of war, particularly by those colonists who were unwilling to grant full agency to the Khoisan rebels. In his 1852 extended poem to the British public back home, the Grahamstown municipal commissioner, William Hartley, maintains,

> some there are
> Who have incited them to War
> By preaching Politics and Rights
> That their oppressors are Whites ...
> Thus some in Holy Orders clad
> Have made the Hottentots go Mad ...
> And why we cannot tell the Reason
> Except thro' London Mission Treason ...
> We think a Renton, & a Niven
> Have with a Read and others striven
> That we should to the sea be driven ...
> The people foremost in Sedition
> Belonging to the London Mission ...
> At a time so critical
> Preached Sermons quite political. (Hartley 1852)[10]

Attorney general William Porter, in 1851, likewise blamed the rebellion on the zeal of the Reads' evangelical gospel (Elbourne 2000, 38). As Elbourne notes, Read Jr represented 'in his very body, the confusions of identity of the Cape Colony'; and, while no one questioned his loyalty to the Colony, many whites tried to blame him and, through him, the LMS for the uprising itself (2000, 37–38). James Read Jr embodied the aspirational normative standards of the colonial ideology of assimilative trusteeship. His betrayal by colonial authorities marks a first turn to segregation.

HISTORIOGRAPHICAL INTERPRETATION AND AFTERMATH OF THE REBELLION

Macmillan sums up the rebellion as 'a reckless and unconsidered protest against unsatisfactory conditions by a people who had only too little to lose' (Macmillan 1968, 280; see also Kirk 1973, 425). As we have noted, Ross argues that the Kat River Rebellion was an early expression of 'Hottentot Nationalism', which developed into 'black and liberation theology' (Ross 2014, 1). Certainly, we agree, black nationalism responds to colonial betrayal.

However, the proto-nationalism evident in the Kat River Rebellion was not a rejection of colonial ideology but an assertion of colonial rights of equal citizenship. Looking back at the notion of *trusteeship*, one is struck by the dishonesty of Kipling's phrase, 'the White Man's Burden', as this dismisses the rationality of colonial subjects who accepted it. By contrast, Homi Bhabha's account of 'sly civility', in the subversive return of the white man's gaze, recognises reason in the colonial conformity of the black Victorian gentleman (Bhabha 1994). Imperial Khoisan loyalism was a reasonable avenue of self-assertion; more reasonable, anyhow, than independence, given the context. On the other side, the burden of colonial trusteeship to secure equal rights imposed an overwhelming military, economic and political cost.

Elbourne makes the compelling argument that the rebellion assisted enemies of the liberal assimilationist project and gave rise to renewed belief in the reality of racial distinctions. The rebellion entrenched prejudices about 'white' and 'black' difference for many participants. Many whites saw the war as 'race warfare' and issued calls for 'white unity' in the face of 'black barbarism' (Elbourne 2000, 17–18). The British cast the war as one of black against white, which proved no black person could be trusted. Thus, writes Hartley, 'while on our Cape Horse Regiment Black / Who fought so well a few years back / No trust at all can now be placed' (Hartley 1852).

The rebellion fed into a colonial narrative of the inevitability of ethnic conflict and the reality of race that haunts South Africa to this day. It also marked a crisis for the assimilationist ideology of imperial government, which utterly depended on indigenous soldiers for the security of the colonies. Concluding that only Europeans could be trusted, white liberalism retreated to a position of careful social distancing and theorising about essential racial difference (Elbourne 2000, 29, 38). All this provoked a 'great fear', in August 1851, of a general uprising of Khoisan farm labourers against their employers to recover their former land in the western Cape, confirming opinion that the Khoisan were fickle, credulous and untrustworthy (Bradlow 1989, 418). Most of the KRS settlers did not rebel, primarily because they saw the war as unwinnable. But in the fog of ideological contestation, the loyalists remained relatively invisible, obscured by polarisation between black and white and fuelled by the desire of the settlers to justify economic exploitation of the Kat River valleys.

The 1820 Settlers in Albany saw themselves as surrounded by Africans whom they feared. By 1840, Fairbairn had rejected the idea of innate similarities of races and insisted on distinctions of race and colour, as well as linguistic and cultural difference between Europeans and Africans (Bank 1999, 370–376). The Kat River Rebellion, which had been a marker of progress for the natives, confirmed such sentiments. The early assimilationist mission model turned, from the 1850s on, towards racial conservatism and paternalism among South Africa's governors and white settlers, as white unity and segregation overcame the early Cape liberal humanitarianism (Bank 1999, 370–376). Widespread expansion in the 1840s led to imperial moves thereafter to abandon costly and awkward responsibilities. As rationalist universalism was overtaken by an historicist, stadial model of civilisation, notions of equal commercial exchange gave way to European management of native labour (Porter 1985, 615–616).

Andrew Bank argues that the Frontier Wars of the 1830s–1850s with the amaXhosa were a formative experience for British imperialism, one that bred pessimism and hostility among colonists in South Africa and engendered a more strident chauvinist racism among the British settler community. The period of 1850–1870 marked a hostile recoil from overseas commitments, while budding anthropologists began applying Darwinian ideas about the survival of the fittest to 'races' in a shift towards colonial ethnology and scientific racism (Bank 1999, 364–366). The language of race warfare became more widespread as the war developed, and served thereafter as a cover for the expropriation of land in the KRS. Bank points out that the liberal abolitionist language of equality had always been inscribed with authoritarianism and hierarchies derived from Scottish Enlightenment models of the progressive stages of societal development. While assimilationism continued through the 1860s and 1870s, segregationist policies were introduced soon thereafter (1999, 370, 380). This interpretation supports our claim that in South Africa, the colonial ideology of trusteeship evolved from (Eurocentric) universalism (which justified direct rule and responsibilities for indigenous civil rights, as espoused by Edmund Burke) towards a relativist justification for indirect rule and cultural pluralism, that is, into a mode of governmentality that deferred accountability for the rights of segregated subjects to political brokers (see Allsobrook and Boisen 2017). This turn to segregated governmentality in trusteeship significantly aligns with the post-Second World War strategic turn to decolonisation taken by the imperial powers.

In her study of the after-effects of the Kat River Rebellion, Katie Carline draws attention to Colonial Governor Sir George Grey's underlying assumption that 'the eastern Cape could only be secure if its black and white population lived separately'. This, she maintains, 'is indicative of a change in the understanding of race in the British empire … The Kat River Rebellion in 1853 was thus one of the earliest causes of this shift', which 'coincided with changes in science and pseudo-science, such as the emergence of evolutionary theory …'. She goes on to argue that the rebellion 'saw the political triumph of white-settler narrative, which rejected the capacity of Africans to become "civilized"' (Carline 2015, 57). But the ideology of trusteeship was not abandoned. Rather, with subsequent neocolonialism and under apartheid, it was typically maintained that Africans should rather civilise along their own cultural lines, in segregated nations, while remaining under the trusteeship of more experienced European powers (Allsobrook and Boisen 2017).

For Read Jr, rhetoric about race warfare and the violence that it permitted was self-fulfilling, and it was this position among influential Grahamstown settlers that turned the rebellion into a race war (Elbourne 2000, 26–27). He wrote:

> Another circumstance which added enthusiasm to the revolters was the position ... some of the whites are said to have taken up against the coloured ... They spoke of bonds, imprisonments, flagellations ... even murders. This, to their ideas, changed the character of their proceedings from a rebellion to a war of races, in which the Hottentots and the Kafirs were against the whites. These things may have been imaginary, but the effects were the same as if they had been real. (Read Jr 1852, 102)

Although various historians repeat the assertion of the Albany settlers that Khoisan nationalism was a major ideological factor behind the rebellion (Elbourne 2000), Read Jr repeats a number of times that the rebels he visited during the war claimed that 'they were not fighting against the Government, and that they were loyal subjects of the Queen' (Read Jr 1852, 24). The Kat River settlers were motivated primarily by colonial disregard for the rights they had earned as respectable British subjects and as defenders of the realm. At the height of the rebellion, during parlay with the Reads, Uithaalder appealed to the justice of their cause:

> Sir, you and Mr Read were both young when you came among us, and now you are both old ... klein Mynheer had no beard when he came to Kat River ... now he is getting advanced in years ...

yet these oppressions won't cease. The Missionaries have for years written, and their writings won't help. We are now going to stand up for our own affairs. We shall show the settlers that we too are men. We are not against the Queen. (Read Jr 1852, 47)

Ross maintains that the Kat River settlers 'developed a powerful critique of colonialism, in which a radical Christianity was central' (Ross 2014, 294). Although he goes on to speculate that this was 'to form the basis of a wide black nationalist ideology,' he admits that 'just how this happened is not clear'. And, in fact, on the contrary, Read Jr observed:

> The majority of them professed loyalty to Her Majesty the Queen, and attachment to her representative, Col. Smith … and would I dare say (like the Irish) at any time have given three cheers for the Queen: and they stated that they were ready to fight under His Excellency, if only the Saxon (as the Irish would say), the settler of gwee [scum of the sea] – for so they styled the English – could only be got to leave the land. (*SACA*, 19 June 1851)

Although Ross repeats the claim for Khoisan nationalism, he admits the rebellion was not against the empire but against the white settlers, and that it was not against Christianity or the mission model of salvation but a defence thereof: 'an attempt to remove the threats to the social conditions of salvation' (Ross 1999, 344). Elsewhere he qualifies the claim for nationalism, arguing that 'the nationalism they propagated was a very Christian nationalism, building on a long tradition of socially engaged mission Protestantism' (Ross 2003, 139). This goes to show that the rebellion was not a rejection of the legitimating ideology of British imperialism; rather, it was an effect of taking this ideology seriously. As Carline explains, 'the rebellion was not an escape from their lives as loyal colonial subjects, but a last-ditch attempt to save the promises of economic independence, political representation and respectability, which the Kat River had at one time offered' (2015, 43).

In a move suggestive of the later turn to what we have termed *segregated* trusteeship (Allsobrook and Boisen 2017), the *RPSCAT* concluded that the success of the KRS showed how much better indigenous people could fare, under colonial stewardship, in separation from Europeans: 'Europeans coming into contact with native inhabitants of our settlements tends (with the exception of cases where missions are established) to deteriorate the morals of the natives ... and to prevent the spread of civilisation, education, commerce and Christianity' (*RPSCAT* 1837, 103). The KRS was emerging as a model of the virtues of separate development, under European trusteeship. This was to influence the institution of an alternative mode of governance over the amaZulu in Natal, after 1849, under the 'Shepstone system', which allocated *separate* land to Africans, in reserves, imposing indirect rule over Africans, under compliant headmen and chiefs, under 'Native Law', which became an important model for racial segregation (Swain et al. 2003, 103). Even within the LMS, an inherent tension took root between the ends of 'emancipation' and 'economic development'. The colonial secretary, Earl Grey, pushed for an informal mode of empire, to integrate spiritual and commercial ideals, arguing that only the 'civilising effect of commerce and of missionary enterprise' could bring security and order in the colony.[11] This sanguine hope was crushed by the rebellion. Ironically, segregation emerges from critique of epistemic injustice in hegemonic Eurocentric normative ideals, failing to appreciate cultural and ethnic diversity. And decolonisation follows through on this insight, as a means to more efficient exploitation.

CONCLUSION

In discourses of colonisation and decolonisation we have attempted to recover the colonial ideological rationale of the Kat River Rebellion by paring off the presentist attribution of a black nationalist rejection of colonial ideology to it. James Read Jr's loyalist account of the Kat River Rebellion appeals to colonial standards of imperial accountability for the rights of subjects under direct rule, showing up the hypocrisy of Cape liberal trusteeship ideology. This sense of betrayal is echoed in rebels' accounts of their cause.

The split at Kat River between black and white that truly doomed the rebellion was not a divide between those who embraced European civilisation and those who rejected it; far from it, it cut at the breach between ideal equality and real domination at the heart of trusteeship. The Kat River settlers demanded recognition that they had reached the standards of independent, rational autonomy that legitimated imperial rule. Loyalists and rebels appealed to the same normative standards of colonial ideology. The ambiguity in the legitimating ideology of colonial trusteeship, of subordination for self-determination, was equally effective for the legitimation of empire as it was for decolonisation.

NOTES

1   The 'coloureds' of South Africa are descended from predominantly monotheistic freed slaves of a mixed ethnic background, of Khoikhoi, San, European and Southeast Asian origin, who speak a language of European origin. The contested term is widely attributed to this historically distinct, culturally discrete social grouping.

2   Godlonton here expresses commonly held nineteenth-century views that all 'primitive' races were doomed to extinction. See also Patrick Brantlinger's excellent study (2003).

3   David Boucher succinctly explains covering law universalism as 'a universal standard for all humanity to which all societies must conform if they are to be redeemed. The is one law, one justice, and one conception of life' (Boucher 1998: 96).

4   Letter to the editor from anonymous Albany settler, 12 March 1829.

5   Lester argues that sympathy between metropolitan and colonial Britain undermined humanitarian influence, with the media depicting half-naked savages mutilating innocent Britons.

6   The Cape Corps was a Khoisan reserve regiment of the British army.

7   Smith to Grey, 18 February 1851 (no. 23): *British Parliamentary Papers: Accounts & Papers, 1851*, XXXVIII (1352): *Further Correspondence Relative to the State of the Kafir Tribes*, 12–13. See also Kirk (1973, 411).

8   Earl Grey cited in Smith to Grey, 8 September 1851 (no. 155), *British Parliamentary Papers* 1852, XXXIII (1428): *Correspondence Relative to the Outbreak on the Eastern Frontier*, 140.

9   Kok to Uithaalder, 27 August 1851 (enclosure 2, no. 26), *British Parliamentary Papers* 1852, XXXIII (1428): *Correspondence Relative to the Outbreak on the Eastern Frontier*, 152–153.

10   W.J. Hartley is author Christopher Allsobrook's grandmother's great-grandfather.
11   Grey to Governor Cathcart, 2 February 1852 (no. 23), *British Parliamentary Papers 1852*, XXXIII (I428): *Correspondence Relative to the Outbreak on the Eastern Frontier*, 256–259.

REFERENCES

Archival sources

British Parliamentary Papers: 1352 of 1851: *Correspondence re: the Kaffir Tribes*; 1428 of 1852: *Correspondence re: the Kafir Tribes*.
Report of the Parliamentary Select Committee on Aboriginal Tribes (British Settlement) (RPSCAT). Published for the Society by William Ball, Aldine Chambers, Paternoster Row and Hatchard & Sons, Piccadilly, 1837.
Report from the Select Committee on the Aborigines (British Settlements), Together with the Minutes and Evidence (RSCA). Printed 5 August 1836.
South African Commercial Advertiser (SACA), 4 April 1829, 15 August 1829, 18 December 1830, 19 June 1851.

Secondary sources

Allsobrook, Christopher and Camilla Boisen. 2017. 'Two Types of Trusteeship: From Subjugation to Separate Development'. *Politikon* 44 (2): 265–285. https://doi.org/10.1080/02589346.2015.1121623.
Bank, Andrew. 1999. 'Losing Faith in the Civilising Mission: The Premature Decline of Humanitarian Liberalism in the Cape, 1850–1860'. In *Empire and the Others: British Encounters with Indigenous Peoples, 1600–1850*, edited by Martin Daunton and Rick Halpern, 364–383. Philadelphia: University of Pennsylvania Press.
Bhabha, Homi K. 1994. *The Location of Culture*. London: Routledge.
Blackbeard, Susan Isabel. 2018. 'Kat River Revisited'. PhD dissertation, University of Cape Town. http://hdl.handle.net/11427/27847.
Boisen, Camilla. 2017. 'From Land Dispossession to Land Restitution: European Land Rights in South Africa'. *Settler Colonial Studies* 7 (3): 321–339. https://doi.org/10.1080/2201473X.2016.1139861.
Boucher, David. 1998. 'British Idealism and the Just Society'. In *Social Justice: From Hume to Walzer*, edited by David Boucher and Paul Joseph Kelly, 80–101. London: Routledge.
Bradlow, Edna. 1983. 'Emancipation and Race Perceptions at the Cape'. *South African Historical Journal* 15 (1): 10–33. https://doi.org/10.1080/02582478308671574.
Bradlow, Edna. 1989. 'The "Great Fear" at the Cape of Good Hope, 1851–52'. *International Journal of African Historical Studies* 22 (3): 401–421. https://doi.org/10.2307/220203.
Brantlinger, Patrick. 2003. *Dark Vanishings: Discourse on the Extinction of Primitive Races, 1800–1930*. Ithaca: Cornell University Press.
Carline, Katie. 2015. 'Undefeated Ambition in an Unsympathetic Empire: The Kat River Settlement in the Cape Colony, 1853–1872'. MA thesis, Dalhousie University. http://hdl.handle.net/10222/72214.

Du Toit, André and Hermann Giliomee. 1983. *Afrikaner Political Thought: Analysis and Documents, Volume 1: 1780–1850*. Cape Town: David Philip.

Elbourne, Elizabeth. 1992. 'Early Khoisan Uses of Mission Christianity'. *Kronos* 19 (November): 3–27. https://www.jstor.org/stable/41033769.

Elbourne, Elizabeth. 2000. '"Race", Warfare, and Religion in Mid-Nineteenth-Century Southern Africa: The Khoikhoi Rebellion against the Cape Colony and Its Uses, 1850–58'. *Journal of African Cultural Studies* 13 (1): 17–42. https://doi.org/10.1080/713674302.

Elbourne, Elizabeth. 2003. 'The Sin of the Settler: The 1835–36 Select Committee on Aborigines and Debates over Virtue and Conquest in the Early Nineteenth-Century British White Settler Empire'. *Journal of Colonialism and Colonial History*, 4 (3). *Project MUSE*, https://doi.org/10.1353/cch.2004.0003.

Hartley, William J. 1852. 'Trials and Troubles of the 1820 Settlers'. Unpublished document.

Kirk, Tony. 1973. 'Progress and Decline in the Kat River Settlement, 1829–1854'. *Journal of African History* 14 (3): 411–428. https://doi.org/10.1017/S0021853700012809.

Lester, Alan. 2008. 'Humanitarians and White Settlers in the Nineteenth Century'. In *Missions and Empire*, edited by Norman Etherington, 64–85. Oxford: Oxford University Press.

Macmillan, William M. 1968. *The Cape Colour Question: A Historical Survey*. Cape Town: A.A. Balkema.

McDonald, Jared. 2010. 'James Read: Towards a New Reassessment'. *South African Historical Journal* 62 (3): 514–533. https://doi.org/10.1080/02582473.2010.519900.

Philip, John. 1828. *Researches in South Africa, Illustrating the Civil, Moral, and Religious Condition of the Native Tribes, Volume 2*. London: James Duncan.

Porter, Andrew. 1985. '"Commerce and Christianity": The Rise and Fall of a Nineteenth-Century Missionary Slogan'. *The Historical Journal* 28 (3): 597–621. https://doi.org/10.1017/S0018246X00003320.

Reid, James Jr. 1852. *The Kat River Settlement in 1851, Described in a Series of Letters Published in The South African Commercial Advertiser*. Cape Town: A.S. Robertson.

Ross, Robert. 1999. 'Missions, Respectability and Civil Rights: The Cape Colony, 1828–1854'. *Journal of Southern African Studies* 25 (3): 333–345. https://doi.org/10.1080/03057070.1999.11742763.

Ross, Robert. 2003. 'Ambiguities of Resistance and Collaboration on the Eastern Cape Frontier: The Kat River Settlement 1829–1856'. In *Rethinking Resistance: Revolt and Violence in African History*, edited by Jon Abbink, Klaas van Walraven and Mirjam de Bruijn, 117–140. Leiden: Brill.

Ross, Robert. 2014. *The Borders of Race in Colonial South Africa: The Kat River Settlement, 1829–1856*. Cambridge: Cambridge University Press.

Stockenström, Andries. 1887. *The Autobiography of the Late Sir Andries Stockenström*, edited by Charles William Hutton. Cape Town: J.C. Juta.

Swain, Shurlee, Julie Evans, David Phillips and Patricia Grimshaw. 2003. *Equal Subjects, Unequal Rights: Indigenous People in British Settler Colonies, 1830–1910*. Manchester: Manchester University Press. http://library.oapen.org/handle/20.500.12657/35059.

Trapido, Stanley. 1992. 'The Emergence of Liberalism and the Making of Hottentot Nationalism 1815–1834'. In *Collected Seminar Papers of the Institute of Commonwealth Studies* 42: 34–60.

4

Decolonisation and the Enduring Legacy of Colonial Borders in Africa

Ian S. Spears

M ost scholars and observers of political and economic history agree that decolonisation is an evolving process that occurs in different forms, waves and layers. Given the complexity of the colonial experience, one can imagine a protracted and ongoing process of unravelling colonial rule in all of its dimensions. It is common knowledge, for example, that there are economic, political, psychological and social aspects to colonial rule and its legacy. It is also possible to identify distinct historical moments when colonial powers accepted the reality of decolonisation and withdrew from territory they once controlled.

But contemporary African states represent only a partial and incomplete decolonisation. The decolonisation of Africa began on a formal political basis with the independence of Sudan in 1956 and lasted to the end of apartheid in South Africa in 1994. In several other respects, however, decolonisation remains unfinished. Since decolonisation produced new states only on the basis of existing colonial territories (as opposed to identity groups or precolonial polities within them), it is difficult to make the claim that Africa has been truly and completely liberated.

Since it is commonly assumed that colonialism is a pejorative term because it is cruel, undemocratic and degrading, further decolonisation must be seen as likely and positive because it is liberating, empowering and just. Indeed, governments, institutions and universities in Africa and much of the world are eager to rid themselves of the remnants of colonial rule and to avoid anything that might be regarded as *re*-colonisation.

But there are also forces and interests that at various times have stalled or prevented decolonisation, sought to maintain the status quo, or regarded colonialism as a salve to insecurity, even while they agreed with decolonisation as an abstract principle. The most obvious remnant of colonial rule in the case of Africa is the grid of borders that form the basis of the continent's contemporary states. This chapter will investigate the factors that obstruct continued decolonisation. In doing so, one uncovers the possibilities and limitations of the contemporary African state for protecting the interests of their citizens as well as the hazards of change. I will briefly consider three waves of decolonisation, identify examples of ongoing colonialism, and then consider three reasons why further border decolonisation is unlikely.

DECOLONISATION IN WAVES

The European colonisation of most regions in Africa was a relatively short affair, at least when it is seen in comparison with the colonisation of other regions. If formal colonisation in much of Africa did not begin until the Berlin Conference of 1884 and had largely ended by the early 1960s, then Africa's colonisation lasted a relatively short 76 years; formal European colonisation of Latin America, by contrast, endured for 250 years.[1] The colonisation of Africa was also late: Africa was the last great region to be dominated by Europeans, beginning more than 60 years after Brazil's colonisation had ended.

These timelines suggest a lack of enthusiasm for the imperial project in Africa on the part of the European colonial powers.

When it came, formal independence for most African states occurred quickly and in sudden bursts. During the first concentrated wave, from 1 January 1956 until 4 October 1966, 35 African states representing nearly 71 per cent of the continent's landmass gained independence from their European rulers. A second wave of decolonisation came as a result of the 1974 fall of the Estado Novo in Portugal, a regime that had resisted the 'winds of change' sweeping through the African continent a decade-and-a-half earlier. The collapse of the Portuguese empire led to the liberation of five Lusophone territories in Africa representing another seven per cent of the continent's landmass. A third wave of decolonisation came with the end of the Cold War, manifesting itself in the liberation of Namibia from South African rule in 1989 and the democratic transformation of South Africa in 1994. With the end of the Cold War came another, more abstract decolonisation when client regimes in Ethiopia, Somalia and Zaire, among others, were liberated from superpower patronage. Regimes that had long been sustained by military and economic assistance from the United States or the Soviet Union soon collapsed, leading to democratic elections in some cases and to continued or renewed instability and war in others.

While each successive experience of liberation was rightly celebrated, for many Africans the expected improvements in their material or political well-being were not immediately realised. In the year 2036 Africa will have been independent longer than it was formally colonised. That is, Africa's borders and the current configuration of states will have existed longer as independent entities than as colonies. Yet, today, few states on the continent are judged to be democratic, and in much of the continent there has been a marked deterioration in their political institutions and economic strength as judged by conventional metrics. According to Freedom House (2022, 20), in 2022 only 8 of sub-Saharan Africa's 50 states could be characterised as 'free'. Consequently, many Africans continue to assume that the source of their problems is related to ongoing forms of colonialism.

Indeed, it is possible to identify manifestations of persistent colonialism in what is ostensibly the postcolonial era. The first of these includes the ongoing exploitation of African resources, unfair trading practices, trade barriers and the accumulation of foreign debt. Alongside those who claimed that Africa was being *robbed* of its resources was the contrary view that claimed Africa suffered from *neglect* because it was not sufficiently *integrated* into the global economy. Either way, African leaders rightly saw no prospect for a more authentic decolonisation as long as African economies remained weak. Indeed, Africa's percentage of world exports has steadily declined from 7.4 per cent in the years immediately after independence, and has more recently hovered around 2 per cent (Drohan 1999). International financial institutions have urged Africa's integration into the world economy and, indeed, many African leaders claim that the continent's most competitive offerings have been kept out of Western markets. Contradicting protesters at the 1999 anti-globalisation protests in Seattle, the Sierra Leone foreign minister demanded *more* globalisation, decrying his country's marginalisation by the world's trading powers. 'As we enter the 21st century,' he declared, 'we are asking for partnership in the trading system' (Sanger 1999).

More recently, renewed interest in Africa and its resources has led to a broader range of connections with the outside world. Accompanying this interest is the promise that Africa will finally benefit from its relationship with the global economy. As *The Economist* magazine observed in 2019, 'this time the winners could be Africans themselves'. Yet, many Africans remain wary of such promises. The desire for integration has long been tempered by a reluctance to be colonised again. The Sudanese scholar T. Abdou Maliqalim Simone has written that the West underestimates Africa's 'fear of a virtual recolonization' and a 'direct reassertion of Western economic domination'. The fear, he writes, 'is that national territory and resources will be taken away once again' (Simone 1994, 8).

Another manifestation of colonialism – one that forms the focus of this chapter – lives on in the borders that remain a passive feature of African contemporary political life. With only a few exceptions, the grid of borders that form Africa's modern state system has remained unchanged since independence. These borders, in turn, reflect the arbitrary lines drawn by Europeans, beginning in earnest at the Berlin Conference of 1884–1885. On a continent where colonialism was relatively brief, and where political institutions have either been weak or unsustainable, Africa's borders – imposed as they were from the outside – have remained its most stubbornly persistent and highly institutionalised legacy. Indeed, frontiers and prohibitions against violating them have been codified in the charters of the African Union and its predecessor, the Organisation of African Unity. The arbitrariness of African borders is substantiated by the fact that nearly half of them – 44 per cent – are straight lines (Herbst 1989, 674; Meredith 2005, 1). In other places, borders are notable for their seemingly random inclusion or exclusion of geographical features (the Caprivi Strip being the most striking example); rarely have the territories they encircle been reflections of state power.

For some observers, it is their very arbitrariness that provides a circular explanation for both the stability of African borders and the weak African state institutions contained within them. The borders are sustained in part *because* the political entities within them are so weak, and thus regimes must rely on them for protection they cannot otherwise provide. Yet, unchallenged as they are from outside, these borders in turn relieve states of the responsibility to engage in domestic institutional development that would make their states strong.

The stability of colonial borders is also notable because political independence only rarely represented the unqualified expression of a single *national* identity. While there was often a common aspiration for political independence, these aspirations were spread across a diversity of language groups, faiths and cultures. When independence came, it was achieved on the basis of the colony and its arbitrary borders rather than the peoples or ethnic or religious groups contained within them. The effect was that, while it was no longer possible for colonial powers to rule colonies or for, say, Zimbabweans to rule Zambians, domestically there was little to prevent Acholi from legitimately ruling Gandans or for Hutu to rule

Tutsi (Jackson and Rosberg 1986, 13). Because borders have proved to be so stable, this dispensation has effectively been made permanent, unless overturned by violence. Indeed, Africa's arbitrary borders – which almost always encircled or joined multiple groups, sometimes with no prior affinity and little in common beyond proximity – have frequently led to armed contestation. In Europe, by contrast, border manipulation or the exclusion of unwanted groups produced increasingly homogeneous states. While in 1900 there were many European states without a single dominant nationality, by 2007 there were two (Muller 2008, 19).

Decolonisation, as it occurred in the 1960s and 1970s, effectively turned newly independent states into black boxes, where the internal matters of who ruled whom were of no concern to outsiders. This was not just an abstract problem. Eritrean leaders claimed that its special status as one of two federal territories was ignored by the international community when the 1952 federal arrangement was dissolved and the territory was fully incorporated into Ethiopia by Haile Selassie in 1962. South Sudan claimed that requests for autonomy were similarly ignored following the second Juba conference in October 1964 (Natsios 2012, 40). Even democracy – to the extent that it was realised in the postcolonial era – provided newly empowered majorities with opportunities to legitimately overrule minorities.

To obscure their internal diversity, ruling groups in much of Africa substituted their own ethnic identity for the national identity. Not surprisingly, minorities became disillusioned with independence, felt alienated by their governments, or regarded their political environment in terms that resembled new forms of colonialism. The Sudanese scholar and diplomat Francis Deng describes the sentiment shared by peoples across the continent towards those in power: those in the government 'are not "its people"; they do not see the government as theirs; they see the government as unresponsive to their needs; [and] the task of the insurgents as they see it is to restructure the country's identity and its leadership or fall back on secession' (Deng 1995, 77–78).

Examples of this kind of alienation and unfulfilled empowerment are endless, and are often reflective of the sometimes bizarre configuration of African borders. In the impoverished (and geographically isolated) Angolan enclave of Cabinda, for example, insurgents have long claimed that their oil wealth has been exploited by foreign oil companies *and* the government in Luanda. Indeed, if so much of its wealth was not transferred to Luanda, Cabindans say, the enclave would be considerably wealthier. The sporadic insurgency that has since emerged to end their domination by Luanda has at times been more violent than the struggle against Portuguese colonial rule (Noble 1992).

Among the earliest and most violent rejections of colonial borders occurred in Nigeria, where political instability and pogroms against the Igbo community led to the 1967 declaration of independence for 'Biafra'. In spite of their liberation from Britain, those who called for Biafran independence regarded Nigeria as merely a 'neocolonial state under the iron grasp of its former colonial master, Great Britain, with a very willing steward at the helm' (Achebe 2012, 124). Few African countries recognised Biafra's declaration, although some did. Among the most eloquent defenders of the region's independence was Tanzanian President Julius Nyerere, who insisted that national unity could only be based on the 'consent of the people'. States and governments, Nyerere claimed, 'exist for no other reason than for "the service of man"'. Biafrans, he said, 'are not claiming the right to govern anyone else ... They have simply withdrawn their consent to the system under which they used to be governed' (Nyerere 1968). Some Igbo continue their rejection of the Nigerian state today. 'What we're fighting [for] is not self-determination for the sake of it,' observes Nnamdi Kanu, one of the region's pro-independence leaders. 'It's because Nigeria is not functioning and can never function' (Oduah 2017).

Elsewhere in Nigeria, the Islamic insurgent group Boko Haram cites the arbitrary division of Africa by the European powers as the cause of the undermining of what was once an Islamic state. The Sokoto Caliphate was West Africa's most powerful state until it was dislodged by British colonialism in 1903 and subsumed into the Northern Nigeria Protectorate and, later, independent Nigeria. Boko Haram's message resonates among northern Nigerians, who see the contemporary state only in terms of its endemic corruption, poverty, unemployment and politicised ethnic groups. The movement has rejected the secular and military regimes that followed independence in 1960, because a regime 'stipulated by Islam ... is the only way that the Muslims can be liberated' (Agbiboa 2013, 4). Decolonisation, then, was merely a continuation of the same Western forces that had undermined Islamic rule in West Africa. 'Our land was an Islamic state before the colonial masters turned it to a kafir land,' observed Boko Haram's founding leader, Mohammad Yusuf. 'The current system is contrary to true Islamic beliefs' (Agbiboa 2013, 17).

In Rwanda, the so-called Hamitic myth sustained the view that the Tutsi minority's dominance over the Hutu majority was also a form of colonial rule. Belgian colonisers viewed the region's Tutsi population as descendants of the biblical figure Ham who had migrated from north Africa, and as more worthy of ruling the more numerous but less politically conscious Hutu population. Other explanations for the superiority of Rwanda's Tutsi population linked the Tutsis to a royal clan who came to dominate Africa's Great Lakes region. The Hutu were not so much an 'ethnic' group as they were the diverse inhabitants of territory colonised by this royal Tutsi clan. The extraordinary violence directed at the Tutsi minority in 1994 was an ill-fated effort by the Hutu majority to prevent further Tutsi domination (Mamdani 2001). The fact that the conflict appears to have been rooted in political and historical grievances rather than geographical ones has not stopped some commentators from proposing a solution that would involve a further redrawing of Rwanda's colonial borders (Matua 2000).

Ethiopia, a state that proudly and successfully stood against European colonialism, nonetheless did not escape the perils of borders that lumped numerous groups together and privileged some over others. Indeed, Ethiopia's constituent groups – Somalis and Oromos among them – argue that a territory that was colonised by Abyssinians or 'highlanders' can rightly be regarded as an 'empire' of the same order as European colonial powers. 'We are colonized,' a spokesman for the Western Somali Liberation Front declared, 'and we do not see why we should be different from the rest of the world in securing our dignity and right of emancipation' (Healy 1983, 105). Similarly, upon its founding, the Oromo Liberation Front dedicated itself to the 'total liberation of the entire Oromo nation from Ethiopian colonialism' (Keller 1995, 628).

Ironically, more recent efforts ostensibly undertaken to decolonise from the existing dispensation – and to liberate groups from their oppressors – often end up reproducing similarly troubled outcomes. In Sudan, southern Christians fought a decades-long war against the Arab-dominated government in Khartoum, rulers that southerners referred to as 'the North'. In 2011, independence from northern rule, and the creation of South Sudan, gave new hope that peace would finally come to the region. But South Sudan contained its own ethnic contradictions between the Nuer minority and the newly dominant Dinka majority. 'By all accounts,' observed Jeffrey Gettleman of the *New York Times*, 'South Sudanese soldiers have become brutal doppelgängers of the widely vilified northern Sudanese forces that they had rebelled against, waging war ruthlessly against their own people' (Gettleman 2017). Once again, a newly empowered government repeated actions first employed by Western colonial powers and then, often, by newly independent states: that is, violently eliminating or dominating those with whom they shared their territory. The Dinka, a minority in Sudan but now a majority in the newly independent South Sudan, are the 'new northerners'. John Gai Joh, an adviser to South Sudan's president, Salva Kiir, reflected, 'we are doing exactly what the north was doing – that is the irony' (Gettleman 2017).

ACCOUNTING FOR THE PERMANENCE OF COLONIAL BORDERS

By one count, at the conclusion of the 'scramble for Africa' in 1904, as many as 10 000 African polities had been incorporated into 40 European colonies and protectorates (Meredith 2005, 2). Consequently, as Robert Jackson has argued, decolonisation, while ostensibly an act of liberation, should more accurately be seen as an 'enclosure movement' insofar as it permanently confined identity groups to their colonial frontiers and required them to adjust to each other in ways that were rarely required inside Western states (Jackson 1990, 151). Currently, as the above discussion demonstrates, there are those who resent or reject the independent African state, or regard it as colonial, dysfunctional, or in need of reform. Given that the ex-colonial state appears to have done so little to stimulate prosperity in Africa (and possibly much to undermine it), how can the adherence to this legacy of colonial rule be explained? If decolonisation is so highly valued, why does it not continue apace to its logical conclusion with respect to the continent's borders?

There are at least three plausible explanations. First, and in spite of the contradiction in logic, Africa's founding leaders deemed that the best defence against fresh colonial incursions was the colonial borders themselves. Newly independent African governments expressly resisted the reformation of colonial borders on the basis that political conflict within their arbitrary states reflected the nefarious machinations of the colonial powers rather than the ordinary politics of ethnic diversity. Secessionism 'is the legacy we have inherited from the colonialists who tried ruling Africans by dividing them', observed the Ethiopian emperor Haile Selassie in 1968. 'We know that secession, if it were to be tolerated on our continent would lead to the destruction of what Africans hold in high esteem – their independence and their progress' (Stremlau 1977, 100). Some defenders saw colonialism in more benevolent terms whereby imperial power had merely and temporarily interrupted Africa's ongoing conflict. In this latter perspective, political conflict is a consequence of the *end* of colonialism, not its commencement (Gilley 2016, 653). Self-determination was seen as a principle to justify independence from colonial rule. But since ethnic conflict was itself assumed to be largely a consequence of imperial machinations, it could not exist outside of colonial rule and thus there was no basis for further liberation from the colonial state.

During the Biafran War, when the Nigerian government sought to reconcile the two principles of liberation and territorial integrity, it chose the latter. Nigerian authorities acknowledged that the 'principle of self-determination in its purely theoretical context may be at variance with the other important principle of territorial integrity', but claimed that the narrower identity-based conception of self-determination 'is not what is meant by the principle in the context of our African policy' (Stremlau 1977, 13). Nigeria's territorial integrity, more so than a multitude of small independent states, was deemed to provide a formidable bulwark against recolonisation.

A second explanation for a limited approach to decolonisation focuses on a group's relative strength and status in the independent state that colonialism produced. Decolonisation produced both status quo groups and revisionist groups; one's views on decolonisation were framed by the real or anticipated condition of the postcolonial state and its ability and willingness to provide security to those who needed it. In some cases, insecurity was precisely what had led some groups to *request* colonial rule in the first place. As Gerald Caplan observes, 'while many African peoples had foreign domination thrust upon them, others seized the initiative and actively *sought* European protection' (1969, 277, author's emphasis). Nineteenth-century Somali herdsmen, for example, welcomed British protection from bandits they encountered as they migrated south to grasslands in present-day Ethiopia, and they codified this relationship in treaties of 1884–1886 (Drysdale 1964, 26). Further south, King Lewanika of Barotseland actively sought advantage over his rivals by securing the protection of the British Crown in the late nineteenth century. According to Caplan, 'unlike many of the powerful kingdoms of south-central Africa – the Zulu, the Ndebele, Mpezeni's Ngoni – colonial rule came to the Lozi peacefully and – for the king at least – *as a great relief*' (1969, 294, author's emphasis).

The end of colonialism, on the other hand, threatened to upend these relationships and, where they existed, perceptions of security and insecurity. This occurred because decolonisation activated and politicised identity groups within each new state by creating new minorities and majorities. But because borders rarely changed, secession was discouraged, minorities could not arm themselves, and few vulnerable groups had the means to seek protection or escape from their enemies. To be sure, dominant groups eagerly awaited independence and insisted on the integrity of colonial borders, believing that they provided a ready-made state that largely safeguarded their interests and relieved them of the need for further institution-building. Small minorities in highly fractured states also favoured independence on the basis of existing boundaries. For these minorities, there was more safety in larger diverse states with cross-cutting cleavages than in smaller ethnic states where they might serve as mere appendages to dominant groups.

This preference for the status quo, however, confronted other politically active minorities who had benefited from colonialism, or found security and political advantage in its power, and who dreaded the implications of its end. In Sudan, for example, decolonisation in 1956 was met with jubilation among the Arab majority in the north and trepidation among the Christian minority in the south. 'We felt this occupation [by the politically dominant Nile River Arabs] indicated a possible renewal of the slave trade after the British left,' wrote Joseph Lagu, a prominent South Sudanese politician and activist (cited in Natsios 2012, 41). 'The southern Sudanese had always regarded the British as their deliverers and protectors, while they viewed the northerners as slave traders and tormentors.' The departure of the British, Lagu concluded, 'was not a true independence for the south but the start of another colonialism by the north, their traditional enemy'.

Other groups pushed hard for independence, only to find that the postcolonial state could not (or would not) safeguard the minority status that independence handed to them. 'We had no doubt where we were going,' observes Chinua Achebe, an Igbo and one of the country's most prominent voices, in his happy reflections on decolonisation. 'We were going to inherit freedom – that was all that mattered' (Achebe 2012, 40). His optimism was in part a consequence of his conviction that Igbos 'were destined to rule' Nigeria (2012, 108). The country's contentious politics and post-independence violence, however, put those aspirations in doubt. Nigerians, he writes, 'found that the independence their country was supposed to have won was totally without content' (2012, 52). The subsequent civil war (1967–1970) laid bare Igbos' fleeting attachment to Nigeria's colonial borders and their new desire to free themselves from northern domination. 'Having spearheaded the fight for Nigerian independence,' Achebe concludes, 'Biafrans were later driven out by the rest of Nigeria, which waged war with the secessionist republic to conserve the very sovereignty of a nation (Nigeria) within whose walls Biafrans did not feel free, safe, or desired' (2012, 97).

Both the 1967 Biafran War and the 2011 independence of South Sudan, then, were acknowledgements that independence on the basis of colonial borders had been an insufficient hedge against the domination of one group by another. On the other hand, Biafra's failure in its efforts to secede was an indication that the international community preferred the status quo. And South Sudan's post-independence violence will not have convinced many observers that redrawing borders is a viable approach to addressing the continent's problems.

Nonetheless, Africans cannot be complacent about the condition of African states. If some groups found security in existing colonial borders, and others found security only in their revision, the complete breakdown of postcolonial state institutions and the consequent brutalities of war led still others to call for a return to the authority that colonialism had produced. When asked what it was like seeing the French return to secure war-affected regions of Mali 53 years after colonialism had ended, one citizen responded: 'it was like a dream. They came to free us, and removed the noose from our necks.' Malians greeted the French with the French tricolor and chants of 'merci France' (Anderson 2013). Similar sentiments were shared in the aftermath of Sierra Leone's civil war when, following a relatively successful British intervention in 2000, Freetown graffiti demanded 'Queen Elizabeth for King' and a plea to 'return us to our colonial mother' (Renton 2010). Evidently, what constitutes liberation, freedom and independence depends on perspective and circumstance.

How, then, can this ambivalence towards colonialism and its legacies best be explained? For Achebe, 'the only valid basis for existence is one that gives security to you and your people. It is as simple as that' (Achebe 2012, 71). In other words, one might be willing to forgo other things – democracy, independence, territorial integrity – even if only fleetingly, if it meant that security could be assured during the uncertainties of the post-colonial era. Alternatively, if the colonial state and its borders were the most promising means to advance an interest, even a narrower, identity-based interest, then there was little value in challenging this convention and much to be said for its retention.

A final (and related) justification for the enduring nature of colonial borders is that the international community tends to see the African state either as an unproblematic and politically neutral entity whose internal conflicts are unrelated to questions of geography and demography, or as an entity that can be reformed within those limitations. Indeed, until recently, few have regarded the nature of the state itself as an irredeemable source of conflict. 'The problems of the Nigerian federation were well-known,' even as the country marched toward civil war, writes Chinua Achebe, 'but I somehow had felt that perhaps this was part of a nation's maturation, and that given time we would solve our problems' (Achebe 2012, 69, 71). In other words, even if political development and the reconciliation of internal conflicts required patience, it was an inevitable process that would occur in the course of time. Until then, political failures in Africa would be dismissed as bad governance, corruption, or incompetence on the part of the ruling class – factors that have no obvious relation to the nature of the state itself.

In recent years and for some scholars, however, it has become evident that the African state *is* a source of conflict. Some critics have even wondered why the international community continues to believe in the viability of the African state in light of so much evidence that it is dysfunctional (Herbst 2004, 308). These critics charge the international community with continuing to invest in peace-building and conflict resolution that are doomed to failure, or with trying to restore or resurrect states that have decades-old track records of failure.

Indeed, they say, the centrifugal forces at work, especially in the largest countries, Sudan, Nigeria and the Democratic Republic of the Congo (DRC), are probably too strong to be held together by enlightened good governance alone. Ethnicity, religion, language and race form a 'set of powerful centrifugal forces', writes the American diplomat Andrew Natsios in regard to Sudan. 'There are 597 tribes and subtribes, which speak 133 languages and even more dialects' (Natsios 2012, 10). Nigeria, too, is conservatively estimated to have 250 distinct linguistic groups distributed among 3 large voting blocs, 2 faiths and contrasting colonial experiences. And the DRC's massive territory endures cycles of war, warlordism and a struggle for resources. With infrastructure almost non-existent, the territory is de facto under the control of more than 40 armed and constantly shifting rebel groups (The New Humanitarian 2013). Given this complexity and the powerful forces at work, and absent juridical recognition provided by the outside world, the very features that many Africans lament – patronage and 'big man' politics – may, ironically, be the only means to keep the contemporary African state whole and orderly.

And yet, even if the African state is a source of conflict, it is not clear what other options exist. In this era of decolonisation, the international community is unlikely to offend the sensibilities of African leaders who have assumed power in once-colonised states by making serious calls for alternatives to the current system of equal and sovereign states. Not even the precolonial African polities provide much guidance for future state-building. While there were important kingdoms, precolonial Africa was generally not organised according to the defined boundaries, mutually exclusive territories and centralised rule that form the bases of the contemporary international system. Advocates of decolonisation, then, must contend with the fact that the modern state is a European import that will be difficult to abandon. The price of today's independent sovereign state, however, is a troubled, sometimes dysfunctional and often corrupt political system where citizens themselves are not necessarily 'free' in the positive sense of the word.

CONCLUSION

As in many other parts of the world, the vast majority of African countries are creations of colonialism. Yet, most African governments are keenly aware that there is no other viable basis for their existence. Indeed, decolonisation was a means to recover sovereignty and reassume control, even if it was on terms different from the precolonial era. The attractions of the status quo of colonial borders, of course, have less to do with colonialism per se than with the power and continuity that colonialism afforded. Consequently, to the detriment of some within the African plurality, decolonisation has effectively stopped at the borders of the contemporary African state. Even amidst a widespread desire to rid Africa of its colonial character, there are limitations to how far decolonisation has been able to proceed. The Westphalian system and Africa's current borders have now become deeply internalised by both the political elite and ordinary Africans who live within their frontiers.

To be sure, there are plenty of Afro-optimists who continue to see signs of hope and progress in African states as they are currently constructed. But these hopes are often tentative, conditional and too often dashed. It may be at the cost of African prosperity that the continent's leaders and commentators (and indeed the broader international community) can only think of the state in terms of mutually exclusive territories and borders that politicise the groups within and undermine a concerted effort towards reform. Even when serious discussions of the contemporary African state are entertained, it is almost always in terms of a redrawing of borders rather than a reconceptualisation of the state itself. Conceptions of statehood that rely only on new lines on a map, rather than institutionalised power, are bound to reproduce the troubled political life that has characterised the continent in the post-independence era. More thinking needs to be done by the continent's intellectuals and statespersons about ways to balance developmental needs with legitimate concerns that the state provides the only basis for interacting with the rest of the world.

The task here has not been to question the sincerity of those calling for decolonisation as much as to highlight the factors that have led citizens to avoid its logical progression. The upheaval and uncertainty that would accompany serious efforts at reform are probably too unpalatable for most of the continent's people. Moreover, such reform would risk undermining the basis for international equality that African leaders rightly see as their last defence against recolonisation. Accordingly, even critics – politicians, stakeholders, citizens – are resigned to the current system of states, in spite of its colonial origins.

NOTE

1   Portuguese Africa is an important exception in this respect, where Luanda and coastal areas were subject to 500 years of foreign rule.

REFERENCES

Achebe, Chinua. 2012. *There Was a Country: A Personal History of Biafra*. New York: Penguin.

Agbiboa, Daniel Egiegba. 2013. 'The Ongoing Campaign of Terror in Nigeria: Boko Haram versus the State'. *Stability: International Journal of Security and Development*, 2 (3): 1–18. 52. https://doi.org/10.5334/sta.cl.

Anderson, Jon Lee. 2013. 'State of Terror: What Happened When an Al Qaeda Affiliate Ruled Mali'. *The New Yorker*, 1 July 2013. https://www.newyorker.com/magazine/2013/07/01/state-of-terror.

Caplan, Gerald L. 1969. 'Barotseland's Scramble for Protection'. *Journal of African History*, 10 (2): 277–294. https://doi.org/10.1017/S002185370000952X.

Deng, Francis M. 1995. 'Negotiating a Hidden Agenda: Sudan's Conflict of Identities'. In *Elusive Peace: Negotiating an End to Civil Wars*, edited by I. William Zartman, 77–102. Washington, DC: Brookings Institution.

Drohan, M. 1999. 'WTO Talks Proving a Rude Awakening for African Minister'. *Globe and Mail*, 3 December 1999.

Drysdale, John. 1964. *The Somali Dispute*. New York: Praeger.

The Economist. 2019. 'The New Scramble for Africa'. *The Economist*, 9 March 2019. https://www.economist.com/weeklyedition/2019-03-09.

Freedom House. 2022. *Freedom in the World, 2022*. Washington, DC: Freedom House.

Gettleman, Jeffrey. 2017. 'War Consumes South Sudan, a Young Nation Cracking Apart'. *New York Times*, 4 March 2017. https://www.nytimes.com/2017/03/04/world/africa/war-south-sudan.html.

Gilley, Bruce. 2016. 'Chinua Achebe on the Positive Legacies of Colonialism'. *African Affairs* 115 (461): 646–663. https://doi.org/10.1093/afraf/adw030.

Healy, Sally. 1983. 'The Changing Idiom of Self-Determination in the Horn of Africa'. In *Nationalism and Self Determination in the Horn of Africa*, edited by Ioan M. Lewis, 93–110. London: Ithaca Press.

Herbst, Jeffrey. 1989. 'The Creation and Maintenance of National Boundaries in Africa'. *International Organization* 43 (4): 673–692. https://doi.org/10.1017/S0020818300034482.

Herbst, Jeffrey. 2004. 'Let Them Fail: State Failure in Theory and Practice: Implications for Policy'. In *When States Fail: Causes and Consequences*, edited by Robert I. Rotberg, 302–318. Princeton: Princeton University Press.

Jackson, Robert H. 1990. *Quasi-States: Sovereignty, International Relations and the Third World*. Cambridge: Cambridge University Press.

Jackson, Robert H. and Carl G. Rosberg. 1986. 'Sovereignty and Underdevelopment: Juridical Statehood in the African Crisis'. *Journal of Modern African Studies* 24 (1): 1–31. https://doi.org/10.1017/S0022278X0000673X.

Keller, Edmond J. 1995. 'The Ethnogenesis of the Oromo Nation and Its Implications for Politics in Ethiopia'. *Journal of Modern African Studies* 33 (4): 621–634. https://doi.org/10.1017/S0022278X00021467.

Mamdani, Mahmood. 2001. *When Victims Become Killers: Colonialism, Nativism, and the Genocide in Rwanda*. Princeton: Princeton University Press.

Matua, Makau. 2000. 'The Tutsi and Hutu Need a Partition'. *New York Times*, 30 August 2000. https://www.nytimes.com/2000/08/30/opinion/the-tutsi-and-hutu-need-a-partition.html.

Meredith, Martin. 2005. *The Fate of Africa: A History of Fifty Years of Independence*. New York: Public Affairs.

Muller, Jerry Z. 2008. 'Us and Them: The Enduring Power of Ethnic Nationalism'. *Foreign Affairs* 87 (2): 18–35. https://www.jstor.org/stable/20032578.

Natsios, Andrew. 2012. *Sudan, South Sudan, and Darfur: What Everyone Needs to Know*. New York: Oxford University Press.

The New Humanitarian. 2013. 'Armed Groups in Eastern DRC'. *The New Humanitarian*, 31 October 2013. https://www.thenewhumanitarian.org/news/2013/10/31/armed-groups-eastern-drc.

Noble, Kenneth B. 1992. 'Cabinda Journal; Oil Rich Yet So Poor: Angolan Outpost Is Restless'. *New York Times*, 24 March 1992. https://www.nytimes.com/1992/03/24/world/cabinda-journal-oil-rich-yet-so-poor-angolan-outpost-is-restless.html.

Nyerere, Julius. 1968. 'Why We Recognised Biafra'. *The Observer*, 28 April 1968.

Oduah, Chika. 2017. '50 Years on: Nigeria's Biafra Secessionist Movement'. *Al Jazeera Online*, 30 May 2017. https://www.aljazeera.com/features/2017/5/30/50-years-on-nigerias-biafra-secessionist-movement.

Renton, Alex. 2010. 'Sierra Leone: One Place Where Tony Blair Remains an Unquestioned Hero'. *The Guardian*, 18 April 2010. https://www.theguardian.com/world/2010/apr/18/sierra-leone-international-aid-blair.

Sanger, David E. 1999. 'After Clinton's Push, Questions about Motive'. *New York Times*, 3 December 1999. https://www.nytimes.com/1999/12/03/world/talks-and-turmoil-news-analysis-after-clinton-s-push-questions-about-motive.html.

Simone, T. Abdou Maliqalim. 1994. *In Whose Image: Political Islam and Urban Practices in Sudan*. Chicago: University of Chicago Press.

Stremlau, John. 1977. *The International Politics of the Nigerian Civil War, 1967-1970*. Princeton: Princeton University Press.

5

Fanon's Challenge: Identity, Recognition and Ideology

David Boucher

In contemporary political theory, the issues of identity and recognition have come to occupy a central place in what had become an obsession with liberalism and social justice. Recently, Amartya Sen has argued that any person who has pre-eminent and grand identities imposed upon them is deprived of other identities that may be as important, if not more so, to whom they think they are. Sen contends that we must insist upon the freedom to conceive ourselves as we would like others to see us, and to decide upon the relative value we attach to membership of the different groups and cultures to which we choose to belong (Sen 2005, 107).

The concept of recognition is integral to this identity formation and the freedom to choose. It is a concept that shoulders a heavy burden in modern political theory and has become the cornerstone of discussions relating to individual, cultural, sexual and state authenticity, as well as to the acknowledgment and conferment of rights (Boucher 2011;

Modood 1998, 2013). One might insist, with Hannah Arendt, on the rejection of the universalism of natural rights, and instead, as citizens and members of groups that comprise multicultural citizenship, on the right to have rights (Arendt 1968).

Recognition is about having a voice, and having that voice heard; an authentic voice that expresses a self-reflective sense of the self, an identity in relation to others, rather than an identity that others impose. In Charles Taylor's view, to misrecognise someone, that is, to impose an identity on someone, is a form of oppression (Taylor 1992, 1999). On the other end of the political spectrum, recognition is the central concept in Francis Fukuyama's championing of liberalism as the only ideology capable of satisfying the basic human need for equal recognition – a struggle for which has characterised human history from the beginning of time (Fukuyama 2018, xiii–xv).

Colonialism is perhaps the most extreme form of identity destruction and the imposition of alien identities designed to deprive peoples of their dignity, language, history, rights and cultural heritage. At the beginning of the First World War, 90 per cent of the world was either occupied by imperial powers or colonised by their settler communities (Young 2001, 2). The work of Frantz Fanon and his allied liberation theorists attempted to identify the elements of the process that dehumanised and degraded the identity and dignity of colonised peoples (Zeilig 2016). Fanon, in particular, explored the cultural and psychological impediments to liberating oneself and one's people from the identities brutally imposed upon them. In the nine years that intervened between the writing of Fanon's two most well-known books, *Black Skin, White Masks* (2008 [1952]) and *The Wretched of the Earth* (2001 [1961]), anticolonial activity around the world had intensified. The maintenance of colonies by force became increasingly difficult for colonial powers to sustain following the Second World War because, like Japan, Italy and Germany, they had either suffered defeat, or like Britain, France and the Netherlands, had been severely weakened by the war. Fanon recognised that no contemporary colonial power had the capacity to engage in protracted conflict to retain their privilege, by sustained large occupying forces (Fanon 2001, 58). The danger was not so much resistance by the coloniser to decolonisation as the collective complicity by the new bourgeoisie and traditional leaders in the values, ideals and governmental structure of the former colonisers, and the immense difficulty of individual psychological liberation from the inferior and subservient identities imposed on the colonised.

In this chapter, I will examine Fanon's engagement with the German philosopher Georg Wilhelm Friedrich Hegel's influential theory of recognition through the master-slave relationship, and how Fanon used it to underpin his contention that violent struggle is a prerequisite of successful decolonisation, collective and personal. He was convinced, however, that a lack of an African ideology would hamper decolonisation and facilitate neocolonialism.

FANON AND HEGEL

Fanon engaged directly with the work of Hegel, particularly with how recognition is achieved in the master-slave relationship. Hegel argued that each state 'has a primary and absolute entitlement to be a sovereign and independent power *in the eyes of others,* i.e. *to be recognised by them*' (Hegel 1991, §331). In this respect colonialism, or imperialism, the subjection of one people by another is the suppression of freedom or national self-consciousness. In Hegel's view, however, Africa and Africans had not developed the consciousness of statehood, and had yet to develop the capacity for demanding recognition. Fanon examined the role of recognition in Hegel's philosophy of Spirit, and how the master-slave relationship – so important to the development of consciousness in Hegel's philosophy – is circumvented in the African colonial context.

Fanon's understanding of the master-slave relationship is heavily influenced by Alexandre Kojève's *Introduction to the Reading of Hegel* (Kojève 1969), which Fanon read and annotated in the original 1947 French edition (Fanon 2018, 13). On Kojève's reading, which was also important for Fukuyama's conception of identity and recognition (Fukuyama 1992), in the *Phenomenology of Spirit* Hegel traces the development of self-consciousness, that is, the awareness of the I and thou. Self-consciousness exists in and for itself only when it exists for another. In other words, it exists only when it is acknowledged (Hegel 1977, §178). This awareness is the result of desire, and consciousness of objects outside of oneself. It differs from animal desire, which is equated with self-preservation. What makes human desire human is the overcoming of animal desire by risking one's life, literally in a fight to the death, for the attainment of recognition of one's value in someone else's eyes. Two desires confront each other, and only in the struggle is human reality born, what Hegel calls recognised reality. If one kills the other the desire for recognition is nullified. When one party to the struggle fears the other to the extent he refuses to risk his life to satisfy this desire for recognition, he recognises the other without being recognised himself.

In the struggle between two identical consciousnesses for mutual recognition one wins out in the battle for domination, giving rise to the master-slave relationship. For Hegel, this is to recognise the one who wins as his master, or Lord, and recognise himself, and be recognised, not as an equal, but as his Slave, or bondsman (Hegel 1977, §192). The master-slave relationship is important in the dialectic of recognition (Sekyi-Otu 1996). Hegel argues that man in his nascent state is never simply man, he is necessarily either master or slave. However, the master does not feel fully recognised because he is not recognised by an equal. For the master, freedom is the most important thing, but paradoxically he becomes totally dependent on the slave for the satisfaction of his needs, becoming enslaved to his own passions and desires.

The slave thinks that the most important thing in the world is to stay alive by anticipating the master's every need. Soon the slave acquires something the master does not have, an understanding of the materials of the world. The slave sublimates his identity through work, diverting the energy of primitive impulses into culturally higher activities – formulating an intention to make a table, for example, and in making it, turning the idea into a concrete object. In the independent being of the object the slave has created, he sees his own independence (Hegel 1977, §195). As Hegel argues, 'it is precisely in his [the slave's] work wherein he seemed to have only an alienated existence that acquires a mind of his own' (Hegel 1977, §196) The slave finds meaning in and through labour, as the master's life devolves into meaningless consumption. Increasingly, the slave becomes an independent self-consciousness, having a mind of his own, and demands equal recognition (see Kojève 1969, 3–30).

Fanon's introduction of race into the master-slave relation exposes weaknesses in Hegel's analysis and its applicability to Africa. Because of the propensity of colonialism to get deeply under the skin of the black person, aspirations, values and perceptions are flawed and perverted. In the first place, *Black Skin, White Masks* reveals the manner in which Fanon worked through the psychic aspects of oppression, and the damage that sublimated stereotypes inflict, along with the resulting alienation. Despite the impediments to liberation, Fanon's stated aim in *Black Skin, White Masks* is 'the liberation of the man of colour from himself' (Fanon 2008, 2), a self that had acquired an inferiority complex primarily for economic reasons, which had been internalised, by what Fanon called the 'epidermalization – of this inferiority' (2008, 4). Fanon argues that the oppressor, through the overbearing all-encompassing character of its authority, imposes on the oppressed 'new ways of seeing, and in particular a pejorative judgement with respect to his original forms of existing' (Fanon 1967, 38), precipitating the belief that the inferiority of natives is the result of their racial and cultural character. The relationship is inevitably racist in that the dominant culture is sustained by the exploitation of other peoples who are made to believe they are inherently inferior. Liberation, for Fanon, involves rejecting the subservient and inferior identities imposed on the colonised by the colonisers and developing a national consciousness to combat cultural genocide. In practice, however, decolonisation, as he sees it, has failed. It did not, for the most part, amount to genuine decolonisation because of the propensity of established black elites to internalise the colonist's values, and to assimilate, conform to and collaborate with established colonial social structures in what was nothing more than a continuation of colonialism under a different guise, and the continuation of the black man to want to be white. Fanon at first explores a form of struggle for recognition that Hegel's theory did not anticipate. It is the consciousness of the man who identifies with being white. This was a consciousness widely theorised and acknowledged among liberation theorists. Albert Memmi, for example, born in the French Protectorate of Tunisia in 1920, maintains that the representatives of the colonisers, recruited from among the colonised, constitute a category that attempted to escape from the subdjugation of colonialism and, in placing themselves in the colonisers' service to protect their own interests, adopted the colonisers' ideology, including its values and aspirations (Memmi 2016, 60).

Fanon speculates on who could provide recognition of the black man who identifies with white, and concludes that it is the white woman. By loving the black man she demonstrates that he is worthy of white love and of being loved like a white man. In marriage, Fanon argues, white culture, white beauty and white whiteness are at once embraced. In grasping the white woman's breasts the civilisation and dignity of the white race are made the black man's (1967, 45). Recognition requires the love of a white woman in order to validate the black man as white, but it is a recognition, or affirmation, that cannot be satisfied by expressions of love alone. It is only when the white woman declares that the black man has opened a wound within her that can be healed by him that her recognition and choice of him becomes real.

This pursuit of white flesh by black men, desperate to identify as white, Fanon describes as a sexual myth precipitated by alien psyches that 'impede active understanding' (1967, 59). Colour, he contends, should in no way be considered a flaw. The inferiority that the colonised feel is the correlative of the European's feeling of superiority; 'let us have the courage to say it outright: *It is the racist who creates his own inferior*' (Fanon 1967, 68–69).

Fanon insists that Hegel's master-slave dialectic has to be reconceived in light of the colonial experience. There is a fundamental difference between the master in imperialism and the master described by Hegel. In Hegel there is reciprocity between the master and slave, but in Africa the master laughs at the slave, demanding of the slave not recognition but work (Fanon 1967, 170–171; Said 1993, 253). Fanon's critique of Hegel emphasises that the black man's consciousness has been suppressed, retarded and denied to the point that the master-slave dialectic cannot even begin to function (Fanon 1967, 168–173; see also Bird-Pollan 2012).

Fanon argues that since the black man is a former slave we should turn to Hegel, among others, to understand his psychology (2008, 44). The foundation of Hegelian dialectic, Fanon argues, is absolute reciprocity. Only by transcending one's own immediate being is the existence of the other recognised as a natural, and more than a natural, reality. It is only in the act of mutual recognition that human reality is realised. When resistance is encountered from the other, self-consciousness experiences desire, the first marker that points the way to spiritual dignity. In the process, the risking of one's life is accepted by self-consciousness, and constitutes a threat to the physical well-being of the other (2008, 169). Fanon argues that 'this risk means that I go beyond life towards a supreme good that is the transformation of subjective certainty of my worth into a universally valid objective truth' (2008, 170).

The black man, in Fanon's view, was set free by the white man, given a place at his table, and allowed to assume the attitude of a master, but there is no master when there are no longer slaves. The black knows nothing of the price of freedom because he hasn't fought for it, that is risked his life in the pursuit of freedom. Occasionally he has fought for white justice and white liberty, but they are the values of his master, not his own. Fanon argues that the former slave needs his humanity to be challenged, 'he wants a conflict, a riot' (2008, 172). To free the negro without a struggle is a hollow, meaningless recognition. As Hussein Abdilahi Bulhan forcefully contends, for Fanon, 'if freedom requires the risk of life, oppression requires the fear of physical death' (Bulhan 1985, 121).

On the basis of Fanon's discussion of Hegel we are able to understand why violence is such an important element in the revolutionary struggle for decolonisation and recognition. In an address, 'Why We Use Violence' (Fanon 2018, 653–659), Fanon argues that colonialism is premised on violence. The colonial regime is always established and sustained by violence. It is three-dimensional in its oppression. First, violence is manifest in the routine behaviour of the coloniser towards the colonised. Fanon points to the examples of apartheid in South Africa, forced labour in Angola and racism in Algeria. In *The Wretched of the Earth*, he makes clear that the preoccupation the settler has with security requires him constantly to remind the native that he alone is master, fostering a festering anger in the native deprived of an emotional outlet (Fanon 2001, 42). Second, colonialism perpetrates violence in its ideological portrayal of the past. The colonised are portrayed as indolent, animal-like, unsusceptible to reason, incapable of directing their own affairs. Fanon goes as far as to suggest that for the coloniser the colonised represents the enemy of values and ethics, constituting absolute evil (2001, 32, 73). The history of the native is characterised by the coloniser as one of meaningless unrest, which has only acquired a sense of humanity with the arrival of the coloniser. Third, colonisation inflicts violence on the future in its claim that Africans are arrested in their evolution and require the permanent guidance of an external ruling power (Fanon 2018, 654). Such violence is provocative of a violent reaction, initially reflecting the quite banal instinct of self-preservation, but capable, as in Algeria, of being elevated into a higher value and truth by heroic struggle, and the crystallisation of national consciousness as African peoples struggle for the future of humanity.

Decolonisation by its very nature is the opposing of two forces in the quest for recognition. Fanon contends that the brutal reality of decolonisation is evocative for us of the blazing bullets and knives dripping with blood that are integral to it. He contends: 'for if the last shall be first, this will only come to pass after a murderous and decisive struggle between two protagonists' (Fanon 2001, 28). The violence that has structured the colonial world is not countered by a redrawing of the boundaries and establishing of new modes of communication. The colonial world has to be destroyed, its values mocked and rejected, and the colonisers expelled from the country in the reclamation of the history of the persons it oppresses. There is no question, Fanon argues, of the mass of the people desiring the position or status of the settler, and unlike the native intellectual who exhibits a thinly veiled desire to assimilate, the people do not want to enter into competition with the settler, they want to supplant him (2001, 47).

In the process of achieving authentic recognition, and not just a gifted acknowledgement by the coloniser, Fanon portrays the peasant as the true hero of revolution, despite the fact that everywhere on the continent of Africa, and even in Vietnam, peasants played an insignificant role in leadership, and were in fact directed by an intelligentsia. Pierre Bourdieu is dismissive of such idealisation of the peasantry, arguing that the peasantry was incapable of formulating its own goals in a rational manner, and instead of determining its destiny awaited its destiny to be dictated to it (2018, 87–88).

Fanon, nevertheless, insists that the peasantry is the only revolutionary force in colonial countries because, having nothing, they have nothing to lose and everything to gain. In fulfilment of the Hegelian struggle for recognition, the destitute peasant standing outside the class system 'is the first among the exploited to discover that only violence pays' (Fanon 2001, 47). In Fanon's view violence has a cleansing effect, liberating the native peasant from his inferiority complex, casting aside despair and inactivity, instilling fearlessness and restoring self-respect in the struggle for recognition (2001, 74).

IMPEDIMENTS TO RECOGNITION AND FREEDOM

The movements for national liberation throughout the world exposed the contradiction inherent in liberal imperialism. In fighting for the very principles of freedom and self-determination advocated by the Allies in their fight against the Axis powers, the Allies themselves continued to deny the same freedoms to their colonies. Hồ Chí Minh was always acutely aware of the contradiction between the ideals of universalism declared by European liberals and the denial of the very same ideals in relation to their colonial possessions. As early as 1922, he maintained that the regime of colonial capitalism, in order to disguise its ugly exploitation of its criminals, always adorned its pernicious banner with the ideals of the great charters of liberation: *liberté, égalité, fraternité* (Hồ 2011, 13). Hồ condemned the French imperialists for violating their own principles in oppressing fellow citizens by acting 'contrary to the ideals of humanity and justice' (Hồ 2011, 51).

For Fanon, writing in 1960 at the height of decolonisation, the immediate and pre-eminent priority and concern for Africans must be the eradication of genocide by the French in Algeria, and of apartheid in South Africa, through violent revolutionary struggle to raise the consciousness of freedom and human dignity (Fanon 1967, 171–172). He urged the oppressed to renounce 'nauseating mimicry', and turn their backs on the murderous European world that never ceased talking of Man, and everywhere murdered men (Fanon 2001, 251).

Early in June 1958, Fanon had accused the United States, England and Italy of clinging to a nascent fascism in supporting General de Gaulle's 'direct methods' in Algeria (Fanon 2018, 607–608). By 1960, the year in which the United Nations passed Resolution 1514, the culmination of a series of resolutions denouncing colonialism (United Nations 1960), nearly all nations still subject to colonial rule had resistance movements inspired by the principle of self-determination. Fanon compares the struggle against colonialism with the Allied resistance to Nazism (Fanon 1967, 170–173). African peoples, he argues, have to emulate the actions of the Allies and fight against the form of Nazism imposed by France, Britain and South Africa, which perpetrated the physical and spiritual liquidation of African and Caribbean peoples. There can be no freedom without recognition, and no meaningful (Hegelian) recognition without violent insurrection.

National struggles for liberation from colonial rule, more often than not, claim intellectual affinities with Marxism. Marxism with its emphasis on class was, however, part of the problem, and had to be reformulated if it was to advance decolonisation (Cabral 2016: 25). There was an ambivalent relationship with Marxism and Leninism, and a belief that Marxism was complicit in the dehumanisation process and an impediment to achieving recognition. The working classes of Europe, who should be at one with the working classes of Africa, were in fact the beneficiaries of colonialism. Although Karl Marx was a source of inspiration in the liberation struggles, his theory, for protagonists, was deficient in theorising colonialist race and racism, and he was as guilty as the colonisers of denying African history. The history of Africa, for him, was a mere extension of European history. However, decolonisation, far from delivering liberation, merely heralded neocolonialism, namely, the collaboration and complicity of native elites in perpetuating the structures and historical narratives of colonialism, and thus inhibiting the necessary confrontation required for recognition.

THE NECESSITY FOR AN IDEOLOGY

A further impediment to a successful revolution and full recognition was the lack of an ideology that gave direction and purpose to the struggle. Both Fanon and the revolutionary leader of the liberation movement in Guinea Bissau and Cape Verde, Amílcar Cabral, for example, recognised the need for an alternative ideology in galvanising the liberation movements in Africa.

A theory of revolutionary insurrection was imperative in transforming the historical reality of colonial imperialism into free societies. Kwame Nkrumah, the first president of Ghana after independence, argued that the Marxist emphasis on the determining force of the material conditions of life was essentially correct, but invoked Friedrich Engels to confirm his own view that this was not the only force. Nkrumah maintained that ideology was also a determining force. He argued that 'a revolutionary ideology is not merely negative. It is not a mere conceptual refutation of a dying social order, but a positive creative theory, the guiding light of the emerging social order' (Nkrumah 2009, 34). Cabral argued that at the heart of this theory needs to be the recognition that 'the motive force of history is class struggle', but its understanding needs to be deepened by being more inclusive of the lived experiences of colonised peoples (Cabral 1979, 123).

The problem, as far as Hồ Chí Minh was concerned, was that the proletariat in the coloniser countries viewed the colonies as alien, exotic and having little affinity with themselves. Without the realisation that the colonial natives were exploited by the same people who exploited them, and only together could they achieve liberation and cast off the common oppressor, they would remain under the iron fist of capitalism (Hồ 2011, 54). He warned that the British and French communist parties had failed to formulate any progressive polices for the colonies, and failed to have any contact with the peoples of the subjected territories. He argued that the programmes of the communist parties were ineffective because they were not consistent with Leninism (2011, 68). In Vladimir Lenin's view, the success of the revolution in Western Europe was dependent on close alliances among liberation *movements* against imperialism in the colonies and nationalist movements, which were part of the same problem of the 'proletarian revolution and dictatorship' (Hồ 2011, 68).

In 1966, Cabral, on a visit to Cuba, told the Cubans that one of the most serious problems to overcome in the struggle for liberation was the struggle against the weaknesses of the colonised people. One of the most pertinent weaknesses was the ideological deficit. The explanation for this was to be found in a basic ignorance of the historical reality that the revolutionaries sought to transform. No one, he claimed, had successfully 'practised Revolution without a revolutionary theory' (Cabral 1979, 122).

No one was more astutely aware of the dangers of decolonisation transforming into neocolonialism without a coherent ideology inclusive of the role of the peasantry than Fanon. He warned of state clientelism, not because the dying colonial powers were able to resist the tsunami of anticolonial sentiment, but because of the lack of a coherent ideology of African liberation. Without such an ideology, the emerging African states would be unable to prevent the degeneration of the ideals of national self-consciousness into narrow factionalism and self-interest. Writing in the summer of 1960, and in the service of the Provisional Government of the Algerian Republic, Fanon contended that the immediate threat to Africa was not a dying colonialism and its derivatives, but the absence of ideology, because the newly independent countries of Africa were as unstable as their middle classes and elevated princes. No longer feeling the threat of their former colonial powers, the middle classes develop enormous appetites, but in lacking political experience they believe that they can conduct politics along the lines of a business, resorting to pleading with their former metropolis to delay its departure. Fanon describes them as 'imperialist pseudo states' with 'extreme militarist' policies that deprive small states, which are in many respects still medieval, of public investment. Within such states, he argues, 'discontented workers undergo a repression as pitiless as that of colonial periods … The people, the people who had given everything in the difficult moments of the struggle for national liberation wonder, with their empty hands and bellies, as to the reality of their victory' (Fanon 1967, 186–187). Countries that attained independence, he lamented, lacked stability, and the unstable middle classes and 'renovated princes' became as rapacious in their conduct of political affairs as they were in their businesses (1967, 186). This was because nationalism was not a political doctrine, nor was it a programme.

For Césaire, Fanon and Cabral, while Marx provided insights into capitalism he was limited in his understanding of Africa, and hence one had to be selective and not treat his philosophy as a religion. Césaire, a committed communist, became thoroughly disillusioned with the French Communist Party's uncritical allegiance to the Soviet Union, and how it failed to address the position of the man of colour. As a man of African descent, he argued, his place in the world was like no other, facing problems that could not be reduced to any others, and with a history constituted by great misfortunes that were the possession of no one else. Because of the uniqueness of their human predicament, black peoples needed their own organisations, established by and for them, adapted to the ends of their own determination. Stalinist fraternalism, with its emphasis on advanced peoples having a responsibility to help those left behind, was nothing more than a form of colonial paternalism (Césaire 2010, 147–149). He called for an African form of communism, a negro rereading of Marx, that at once avoided burying oneself in a narrow particularism, and losing oneself in a malnourished universalism.

As Fanon suggests, 'Marxist analysis should always be slightly stretched every time we have to do with the colonial problem. Everything up to and including the very nature of pre-capitalist society, so well explained by Marx must here be thought out again' (Fanon 2001, 31). In a pre-capitalist society, the serf is different from the knight, but the relation is legitimised by some such notion as divine right. In the colonies, rule is imposed by the force of a foreigner, although a settler always remains a foreigner. The governing class is not distinguished by its estates, wealth, or factory ownership, but primarily because it is a race that has come from elsewhere (2001, 31). Fanon, like Hồ Chí Minh, believed that the European, and particularly the French, working class benefited from colonialism. Urban workers, Fanon and Hồ Chí Minh believed, were parasitic on Third World colonies. Unlike Hồ Chí Minh, however, Fanon argued that in capitalist countries the working class has everything to gain from revolution, but in colonial countries it has everything to lose. The working class is the fraction of the colonised nation upon which the whole structure depends. He included within this class such occupations as doctors, nurses and interpreters, as well as miners, tram conductors, taxi drivers and dockers, who constitute a bourgeois element within the colonised population (2001, 66, 86).

Fanon argued that within the colonies the white and black urban working class occupied privileged positions, and played no positive role in revolution and decolonisation; they inhibited rather than facilitated recognition. Such stark overstatements are, of course, made for political and rhetorical effect. For the most part in Africa, the indigenous working class was small and lived in poverty. Its composition was diverse, spanning different ethnic and tribal groupings, working in diverse conditions and earning differential rates of pay. It was, nevertheless, involved in 'widespread and protracted class struggle throughout the colonial period and thereafter' (Seddon 2009, 59–60). In the case of Algeria, for instance, the working class had developed a politically heightened sense of solidarity and internationalism, and from the early days of the communist insurgency in Vietnam, Algerian dockers boycotted the loading of war supplies and trade goods en route to and from Vietnam (Woddis 1972, 139).

FANON AND IDENTITY

Pace Sen and Taylor, with whom I began this chapter, it is the subversion and eradication of the ability to make choices of identity because of the psychological trauma of alien subjection that preoccupies Fanon, particularly in *Black Skin, White Masks* (2008), whereas in *The Wretched of the Earth* (2001) he is more optimistic about the emergence of freedom among black peoples to enter into the violent struggle for liberation against their colonial oppressors and achieve the type of recognition of which Hegel spoke when presenting the master-slave relation. He is not talking about a convergence of values between the oppressed and their oppressors, but about their rejection and replacement wholeheartedly and uncontaminated. Fanon's most famous book, *The Wretched of the Earth*, hurriedly dictated to his wife, friends and secretary while his health rapidly deteriorated, was his attempt to fill the ideological void he had identified.

To prevent the regression and uncertainty that follows independence, national consciousness, not nationalism, had to be rapidly elevated to political and social consciousness, Fanon argued. He maintained that 'the nation does not exist except in a programme which has been worked out by revolutionary leaders and taken up with full understanding and enthusiasm by the masses' (2001, 163–164).

For Fanon, there was an internal dynamic in revolutionary movements. He began with an analysis of the psychological and social effects of colonialism, and then examined the struggle for independence, and the problems of the transition from collective to individual self-rule. Violence, he argued, is the vehicle for transforming the nation as collective subjects of history into its agents or creators (Kohn and McBride 2011, 69). The necessity for a collective movement of revolution to decolonise later becomes an impediment to the achievement of individual freedom. After the collective surge against the oppressor, the myth of the group has to be expunged and replaced by the idea of the individual reintroduced to, or reclaiming, the world (2011, 70–71), and achieving recognition in his or her own right and not just as a group member.

Fanon wanted to go beyond the language of liberal humanism that focused on the ending of particular abuses, amounting to little more than asking the colonial master for better treatment. On the Hegelian model, this would not attain the desired recognition. Authentic national consciousness entailed going beyond rights discourse, beyond nationalism and beyond pan-Africanism, extending to all 'underdeveloped people' and offering a truly human prospect for all the 'wretched of the earth', in the struggle for recognition. This entailed ceasing to emulate Europe, and refusing to pay tribute to it by creating states, institutions and societies inspired by it. Fanon contended that in response to European expectations it is futile to '[send] them back a reflection, even an ideal reflection, of their society and their thought'. He maintained that 'for Europe, for ourselves and for humanity, comrades, we must turn over a new leaf' (Fanon 2001, 255).

The difficulties, however, are immense, and Fanon and his revolutionary contemporaries, such as Hồ Chí Minh and Amílcar Cabral, warned of the propensity for corruption and social division by cultural assimilation. Cabral, for example, contended that the urban and peasant petite bourgeoisie 'assimilates the colonizer's mentality, considers itself culturally superior to its own people and ignores and looks down upon their cultural values' (Cabral 1973, 45). Both Fanon and his Vietnamese near contemporary, Hồ Chí Minh, feared the transformation of the decolonised state into a tyrannical dictatorship. Both were subjects of the French state, the product of revolutionary insurrection, that had degenerated into the Terror and the emergence of Napoleon Bonaparte, who by conquest created a French empire. The political determination of both Fanon and Hồ Chí Minh was to create an unequivocal break with the French colonial system that dominated their countries, in order to protect against the predominant tendency of revolutions to reappropriate the past, on the model of the Russian revolution, which produced Lenin and Stalin as the new tsars (Kohn and McBride 2011, 56). The war of liberation was not the pursuit of reform, but the extraordinary endeavour by an ossified people to rediscover its own genius, retrieve its own history and reassert its sovereignty (Fanon 1967, 84).

The current beneficiaries of past colonial exploitation, Fanon reminds us, have become complicit in deeply entrenched practices of domination and will not step aside willingly (Fanon 2001, 131). While he is critical of those Africans who before the collapse of colonialism insisted on the absolute necessity of Europe to African development, he does not regard them as traitors because, to a large extent, they had been psychologically brainwashed by their colonisers. They exhibited tendencies towards fawning in their dependency and inferiority complexes, as indicated by the example discussed earlier in this chapter of the black man seeking validation by the white woman. There could be no excuse, however, at the height of decolonisation, for African leaders such as Mamadou Dia, the first prime minister of Senegal (1958–1962), who was complicit in continued French domination in Senegal and supported French resistance to decolonisation in Algeria. Fanon is at his most caustic in his condemnation of such counter-revolutionaries, branding them traitors, 'odious creatures' and 'stooges of imperialism'. Of Mr Dia, who 'defended colonialist theories with ardour', he venomously remarks that he was a miserable puppet, 'disavowed by History and waiting to be sent to the Chamber of Horrors' (Fanon 2018, 662–666).

Cabral, too, like Fanon, recommended the liquidation of the colonial culture. At the same time, he wanted to eradicate the negative aspects of the colonised culture. His intention was to create a new culture that emerged out of African traditions, but also incorporated what the contemporary world had attained in the service of the people (Cabral 2016, 117). The assertion of African culture, Fanon maintained, will not be achieved by reflecting back to Europeans their own expectations, but instead will have to 'work out new concepts, and try to set afoot a new man' (Fanon 2001, 255).

Both Fanon and Cabral rejected the idea of overcoming cultural incomprehension by assimilation and convergence. There is no desire for what Hans-Georg Gadamer calls a fusion of horizons (Gadamer 2013), but instead a rejection of the horizon of the oppressor. The desirability of overcoming cultural incomprehension which both Fred Dallmayr (2014) and Charles Taylor (1999) promote, in their different ways, assuming as Michael Walzer does (Walzer 1990, 1994), that above the particularity of different cultures there is a thin universalism which somehow embodies liberal values, is absolutely rejected by Fanon. Dallmayr, for example, suggests that cultural incomprehension may be overcome by the idea of a conversation between civilisations, in opposition to Samuel Huntington's metaphor of a 'clash' (Dallmayr 2014). Central to Dallmayr's image is Michael Oakeshott's idea of the conversation of humankind in which no voice is privileged over the others, and each respectfully listens to the interjections of the interlocutors, without trying 'to persuade, or refute one another, and therefore the contingency of their utterances does not depend upon their all speaking in the same idiom; they may differ without disagreeing' (Oakeshott 1991, 489).

Dallmayr premises the idea of a conversation among civilisations on a common commitment to global civility, social justice, the rule of law and the demands of 'civic prudence' or reflection, that is, *phronesis* (Dallmayr 2014, 365–378). Central to this engagement is the absence of a symposiarch acting as a master of ceremonies. However, the terms of reference of the conversation, as Dallmayr characterises them, privilege the liberal view of the world and its universal set of values that both Fanon and Cabral reject. Dallmayr's conditions for conversation require the non-European cultures to reflect European values back to those who initiate the conversation.

In abjuring Western universalism Fanon rejects the tyranny of the Enlightenment. He mocks colonised intellectuals for having deeply implanted in their minds the view that the essential qualities of mankind are universal: 'the essential qualities of the West, of course' (Fanon 2001, 36). He begins *Black Skin, White Masks* with the words, 'I do not come with timeless truths' (Fanon 2008, 1). Central to understanding what Fanon is doing is the claim that we are unable to stand outside of the Western grand narratives of its cultural and racial superiority, or avoid being contaminated by them. The only way to regain history, self-respect and full recognition is the destruction of Western culture and its values in its domination of Africa.

One of the ways to prevent complicity, he argues, is to circumvent the aspirations of the national petite bourgeoisie by mobilising the masses in violent struggle against them to avoid 'the vicissitudes of new-found independence,' such as declining morals, the installation of corruption, 'economic regression, and the immediate disaster of an anti-democratic regime depending on force and intimidation' (Fanon 2001, 143).

CONCLUSION

There was little in the practice of Western European states in their relations with Eastern Europe, for example, let alone with non-European polities, over the last 600 years of colonisation and decolonisation to establish the trust that Dallmayr's conversation and cross-cultural comprehension requires. Experience tells us, argues Amílcar Cabral, that the domination of the foreigner was accomplished and maintained by the permanent and organised repression of the culture of the colonised, and in order to free themselves they must reappropriate their upward cultural trajectory in the 'living reality of its environment'. Liberation from imperialist domination is 'necessarily an act of *culture*' (Cabral 1973, 39, 43). This liberation is for Fanon necessarily a violent struggle, because rational discourse has elicited nothing but violent responses that may only be countered by violence in the quest for recognition.

Given the apparent disingenuousness of the conciliatory overtures of Western civilisation to former colonial territories, whose leaders are frequently accused of complicity in prolonging imperialism under a different guise, it is hardly surprising that there is considerable distrust of attempts to facilitate greater cross-cultural comprehension (Galtung 1981). Margaret Kohn and Keally McBride, for example, argue that modern theories of global justice, which provide normative arguments for more cosmopolitan approaches to moral obligation and redistribution of wealth, stand in contrast to postcolonial political theories that cast the developed world as the exploiter rather than the saviour (Kohn and McBride 2011, 7; see also Go 2013).

Fanon's depiction and analysis of the colonial and postcolonial condition is a deep-rooted exposure of the impediments indelibly ingrained in black identity by Western civilisation, which serve to militate against recognition and the freedom Sen prizes for choice in cultural identity. Colonialism, with its accompanying racism, constitutes for Fanon the 'systematised oppression of a people,' which destroys ways of life and cultural values, and demeans language, cultural practices and dress (Fanon 1967, 33). Colonialism is a collective relationship between peoples, or nations, and not between individuals. It is, Fanon argues, 'the conquest of a national territory and the oppression of a people: that is all' (1967, 81). No personal relations between individuals can negate the basic fact that the French nation, for example, 'through its citizens opposes the existence of the Algerian nation' and is an accomplice in the acts of murder and torture that are endemic in the Algerian war (Fanon 1967, 83).

REFERENCES

Arendt, Hannah. 1968 [1951]. *The Origins of Totalitarianism*. London: Penguin.

Bird-Pollan, Stefan. 2012. 'Fanon: Colonialism and the Critical Ideals of German Idealism'. *Critical Horizons: A Journal of Philosophy and Social Theory* 13 (3): 377–399. https://doi.org/10.1558/crit.v13i3.377.

Boucher, David. 2011. 'The Recognition Theory of Rights, Customary International Law and Human Rights'. *Political Studies* 59 (3): 753–771. https://doi.org/10.1111/j.1467-9248.2011.00890.x.

Bourdieu, Pierre. 2013. *Algerian Sketches*. Edited by Tassadit Yacine. Translated by David Fernbach. Cambridge: Polity Press.

Bulhan, Hussein Abdilahi. 1985. *Frantz Fanon and the Psychology of Oppression*. New York: Springer.

Cabral, Amílcar. 1973. *Return to Source: Selected Speeches of Amílcar Cabral*. Edited by Africa Information Service. New York: Monthly Review Press.

Cabral, Amílcar. 1979. *Unity and Struggle: Speeches of Amílcar Cabral*. Texts selected by the African Party for the Independence of Guinea and the Cape Verde Islands (PAIGC). Translated by Michael Wolfers. New York: Monthly Review Press.

Cabral, Amílcar. 2016. *Resistance and Decolonization*. Translated by Dan Wood. New York: Roman and Littlefield.

Césaire, Aimé. 2010. 'Letter to Maurice Thorez'. Translated by Chike Jeffers. *Social Text* 28 (2): 145–152. https://doi.org/10.1215/01642472-2009-072.

Dallmayr, Fred. 2014. 'After Babel: Journey toward Cosmopolis'. In *Intercultural Dialogue: In Search of Harmony and Diversity*, edited by Edward Demenchonok, 365–378. Newcastle upon Tyne: Cambridge Scholars Press.

Fanon, Frantz. 1967 [1964]. *Toward the African Revolution*. Translated by Haakon Chevalier. New York: Grove Press.

Fanon, Frantz. 2001 [1961]. *The Wretched of the Earth*. Translated by Constance Farrington. London: Penguin.

Fanon, Frantz. 2008 [1952]. *Black Skin, White Masks*. Translated by Richard Philcox. London: Pluto Press.

Fanon, Frantz. 2018. *Alienation and Freedom*. Translated by Steven Corcoran. London: Bloomsbury.

Fukuyama, Francis. 1992. *The End of History and the Last Man*. London: Hamish Hamilton.

Fukuyama, Francis. 2018. *Identity: Contemporary Identity Politics and the Struggle for Recognition*. London: Profile Books.

Gadamer, Hans-Georg. 2013 [1960]. *Truth and Method*. Translation revised by Joel Weinsheimer and Donald G. Marshall. New York: Bloomsbury.

Galtung, Johan. 1981. *The European Community: A Superpower in the Making*. New York: Harper Collins.

Go, Julian. 2013. 'Fanon's Postcolonial Cosmopolitanism'. *European Journal of Social Theory* 16 (2): 208–225. https://doi.org/10.1177/1368431012462448.

Hegel, Georg Wilhelm Friedrich. 1977 [1807]. *Hegel's Phenomenology of Spirit*. Translated by A.V. Miller. Oxford: Oxford University Press.

Hegel, Georg Wilhelm Friedrich. 1991 [1820]. *Hegel: Elements of the Philosophy of Right*. Edited by Allen W. Wood. Translated by Hugh Barr Nisbet. Cambridge: Cambridge University Press.

Hồ, Chí Minh. 2011. *The Selected Works*. New York: Prism Key Press.

Kohn, Margaret and Keally McBride. 2011. *Political Theories of Decolonisation*. Oxford: Oxford University Press.

Kojève, Alexandre. 1969 [1947]. *Introduction to the Reading of Hegel: Lectures on the Phenomenology of Spirit*. Edited by Allan Bloom. Translated by James H. Nichols Jr. Ithaca: Cornell University Press.

Memmi, Albert. 2016 [1957]. *The Colonizer and the Colonized*. Translated by Howard Greenfeld. London: Souvenir Press.

Modood, Tariq. 1998. 'Anti-Essentialism, Multiculturalism and the "Recognition" of Religious Groups'. *Journal of Political Philosophy* 6 (4): 378–399. https://doi.org/10.1111/1467-9760.00060.

Modood, Tariq. 2013. *Multiculturalism: A Civic Idea*. 2nd edition. Cambridge: Polity.

Nkrumah, Kwame. 2009 [1964]. *Consciencism: Philosophy and Ideology for De-Colonization and Development with Particular Reference to the African Revolution*. New York: Monthly Review Press.

Oakeshott, Michael. 1991 [1962]. *Rationalism in Politics and Other Essays*. New and expanded edition, edited by Timothy Fuller. Indianapolis: Liberty Fund.

Said, Edward W. 1993. *Culture and Imperialism*. London: Vintage Books.

Seddon, David. 2009. 'Popular Protest and Class Struggle in Africa: An Historical Overview'. In *Class Struggle and Resistance in Africa*, edited by Leo Zeilig, 57–86. Chicago: Haymarket Books.

Sekyi-Otu, Ato. 1996. *Fanon's Dialectic of Experience*. Cambridge, MA: Harvard University Press

Sen, Amartya. 2005. 'Civilizational Imprisonments'. In *The Philosophical Challenge of September 11*, edited by Tom Rockmore, Joseph Margolis and Armen T. Marsoobian, 96–107. Oxford: Blackwell.

Taylor, Charles. 1992. *Multiculturalism and the Politics of Recognition*. Princeton: Princeton University Press.

Taylor, Charles. 1999. 'Conditions of an Unforced Consensus on Human Rights'. In *The East Asian Challenge for Human Rights*, edited by Joanne Bauer and Daniel Bell, 123–144. Cambridge: Cambridge University Press.

United Nations. 1960. 'Declaration on the Granting of Independence to Colonial Countries and Peoples, General Assembly Resolution 1514 (XV) of 14 December'. https://www.ohchr.org/en/instruments-mechanisms/instruments/declaration-granting-independence-colonial-countries-and-peoples.

Walzer, Michael. 1990. 'Nation and Universe'. In *Tanner Lectures on Human Values*, edited by Grethe B. Peterson, 509–556. Salt Lake City: University of Utah Press.

Walzer, Michael. 1994. *Thick and Thin: Moral Argument at Home and Abroad*. Notre Dame: University of Notre Dame Press.

Woddis, Jack. 1972. *New Theories of Revolution: A Commentary on the Views of Frantz Fanon, Règis Debray and Herbert Marcuse*. New York: International Publishers.

Young, Robert J.C. 2001. *Postcolonialism: An Historical Introduction*. Malden: Blackwell.

Zeilig, Leo. 2016. *Frantz Fanon: The Militant Philosopher of Third World Revolution*. London: I.B. Tauris.

6

Beyond Redemption: Unsettling Progressive-Romantic Storyings of Colonial Injustice in Western Critical Thought

Michael Elliott

I n the opening pages of *Black Skin, White Masks*, Frantz Fanon issues a call to his readers to consider every human problem from the standpoint of time. The present, Fanon contends, must be understood as contributing to the building of the future, and the future, in turn, as an edifice supported by the living. In locating the 'structure' of the future in an imagining of the present as 'something to be exceeded', Fanon (2008, 6) expresses a familiar idea, present also in Karl Marx's characterisation of critique as 'the self-clarification of the struggles and wishes of the age' (see Fraser 2020, 25). This idea, as glossed by Boaventura de Sousa Santos, is that 'there is no way of knowing the world better than by anticipating a better world', and that when critical work is detached from hope for transcendence of the present it risks becoming meaningless (Santos 2016, viii). When interventions fail to help us imagine, glimpse, or reach for something better, they appear as something other than critical – conservative or irrelevant, for instance – still with the power to disturb perhaps, but not in a way that promises to *take us anywhere*. They lack criticality, we might say, by virtue of their apparent disassociation from progressive hope.

In one way or another, this idea permeates all that we would today label as critical. It is so ingrained, in fact, as to usually be taken for granted. Nevertheless, it has been brought into sharper focus by work exposing the role that progressive imaginaries have played in the history of Western colonialism and imperialism (Mignolo 2011; Mignolo and Walsh 2018; Ndlovu-Gatsheni 2013; Quijano 2000). Charting how narratives of modernity, enlightenment, forwardness/backwardness, divine providence, salvation and development have been central to the enactment and rationalisation of colonial injustice, scholars in this vein establish direct connections between Western ideas of progress and the suffering of colonised and racialised populations. While exceeding the critical branches of Western thought in any specific way, these charges nevertheless weigh especially heavily here. They reveal how Western critical work has, in seeking to set itself up in opposition to injustice, more often implicitly supposed – or explicitly defended – notions of Western superiority than served to disrupt them. Moreover, it has done so even while opposing the micro and macro politics of colonialism. At the same time, it has benefited in material ways from the processes of genocide, enslavement, oppression, theft and exploitation that those ideas have served to support. It is notable in this regard that when Fanon pointed to Europe as 'literally the creation of the Third World', he was not minded to bracket its more critical elements (Fanon 1963, 102). Western critical thought thus stands implicated not only for contributing to discourses of progress that have brought considerable suffering to large sections of humanity but for the ways it has fed – whether willingly or unwillingly – on that suffering. The ramifications could hardly be more profound. It is not an exaggeration to say that the entire enterprise of

Western criticality is called into question by virtue of its deep-seated complicity in colonial injustice. At the very least, the prospect of advancing any kind of robust anticolonialism through Western epistemological traditions is cast into serious doubt.

This has helped to elevate progress (and its cognates) to a position of prominent concern among recent efforts to respond to Western critical thought's implication in colonial, imperial and racial injustice (see for example Allen 2016; Ciccariello-Maher 2017; McCarthy 2009; Young 1990). Work in this vein has consisted both in attempts to revise the 'content' of progressive imaginations, for example, by unpacking hidden (along with more visible) forms of racism inhabiting ideas of better worlds, and in a deeper exploration of the structural relationship between critique and progress. The common aim is to carve out modes of criticality that are more consciously attuned to the progressive imaginaries they inherit, and be vigilant of how these might serve to reproduce injustice in some respects, even while helping to address it in others.

However, while rigorously problematising progressive hope in some ways, these contributions towards developing more robust forms of Western anticolonialism have tended to neglect it in others. In particular, they have ignored its role amid the storyings of colonial injustice that their interventions participate in and depend upon. In almost uniform fashion, work in this vein has assumed a narrative structure in which the transcendence of colonial injustice and the redemption of Western critical theory are not only presumed possible but conspicuously linked. In other words, at an underlying, structuring level of critique, the role of progressive hope has largely escaped attention.

I argue in this chapter that this neglect has damaging and disabling consequences. This is because it serves to obscure a range of questions that, while threatening to further unsettle Western critical ambitions and self-understandings, might nevertheless be considered necessary to addressing contemporary forms and contexts of colonial injustice. My suggestion, accordingly, will be that if Western critical thought is to give these questions the space and attention they deserve, rather than work to bury them, a reconfiguration – or at least diversification – of the narrative structure of its interventions is needed. Specifically, it must undertake to disrupt existing tendencies towards reproducing essentially progressive-romantic storyings of colonial injustice, which tend to unreflectively fixate on a promise/moment of overcoming, with tragic alternatives. By bringing these conflicting narratives together and endeavouring to hold them in tension with one another, Western critical thought might succeed in contributing more relevant and valuable insights to contemporary contexts of struggle. Whether or not this can (or needs to) coincide with its 'decolonisation' remains an open question.

THE TEMPORAL-HISTORICAL ENTANGLEMENT OF CRITICAL THOUGHT

The observation that criticality depends on hope for a better world might seem to risk banality. After all, the connection it describes is so ingrained in our thinking as to be a truism. Indeed, it is difficult to even imagine how one could go about challenging this claim (that is, critiquing this idea of criticality) without inadvertently inscribing it anew. Criticality, then, *as it exists for us*, appears necessarily and inextricably linked to a progressive imaginary. What is easily overlooked, however, is the essentially historical character this also brings to critique. By historical here is meant not just that critical work necessarily takes place 'in time', as a kind of unfolding of events in its own right, but that in order for it to function in a critical way it depends on some kind of storying of how things are, how they have come to be, and how they could be otherwise. To rephrase this just slightly: by virtue of its connection with progressive hope, the critical endeavour seems to fundamentally depend on some kind of narrative structure for its theoretical and affective success. It is in telling a certain story of things that a critical work is able to imbue a feeling of direction and purpose, enabling us to connect with it on an emotional (even libidinal) level and perhaps find within it a stimulus to action.

If elemental to the appearance of critique as such, what need is there (beyond purely academic interest perhaps) to attend to practices of storying? I think that in view of exposures of Western progressive thought's role in perpetuating suffering and injustice, the need is considerable – especially if those operating in this vein seek to offer consistent support to anticolonial movements. For as Mark Currie observes, while 'time is a universal feature of narrative ... it is the topic of only a few' (2007, 2). Which is to say, with Paul Ricoeur (1988), that while all stories (including critical ones) are 'of time', comparatively few are explicitly 'about time'. Accordingly, part of the answer I want to give as to why we need to attend more closely to the practices of storying that underpin Western anticolonial interventions relates to a current tendency to exclude a key aspect of their temporal-historical entanglement from view – a tendency, that is, to be merely *of* time rather than self-consciously *about* it, and in particular to treat a narrative structure of progressive overcoming in respect of colonial injustice as entirely natural or necessary and therefore undeserving of examination. There is at least a prima facie reason to think that these aspects of critical work deserve the same kind of scrutiny that other sorts of claims and assumptions receive. Just because a story is not explicitly 'about' time does not mean it is not 'of' it in ways that need to be carefully unpacked.

This becomes all the more important once we consider that, as Currie points out, the line between 'of-ness' and 'about-ness' is not as stable as it may initially appear. In fact, viewed in a particular way, *all* narratives are really about time even if they do not explicitly acknowledge it. And when we think that they are not, we are really just succumbing to the temporal naturalisation they perform. Failure to recognise a narrative's about-ness of time (whether in the act of writing or of reading) therefore indicates not a form of absence but acceptance, specifically, acceptance of 'the way that conventional narrative temporality has embedded a certain view of time in our universe' (Currie 2007, 4). Perhaps the greater part of the reason we should attend to the practices of storying, then, is not for how they might serve to limit or undermine individual critical interventions but for the capacity they have to reflect much broader social and cultural patterns and norms concerning how we 'imagine [ourselves] into time' (Johnson 2000, 494), and how they might serve to reinforce or disturb those norms accordingly. Let me to try to develop and substantiate these ideas by way of an example.

PROGRESS AND CRITIQUE

The one I have in mind comes with the recent contribution to Western anticolonialism made by Amy Allen in her book *The End of Progress: Decolonizing the Normative Foundations of Critical Theory* (2016). What makes this a particularly useful case for my purposes is that it is a critical work about time in a very pronounced sense: Allen's aim is to confront what she considers to be a persistent and problematic reliance within Western (and particularly Frankfurt School) critical theory on progressive and Eurocentric normative strategies. Though largely disabusing itself of strong progressive notions of history found in the philosophies of Immanuel Kant, Georg Wilhelm Friedrich Hegel and Marx, for example, and so leaving behind explicit assumptions of European developmental superiority, certain vestiges remain in the normative strategies of critical theory's major contemporary proponents – most prominently, Jürgen Habermas and Axel Honneth.[1] More specifically, each remains wedded to a claim that certain practices and values found within Western modernity can be shown to be the result of cumulative and progressive learning processes that render them superior to pre-modern, non-modern and traditional forms of life, such that they can be defended as worthy of our allegiance and relied upon as a basis for context-transcending forms of critique. For Allen, though, the effect is to reproduce through their theories a form of Eurocentrism that threatens not only to limit critical potency in some significant respects but to generate fundamental conflict with anticolonial agendas. If critical theory is to truly live up to that name – in the sense proposed by Marx (and affirmed by Nancy Fraser [2020]) of contributing to the demystification of the struggles and wishes of the age – new normative footings must be fashioned.

This, however, delivers Allen to a dilemma linked back to the critical belief expressed by Fanon and Santos. For Allen, the route into this lies with Kant and particularly with his third question from the *Critique of Pure Reason*: 'what may I hope?' As Allen puts it:

> For a theory to be critical, it must be connected to the hope for some significantly better – more just, or at least less oppressive – society. Such hopes serve to orient our political strivings, and in order to count as genuine hopes, they must be grounded in a belief or a hope in the possibility of progress. (2016, 12)

To simply turn away from progress in view of its implication in colonial injustice, therefore, would equally be to retreat from criticality as such, and so slip into another kind of complicity. The only way out of this dilemma, if progress can neither be straightforwardly accepted nor abandoned, is therefore to try to reset the relationship with it.

This Allen proposes to do by disentangling what she calls a 'forward-looking' notion of 'progress as a moral-political imperative' from 'backward-looking' ideas of 'progress as a "fact"'. If the former appears utterly essential to the critical endeavour, however conceived, an expression of what I have called the critical belief, the latter always threatens to turn problematic, to bleed beyond mere suggestion of 'our' apparent superiority in relation to something or someone truly prior to influence views also about contemporary 'Others'. Since critical theory cannot leave behind progress entirely, finding a more positive role for it among contemporary anticolonial struggles depends on reconfiguring its normative footings towards a resolutely forward-looking, imperative conception of progress, shedding any latent reliance on claims of European or Western developmental superiority in the process.

While hardly doing justice to the complexity of Allen's investigation, this brief schematic suffices to demonstrate the extent to which it is a work self-consciously *about* time. Here, the question of criticality's temporal-historical entanglement is foregrounded in a very vivid and open way, and subject to sustained analysis from multiple directions. Yet, it is notable that, for all this, Allen's intervention is also of/about time in a way that it fails to suitably acknowledge or draw into the process of critical reflection. Which is to say that while the question of temporal-historical entanglement is foregrounded here on one (or indeed multiple) level(s), and vividly so, it is nevertheless naturalised on another. This becomes evident when we consider the background storying of colonial injustice and decolonisation taking place, which can be reconstructed in the following terms.

Contemporary critical theory, partly as a result of its inheritance of problematically Eurocentric theories of history and progress, stands implicated in experiences of colonial, imperial and racial injustice. Though now often opposing such forms of injustice politically, it remains complicit in their reproduction and concealment at the level of theory. This represents not merely an important moral concern but also brings into question the fundamental identity or self-image of critical theory itself, for it suggests that all claims to and presumptions of true criticality have hitherto been dubious at best and more likely fallacious in some elemental respect. What is now required, then, on both counts, is an honest reappraisal of contemporary critical theory's normative core and a concerted effort to reconstruct its foundations. The result, supposing all goes well, would be a brand of critical theory that avoids participating in the easy reproduction of colonial injustice and its cognates, and emerges as a positive force among efforts to overcome them. This 'decolonised' brand of critical theory might, accordingly, become an important part of a much wider transformation of contemporary social and psychological landscapes.

In more or less authentic (if abbreviated) terms, this is the narrative underpinning Allen's intervention; this is the *storying* of colonial injustice and anticolonialism in which her examination of criticality's temporal-historical entanglement takes place. What is most interesting about it, I think, is not just the obviously progressive undercurrent it displays but what David Scott (2004) would identify as its 'Romantic' form.

For Scott, the romantic anticolonial story is one that moves 'in sequential and processual form ... steadily and rhythmically (one might even say, teleologically) in the direction of an end already in some sense known in advance', namely, a world or a time beyond injustice/suffering/violence (2004, 70). The story is, as such, carried along by rhythms that replicate familiar metaphysical movements, for instance 'from Darkness to Light, Bondage to Freedom', each of which is anchored by, and reinforces in turn, a sense of progressive overcoming, a sense of leaving injustice and its various toxicities in the past (2004, 47).

The storying of colonial injustice and decolonisation that Allen (2016) partakes in through her discussion of progress is consistent with this rendering of anticolonialism as a 'drama of redemption' (Scott 2004, 47). Allen's analysis takes place within a narrative frame characterised by a linear temporal-historical path that leads from a morally impeached present (itself, notably, something of an improvement on an even more objectionable past) towards a better future – a future that, not incidentally, consists not just in the overcoming of colonial injustice but in Western critical theory's transformation from a force obstructing that overcoming to one now enabling it. The governing temporal logic is, accordingly, of gradual, progressive movement along a path towards overcoming and heroic redemption.

But what could be problematic about this? Well, in one respect, perhaps not very much. If we agree that critical work must always reflect progressive hope in some sense if it is to avoid meaninglessness, then a directional narrative structure of some kind is necessary, and probably inescapable anyway. But what is cause for concern is the extent to which this path and its temporal logic – which, remember, constitute the frame within which our thinking of the problem of Western anticolonialism is supposed to take place – are *naturalised*, reproduced as if they were simply part of the lay of the land and a force of nature, in short, a direct representation of some objective reality, rather than artefacts of cultural and political construction. But, consider what this naturalisation depends on and what it does. What it depends on is a set of assumptions about the nature of colonial injustice and anticolonialism – for example concerning the form that such injustice takes (or could take); some basic requirements of addressing it; its relationship with other trajectories of political struggle; and so on. What it *does* is diminish the likelihood of us noticing these assumptions *as assumptions* and asking difficult questions of them accordingly. To put the point another way: the naturalisation of this progressive-romantic anticolonial frame not only leaves some important questions unasked but contributes to rendering them *unaskable*, whether because they are literally unthinkable or meaningless within that frame or because its hold over us makes them seem silly, misguided, incoherent, or irrelevant. Some examples here might include:

- Must we think of colonial injustice as impermanent in principle in order to critically oppose it; or at least (and perhaps more importantly), does it serve critical ambitions to *always* think of it in this way?
- Can we presume that a unification of anticolonial desire and the self-understanding/internal trajectory of Western criticality is possible, and what are the potential costs of doing so?
- And if such a unification can, in the end, be defended as possible, whom would it benefit and how?
- To what extent might our thinking of the problem of anticolonialism remain an expression of specific anxieties (as well as conceits)? And what are the moral and practical implications of allowing these to commandeer space, energy, time and other resources within the discursive field of struggles against colonial and related forms of injustice?

I pose these questions not (or not just) because they seem provocative but because they are already implicitly answered through Allen's naturalisation of a progressive-romantic framing of the anticolonial problem. And this is what I am trying to get at in speaking of the ways we 'imagine ourselves into time' in the process of storying colonial injustice and anticolonialism. It is an honest move to ask: are we truly satisfied by the answers we possess to such questions? If not, or if we think criticality is enriched by holding them open regardless of any personal content-ment, then we have reason to be wary of how our critical engagements would implicitly perform answers to them, and how those performances might serve to block off or silence lines of questioning we would do better to enliven.

It is worth stressing that, in saying this, I do not mean to imply that lines of questioning such as those described above should necessarily be regarded as the most important ones for contributions to anticolonialism coming from or through a Western epistemic locality, and still less that they should supplant other pressing issues of political, economic and social transformation. But I am suggesting that they are important lines of questioning nonetheless and that we neglect them at our peril (if also our convenience). So when I say that Western anticolonialism risks faltering insofar as it allows itself to be consumed by narrative forms that would silence such directions of critique, I am saying it risks faltering in two respects at once: by arbitrarily predetermining the boundaries of the domain of colonial injustice and therefore (at best) limiting its capacity to contribute to efforts to understand, expose and address such injustice; and by thereby (once again) negating its own internal ambitions of criti-cality in general. If I pick on Allen for the sake of illustrating this, it is not because I find hers to be a unique or particularly damaging expression but because she shares exactly these same concerns. Moreover, the naturali-sation she performs comes amidst an unusually close and erudite explo-ration of the temporal-historical entanglement of criticality. That it could escape notice even here – and I mean as much in the act of reading as of writing, for this was not something that was, for me at least, obvious on first reading (or second, or maybe third ...) – perhaps indicates something of its pervasiveness as a problem and therefore the difficulty likely to be faced in trying to seriously confront it.

It will though, I'm sure, be apparent that in raising this concern I nevertheless operate in the same spirit of criticality. Which means that if I am attempting to articulate a potential problem located in the ways that we conventionally 'do' anticolonialism from Western theoretical stand-points, it is not with the intention of proposing that we therefore stop doing it. On the contrary, the aim is to generate movement towards improved methods of engagement and thereby increase the value of broader efforts to expose and address colonial injustice in contemporary forms. This bears witness to two things. First, in keeping with this spirit, what I want to do next is consider how a suitable method of response might be conceived and implemented. Second, I, too, in this sense, partake in a storying of Western anticolonialism that betrays a certain progressive-romantic undercur-rent. And how could I not? Just as Allen faces, in the act of critiquing progress, the impossibility of leaving it behind, so, too, and for essentially the same reasons, does an imperative of overcoming (and also redemp-tion?) remain integral to the kind of critical engagement I am undertak-ing here. But if this reflects what I have characterised as the unavoidable temporal-historical entanglement of criticality – at least as it exists for us – then this still leaves the question of how we would *allow* that entan-glement to inform and shape critical practice once we better realise it. And it is in this domain, I think, that a productive form of response might be found (or fashioned). By working to consciously integrate forms of counter-narrative into our storyings of colonial injustice, we might bet-ter resist the naturalising tendencies and forms of critical retreat that our temporal-historical entanglements would otherwise pull us towards. Let me try to explain what I mean by this.

FROM ROMANTICISM TO TRAGICISM

The dilemma Allen (2016) encounters in view of the implication of progress in colonial injustice stems from its simultaneous, and seemingly unavoidable, presence as a motif of critique. In retracing the outline of this dilemma in discussion of and with Rainer Forst, however, she makes an important qualifying observation: if it is true that we cannot, therefore, be 'against' progress without also somehow being 'for' it, the opposite does not hold: one clearly can be 'for' progress without being 'against' it.

And captured in this asymmetry is a difference of critical consistency. For it would seem that being for progress but not against it can only be maintained (today at least) by bracketing some relevant issues of power and injustice from full examination, that is, through calling a halt to the internal motions of critical investigation at a certain arbitrarily determined point. To be against progress and therefore also for it, in contrast, is to engender a willingness to follow the critical belief wherever and as far as it leads, including to the very grounds from which work in its honour springs.

Allen's response to this, as I have noted, is to pursue a form of conceptual innovation, separating out progress as a moral-political imperative from progress as a 'fact'. She thinks that this not only promises a more reliable basis for critique but, just as importantly, reflects the application of a more thoroughly critical ethos. While I have suggested that an important form of critical failure is preserved in this move given its confinement to a naturalised progressive-romantic story of overcoming, I think it can nevertheless be considered instructive. First, it affirms a few key things that I have already implied but which are worth stating more directly in summary: that even if we cannot radically escape the temporal-historical entanglements that make critique possible, this does not render us mere passive captives to them; that in choosing to directly engage those entanglements we might stand to find a more consistent and richer form of criticality; and that we can apply ourselves to devising strategies or methods that would both reflect such engagement and foster it in turn. Of perhaps greater immediate importance, though, is that this move also underlines that, from a critical point of view at least, the focus of our concern for progressive-romantic storyings of colonial injustice should not be the mere presence of progress as a structuring force but the unrealised and/or unchecked nature of that presence. In other words, the problem is that our usual storyings of colonial injustice are unrelentingly 'for' progress and insufficiently 'against' it. If we want to increase critical reach and consistency, then, we might look for ways to upset – and ideally reverse – this arrangement. One option lies in a turn towards the tragic.

In identifying the internal features of the romantic anticolonial narrative that I draw on above, Scott (2004) wants not only to illuminate but to problematise. Specifically, he means to bring into question the validity of this way of talking or thinking about colonial injustice as a strategy of opposition. While unwilling straightforwardly to deny that validity, Scott is of the view that it might need to be understood as more contextually limited than is often presumed, and part of a problem-space now itself desperately in need of problematisation. By 'problem-space' Scott means a discursive context consisting not just in particular arrangements of concepts, ideas, images, meanings and so on, but also particular expectations and norms of argumentation and intervention. The term refers, as such, to the entire arena in which moral-political disputes arise and are staged, and in which some particular kinds of question come to seem more worthy of being answered than others, and some kinds of answers more useful than others. Scott worries that contemporary anticolonial thought too readily inherits a problem-space forged through past eras, contexts and notions of struggle, and which is ill-suited to present circumstances in at least some crucial respects. He asks, accordingly:

> Does the political point of anticolonialism depend on constructing colonialism as a particular kind of obstacle to be overcome? Does the purchase or salience of anticolonialism depend on a certain narrative form, a certain rhythm, and a certain conception of temporality? Does the anticolonial demand for a certain kind of postcolonial future oblige its histories to produce certain kinds of pasts? (Scott 2004, 7)

In the manner in which I have been talking here, Scott's worry is that the general dominance and naturalisation of progressive-romantic storyings of colonial injustice contributes to a silencing of questions that, perhaps today more than ever, need to be posed rather than presumptively answered. If coloniality in its contemporary forms is to be explored in the manner required, which is to say in a thoroughly critical manner, Scott suggests that we would benefit from upsetting our romantic inclinations and pursuing a more tragic narrative form.

What is meant by the tragic in this instance? Well, opposed to 'the confident hubris of teleologies that extract the future seamlessly from the past', the tragic is, in Scott's conception, more attuned 'to the intricacies, ambiguities, and paradoxes of the relation between actions and their consequences, and intentions and the chance contingencies that sometimes undo them' (2004, 210). In this sense, it consists in a 'more respectful attitude to the contingencies of the past in the present' and a greater sensitivity to the ways in which the past's remains 'come back to usurp our hopes and subvert our ambitions' (2004, 220). Perhaps most importantly, it consists in confronting a hard truth: 'the colonial past may never let go' (2004, 220). Against the self-confidence that saturates the romantic frame – which always threatens to become, at a certain point or in certain ways, a blinding confidence – the tragic is openly permeated by uncertainty, doubt, anxiety, and in being so opens up space for alternative expressions of criticality, expressions that might be crucial in moving to reimagine contemporary dilemmas of coloniality.

What I find most compelling in this call for a turn towards the tragic as a technique of anticolonial storying is that, while clearly taking issue with the kind of progressive and romantic inclinations about which I have raised concern, and for similar reasons, contact is nevertheless maintained with the sense of hope that energises those progressive-romantic forms. For I think it would be wrong to read progressive hope and desire as having no place in the kind of tragicism Scott proposes. More accurate would be to say that these find a different inflection here.

One can see this, perhaps, in the fact that Kant's question 'what may I hope?', employed by Allen (2016) amidst a progressive-romantic storying of anticolonialism, can be sensibly recast within the atmosphere of Scott's tragicism. If in Allen's hands this question is notable for the futural light it is imbued with, illuminating before us a path of overcoming, it can also be read in a darker and much weightier way, for instance, as muttered solemnly into one's chest or even perhaps expelled breathlessly as we slump before an obstacle of seemingly insurmountable proportions. Yet, if darkness appears the more dominant presence on this recasting, it must be considered that this is not so much an originary or pure darkness as one manifested through a *loss* of light (whether through a turn away, its obstruction, or its extinguishment). In other words, it is a darkness *that knows* light. There is, as such, not a simple presence of progressive hope in one and a simple absence in the other. Rather, what we have is a contrast in predilections of hope. A certain contact or correspondence with hope is maintained in the tragic.

In terms of our discussion, of course, the most relevant factor here would be hope for overcoming colonial injustice. And so what I am saying is that if the tragic way of storying anticolonialism starts with the idea that the colonial past may never let go, it nevertheless maintains a residual contact with the hope that it will. Indeed, it is not incidental that in urging us to consider this alternative, Scott places us firmly in the domain of the possible: the colonial past *may* never let go. *But then it may.* This is a mode of storying, then, that is not radically detached from progress or overcoming, and if it does move to abandon them, it is more by way of disillusionment with or doubt in the promises they hold than through ignorance of them.

The tragic anticolonial story remains, in this sense, 'for' progress even as it mobilises 'against' it. To be sure, it engenders a form of scepticism about the possibility of overcoming colonial injustice and elevates this scepticism (or doubt or uncertainty) to a prevailing theme. But in doing so, it nevertheless tacitly retains that possibility and the hope that accompanies it, differently inflected of course, but no less vividly. And this should be no surprise. The tragic anticolonial story remains, after all, *anti*colonial. It does not set out to render colonial injustice unnecessarily permanent or refigure it as inert, and still less to divert interest from it or undermine efforts to understand and confront it. What it aspires to is a different, and in fact more thoroughly critical, direction of view onto the colonial – one that, in Scott's terms, might assist in productively reimagining the contemporary problem-space.

It is worth noting a threat that perhaps inhabits a turn towards tragicism of this kind. This lies in the fact that, just as a romantic fixation on a better future might, ironically, have the tragic consequence of confining us to a colonial present, there is a danger that our embrace of the tragic might start to verge on the romantic, that is, to become a matter of fixation that would lead us towards new presumptive answers to the very questions it originally helped to open up. *Does* anticolonialism depend on constructing colonial injustice as a particular kind of obstacle to be overcome? *Is* anticolonialism somehow reliant on a certain rhythm of critique and/or a certain conception of temporality? Upsetting naturalised answers to such questions is important, but the point surely cannot be to simply institute new (inverted) answers in their place. Keeping in view the full extent of the tragic's relationship with contingency, possibility and hope is, then, I would hazard, crucial to realising the truly critical benefits it promises, not only initially but in ongoing fashion.

What this amounts to is a suggestion that the incorporation of tragic narrative forms into practices of anticolonial storying holds potential to expand the domain of questions that can be sensibly posed and explored, and can alter orientations to such lines of questioning in the process (that is, by figuring relevant objectives of investigation as irresolvable openings or prompts to critical work rather than in principle closable through it). In particular, the tragic narrative agitates against the easy naturalisation of presumptive answers concerning the nature of colonial injustice (and struggles against it), and so offers enhanced opportunities to realise and resist the critical retreats or failures this might otherwise lead to. In the concluding section I want to take a few tentative steps – progressive imagery notwithstanding – towards considering what this means for Western anticolonialism in a practical sense.

CONCLUSION: UNSETTLING NARRATIVES

It seems plausible that all meaningful critical engagements depend on a certain storying of injustice. They face, that is, a need to establish (or accept) a narrative frame within which the intended object of study acquires form and significance. Accordingly, they must proceed in view of some basic assumptions or claims about the form that thing takes, its significance, its moral status, its relationship to us and so on. Sometimes these will be openly acknowledged along the way, held up as contestable perhaps, or defended in one way or another; at other times they will remain unacknowledged or unrealised. But a form of storying will be evident nonetheless. It is what carries along a critical engagement, indeed, makes it an engagement at all.

My interest here has been in how efforts to develop anticolonialism with/within/through the Western critical tradition might falter in their ambitions by virtue of practices and patterns of storying. The argument I have tried to develop is that while a progressive structure of overcoming might in some sense be integral to all such work, given the temporal-historical entanglements of the critical belief that underpins it, when left unchecked this can have an undermining effect. It leaves us vulnerable to a form of critical failure that is not merely technical but results in the very real refusal, silencing, or closure of some pertinent lines of questioning, indeed, lines that might actually prove some of the most difficult but important Western anticolonialism has to face. Included here are questions about the impermanence or permanence of colonial injustice; the eliminability of complicity and guilt associated with it; the damage caused by Western anticolonialism even when succeeding by its own standards; and Western anticolonialism's reduction to a form of self-therapy. A self-conscious turn towards more tragic storyings of colonial justice, I have suggested, offers possibilities for upsetting the kind of naturalised romanticism that inhibits such questioning and therefore signals a pathway of greater critical consistency. But what does this really mean for the practice and development of Western anticolonialism? Does this mean we should aim to make *all* anticolonial stories tragic ones?

The perhaps somewhat frustrating answer I want to close on is 'yes' and 'no'. Let me try to explain the 'no' part first.

I think that were the conclusion to be taken from the preceding argument that we should now move to recast all storyings of colonial injustice in an expressly tragic mould, this would not only be probably unworkable but to set our sights on a different kind of impoverishment of the critical terrain. This is because it would in effect aim to supplant one restricted frame with another. Granted, it might be argued that tragicism tends to be more hospitable to complexity, nuance and contingency than romance typically shows itself to be, and so if our choice is between one or other of these narrative forms then, from a critical point of view at least, tragicism might be the preferable option. But even if this is so (and I think a convincing challenge could be made to that claim), in reality we do not face a trade-off of this kind. First, the field of Western anticolonialism can clearly support varied and opposing forms of storying and has no requirement to commit to a single model; second, even individual storytellers are perfectly able to move between narrative forms, either between critical interventions or within them, for the sake of opening different sets of questions and considering different kinds of answers, and subjecting existing questions or answers to more rigorous scrutiny. The point of calling for a turn to the tragic is therefore not to say that we *all* need to tell tragic stories *all* of the time. Moreover, it is worth noting that much of the power of tragicism – it is tempting to get a little carried away here and say even its whole *point* – is precisely that it troubles the norm, that it jars, offers an unfamiliar reflection of our hopes, expectations and desires, exposing some of their more unfounded, ridiculous or even violent aspects. To saturate the discursive field with the tragic would be to risk, ironically, compromising this power. If the point is, as Scott (2004) suggests, to help us reimagine the contemporary problem-space of colonial injustice, the call for a turn towards the tragic seems most convincing when taken as a call for greater *inclusion*, not as endorsing a new all-encompassing cult of the tragic. Criticality is enhanced when naturalisation is resisted, and so a vibrant plurality of perspectival positions and techniques of representation is most conducive to this. So, *no*, not all storyings of colonial injustice need to be expressly tragic.

And yet, I would say that there is a need to promote greater contact with the tragic across critical engagements in general, including where these remain, at heart, romantic. And this is the 'yes' part of my answer.

The critical inconsistency that arises when we are 'for' progress but not against' it is most acute when even the possibility of being 'against' it is obscured. It is at this point that the naturalisation of the temporal-historical is most complete and finds greatest freedom to configure our understanding of justice and injustice, and our relation to it. Yet, we know that the best romances are those that trade in jeopardy, that is, that are willing to tread a fine line between fear and desire and to play on the possibility that the ending, when it does come, will be an unhappy one. By its own standards, then, the romantic story is enhanced by flirtation with the tragic. And so it is with anticolonial storyings. Even when the governing theme remains, essentially, one of overcoming, the more plausible and tangible the *possibility* of failure, the more powerful that story becomes. Put a little less indirectly: the more serious and comprehensive the engagement with questions concerning the possibility and morality of overcoming itself, the more satisfying will be any resolution in its favour. A discursive field characterised by greater contact with the tragic, then, even amidst its continuing romanticism, would seem more in keeping with a thorough and consistent critical ethos. In contributing to this, Western critical work might better serve and engender forms of anticolonialism suited to the present age.

NOTES

*   I am grateful to Lawrence Hamilton and the NRF/British Academy Chair in Political Theory for supporting the initial phase of research for this chapter, and to the organisers and participants of 'After the Prelude: Decolonisation, Revolution, and Evolution?' at the Johannesburg Institute for Advanced Study, 9–11 July 2018, where a first draft of these ideas was presented.

1   There are in fact three focal points in Allen's analysis, the third being Rainer Forst. I have chosen not to include Forst here given that the charge against him is slightly different. In contrast to the neo-Hegelian reconstructivism of Habermas and Honneth, Forst adopts a neo-Kantian constructivist normative strategy, centred on a universal basic right to justification. On Allen's account, this arguably offers better protection against charges of ethnocentrism, but does so by sacrificing too much in the way of critical potency in respect of the kinds of power relations that anticolonialism must engage. If in a somewhat different way, then, here, too, critical theory stands accused of failing to offer a suitable basis for opposing colonial and cognate injustices, and perhaps remaining indirectly complicit in their perpetuation.

REFERENCES

Allen, Amy. 2016. *The End of Progress: Decolonizing the Normative Foundations of Critical Theory.* New York: Columbia University Press.

Ciccariello-Maher, George. 2017. *Decolonizing Dialectics.* Durham, NC: Duke University Press.

Currie, Mark. 2007. *About Time: Narrative, Fiction and the Philosophy of Time.* Edinburgh: Edinburgh University Press.

Fanon, Frantz. 1963 [1961]. *The Wretched of the Earth.* Translated by Constance Farrington. New York: Grove Press.

Fanon, Frantz. 2008 [1952]. *Black Skin, White Masks.* Translated by Richard Philcox. London: Pluto Press.

Fraser, Nancy. 2020. *Fortunes of Feminism: From State-Managed Capitalism to Neoliberal Crisis.* London: Verso.

Johnson, Walter. 2000. 'Possible Pasts: Some Speculations on Time, Temporality, and the History of Atlantic Slavery'. *American Studies* 45 (4): 485–499. http://www.jstor.org/stable/41157603.

McCarthy, Thomas. 2009. *Race, Empire, and the Idea of Human Development.* Cambridge: Cambridge University Press.

Mignolo, Walter. 2011. *The Darker Side of Western Modernity: Global Futures, Decolonial Options.* Durham, NC: Duke University Press.

Mignolo, Walter and Catherine Walsh. 2018. *On Decoloniality: Concepts, Analytics, Praxis.* Durham, NC: Duke University Press.

Ndlovu-Gatsheni, Sabelo. 2013. *Coloniality of Power in Postcolonial Africa: Myths of Decolonization.* Dakar: Council for the Development of Social Science Research in Africa.

Quijano, Aníbal. 2000. 'Coloniality of Power and Eurocentrism in Latin America'. *International Sociology* 15 (2): 215–232. https://doi.org/10.1177/026858090001500 2005.

Ricoeur, Paul. 1988. *Time and Narrative: Volume 3.* Translated by Kathleen Blamey and David Pellauer. Chicago: University of Chicago Press.

Santos, Boaventura de Sousa. 2016. *Epistemologies of the South: Justice against Epistemicide.* Abingdon: Routledge.

Scott, David. 2004. *Conscripts of Modernity: The Tragedy of Colonial Enlightenment.* Durham, NC: Duke University Press.

Young, Robert. 1990. *White Mythologies: Writing History and the West.* London: Routledge.

7

The Limits of Decolonisation
and the Problem of Legitimacy

Paul Patton

I ndigenous peoples have long challenged the claims of European states and their settler colonial successors to exercise sovereignty over their territories. Ever since the 1960 United Nations (UN) 'Declaration on the Granting of Independence to Colonial Countries and Peoples', General Assembly Resolution 1514 (XV) (United Nations 1960) limited the right of self-determination to subjugated territories that were 'geographically separate' – a requirement often misleadingly referred to as the 'blue water' or 'salt water' thesis, suggesting the need for there to be ocean between the colonial power and the territory in question – their path towards decolonisation has been different from that of the territories decolonised during the 1950s and 1960s. Up until the adoption in 2007 of the UN 'Declaration on the Rights of Indigenous Peoples', General Assembly Resolution 61/295 (UNDRIP, United Nations 2007), it has largely been pursued through the domestic courts and legislatures of the settler colonial countries. These countries developed a range of constitutional and legal settlements that determined the status of the Indigenous peoples, from domestic dependant sovereignty to treaties and the recognition of common law rights to land and other resources. A variety of arguments have been put forward in support of special status and specific rights for such colonised Indigenous peoples, in the ongoing effort to 'decolonise' their relationship to the liberal democratic states that have inherited these constitutional and legal settlements. One such argument raises questions about the legitimacy of government by such states (Ivison 2017; Moore 2010; Patton 2009, 2019).

There are two distinct approaches to the question of legitimacy in contemporary political philosophy. One approach builds on the tradition from John Locke to Immanuel Kant and John Rawls in supposing that government is legitimate when it produces the kinds of moral goods expected of government, such as justice. In these terms, it may be argued that citizens who benefit from the protections of a just social order tacitly consent to the government that provides those protections. Rawls argues that the exercise of (coercive) political power is legitimate when it produces justice, or at least a political regime that is not too unjust.[1] Building on his account of how principles of justice are produced, he proposes as a criterion of legitimacy that power be exercised 'in accordance with a constitution the essentials of which all citizens as free and equal may reasonably be expected to endorse in the light of principles and ideals acceptable to their common human reason' (Rawls 2005, 137, 393).

Another approach, recently defended by Philip Pettit, builds on an actualist conception of the citizen–state relation and the work of Alan John Simmons to reject all forms of hypothetical contract or consent as a basis for legitimacy (Simmons 2001). The 'hypothetical' approach is rejected on the grounds that it allows a social and political order to count as legitimate if it satisfies terms that people would endorse if they were sufficiently reasonable and rational, thereby shifting focus from the relation of people to their government to the nature of the social order established by government. In these terms, a benevolent dictatorship or a well-intentioned colonial regime might count as legitimate. Pettit follows Simmons in arguing that, by contrast, legitimacy concerns 'the actual world' and the contingent relationship between a people and their government (Pettit 2012, 141). Tacit consent or a hypothetical contract would allow forms of government to count as legitimate even though they are not supported by those governed 'as they are actually disposed' (2012, 144).

Pettit argues that justice and legitimacy are distinct concepts that impose distinct demands. He suggests that the difference between legitimacy understood in terms of the actual relation between a people and their government and legitimacy understood in hypothetical terms marks a deep divide in contemporary political thought.[2] However, both approaches proceed on the assumption that they are dealing with a more or less homogeneous people on a given territory. When we take into account the situation of colonised peoples as more or less permanent minorities in settler states, both tend to support the conclusion that these are illegitimate regimes. The question then arises of what, when the history and circumstances of colonised peoples are taken into account, these approaches can tell us about the kinds of constitutional, legal and policy arrangements that might ensure legitimacy. The aim of this chapter is to explore this question by comparing Pettit's neo-republican conception of legitimacy with that of Rawls, from the perspective of how they might respond to the situation of colonised Indigenous peoples.

PETTIT'S NEO-REPUBLICAN CONCEPTION OF LEGITIMACY

All governments should and do set limits to the freedom to act on the part of citizens. In the terms of Pettit's neo-republicanism, the problem is to reconcile the coercive power of government with the freedom as non-domination of citizens. His core idea is that where state interference with the freedom of citizens remains under their control it no longer counts as domination. He argues that a government that is subject to the democratic will of the people will be legitimate:

> If the people governed by a state control the ways in which government interferes with their freedom – if they control the laws imposed, the policies pursued, the taxes levied – then they may not suffer domination at the hands of their rulers and may continue to enjoy their freedom in relation to the state. A state that was suitably controlled would be legitimate in the required sense of not exercising domination over its people. (Pettit 2012, 153)

A state that is suitably controlled by its citizens is one in which the people are able to influence the process that leads to particular outcomes, and one in which they exercise that influence in a manner that imposes a direction on the policies of government that is acceptable to all. Pettit devotes two chapters of *On the People's Terms* to outlining the institutional mechanisms through which such control might be achieved. The first is a system of representative democracy in which members of the ruling assembly are elected on the basis of their electoral promises and commitments to govern in the interests of all. This form of 'responsive' assembly, in the context of a mixed constitution that separates the legislative, executive and judicial powers of the state, is presented as the best way to achieve individualised, unconditioned and effective control over government. The second is a 'dual aspect' model of democracy in which the day-to-day deliberations over policy are supposed to elicit norms of public policy-making in the common interest. To the extent that the process of policy-making is actually carried out in accordance with such norms, the policy outcomes will be acceptable to all.

I will come back to the question of how popular influence is supposed to impact on the direction of government policy. For the moment, I focus on Pettit's account of the nature of popular control. This is supposed to satisfy three conditions. First, it must be democratic, in the sense that it is equally shared among all citizens. All must have equal access to participation in a system of government that gives people control over the direction of public policies. This commitment to democratic decision-making must involve a readiness to accept outcomes that are not in accordance with one's personal preferences. Pettit's rejection of contractualist approaches that give a normative sense to 'acceptability' implies that this readiness means that people are actually disposed to accept a given outcome, whether or not it is their preferred option (Pettit 2012, 170). Living with others on equal terms means that sometimes the views of others prevail.

Second, the required form of control must be unconditioned, in the sense that it depends on no will other than that of the people concerned. It cannot depend on the will of a governing body, individual, or group that merely humours the electorate in acting in accordance with their will. Nor can it be the will of any alien power that exercises some form of colonial or neocolonial influence over the direction of government.[3]

Third, the required form of control must be effective in the sense that individuals have no cause to complain if the outcome is a form of government intervention in their lives that they do not approve. As noted above, the fact of living in political society on equal terms with others means that no individual can expect to exercise personal control over the direction of government. Part of what it means to live in a democracy is that the control exercised over government will be shared with others and that, as a consequence, individuals may not always get the policy result they desired.

Given that there will be many situations in which 'the people' are divided on the appropriate policy, effective popular control must include mechanisms for resolving such differences: elections of course, but also referral to independent tribunals including courts, referenda and majority votes in elected assemblies. Whatever the procedure, it has to be such that all individuals are actually disposed to accept the outcome. If a decision of government is not in accordance with your wishes, you must be able to think that it was just 'tough luck' that the decision went that way:

> The point of legitimacy is to ensure that you and your fellow citizens are not subject to an alien, controlling will, despite the fact that there may be a good deal of discretion exercised by those in power. Such legitimacy will be adequately ensured … to the extent that you and your fellows have good grounds to think that any unwelcome results of public decision-making are just tough luck. (Pettit 2012, 177)

Judgements of 'tough luck' thus provide a test for assessing how far the democratic control over government is effective. When there is no ground for resentment at the outcome, we can suppose that the test is passed. There is still scope for resentment at the ignorance, indifference, or even stupidity of your peers for failing to perceive the merits of good policy, but on Pettit's view such resentment at fellow citizens is consistent with supposing that government itself is legitimate because subject to the shared, unconditioned and effective control of citizens.

MINORITIES AND THE PROBLEM OF STICKY DIVIDES: 'THOSE OF OUR KIND'

The 'tough luck' test raises a number of issues that turn around the different ways that the subject of democratic control may be divided. Pettit acknowledges that minority groups are vulnerable to domination by majority government when he notes that 'if we are subject to a government that can dominate us, as in an illegitimate regime, then we are going to lack control over changes in that government's will towards us and towards *those of our kind*' (Pettit 2012, 24, author's emphasis).

The italicised phrase suggests that the 'we' that is dominated is a particular kind of citizen. There are many ways in which 'the people' who exercise control over a government may be divided on the basis of ethnicity, religious belief, historical experience, or other factors. Consider the division in countries established by colonisation between descendants of the colonisers, along with subsequent immigrants, and the descendants of the colonised. Where the latter are a minority, and where there is a long history of prejudicial beliefs and deeply ingrained racist attitudes, they are all too often subject to decisions of government that they opposed, or would have opposed if they had been consulted. Ignorance of their culture and hostility towards them is deeply entrenched. In many cases, they have been subjected to colonial and postcolonial policies of assimilation designed to eliminate their language and their culture. They consistently experience the frustration of their hopes and desires in ways that lead to suspicion and resentment of the state as well as of their fellow citizens. Social indicators such as high rates of suicide, alcoholism, drug use and penal incarceration are among the signs of this frustration and resentment.

From the perspective of minorities such as these, the idea that they participate equally in the effective control of government appears at best a hollow ideal. It is not just a matter of tough luck that a majority of their fellow citizens harbour active or passive racist beliefs that lead them to consistently oppose the full and equal enjoyment of basic rights by Indigenous people. It is a matter of aspects of individual and collective colonial identity that are not readily subject to change. It is not the case that members of such minorities could just as easily have been on the winning side. On the contrary, they are consistently and systematically on the losing side in majority decision-making processes.

Pettit acknowledges this problem in discussing the phenomenon of different kinds of 'sticky divide' between majorities and minorities. Where there are entrenched differences of the kind that we see in countries established by colonisation, equal individual votes are not sufficient to ensure equally accessible influence over government policy:

> On one or another range of issues there may always be a more or less sticky divide between a majority and a minority and, if there

is, then on that range of issues people will not enjoy equal access to influence, not having the same *ex ante* chance of being on the winning side; the patterns of electoral or legislative voting may shut out the minority. (Pettit 2012, 212)

Sticky divides pose a problem for the 'tough luck' test. They expose the fact that not all individuals and groups have the same *ex ante* chance of being in the majority on certain issues. In response to this problem, Pettit allows for the possibility of other decision-making procedures to ensure equal, unconditional and effective control over government. Institutional responses might include forms of relatively independent regional or cultural self-government, or the establishment of independent bodies with whom governments are supposed to consult on issues relating to the interests of the minorities concerned. Such institutional responses might well be 'messy', but a republican conception of legitimacy could not take that as a reason to exclude them (Pettit 2012, 214).

The case for such institutional changes to simple majority decision-making would have to be made in terms that appeal to the common good, for example by arguing that failure to make such changes would expose the minority to disadvantages to which no one should be exposed (Pettit 2012, 16). However, it is plausible to think that the case could be made in relation to a range of issues such as cultural heritage, cultural identity, or title to traditional lands or waters. Will Kymlicka's argument for minority cultural rights is of this form: without such rights, minorities would be subject to a loss of context of choice that all should enjoy (Kymlicka 1989). However, as the debate over Kymlicka's argument shows, it remains at best an open question whether the kinds of measures that could be defended in such terms would be sufficient to maintain equality of influence on the part of Indigenous people (Patton 2019: 1267–1269).

Proposals for distinct status and for special forms of consultation with Indigenous people have been put forward in the context of Australian debates about reconciliation or constitutional recognition

(Dodson 2000; Lino 2018; Pearson 2014). It is a strength of the republican conception of legitimacy that it supports consideration of such proposals, to the extent that it seeks to maintain the principle of equal influence over government for relatively permanent minorities. However, it is doubtful whether the mere presence of mechanisms of contestation or alternative decision-making would be sufficient to overcome the problem of sticky divisions among the people. Pettit's insistence that legitimacy concerns the *actual* relationship between the state and the people further raises the bar. It implies that legitimacy will not be assured by the existence of a regime in which citizens *could* exercise the requisite control over government. Rather, the mechanisms must work and citizens must be able to effectively exercise a certain degree and kind of control over the state and its policies. This brings us back to the question of the actual influence of people over the nature and direction of public policy.

REPUBLICAN PUBLIC REASON AND THE LIMITS OF LEGITIMACY

As noted earlier, the control theory of legitimacy requires influence over the process that leads to government policy, but also the exercise of that influence in a manner that imposes a direction on government that is acceptable to all. This implies that it should not be possible for a permanent majority to impose policies that are unacceptable to a minority. But this is precisely what has happened in societies established by colonisation. They involve deep and abiding differences about what the public interest requires and the manner in which government should be conducted. Pettit's answer to the question of how, in the face of deeply entrenched differences of way of life, outlook, or beliefs, a people may nonetheless exercise control that imposes a direction equally acceptable to all is complex. It relies on the idea that a republican system of democratic influence over government will produce norms of public deliberation and policy-making acceptable to all and that, over time, these will constrain the policies of government to develop in a direction acceptable to all. Briefly, the argument for this dual aspect or two-speed conception of democracy goes as follows. A republican system of democratic influence is supposed to include a responsive representative assembly with periodic elections, a complementary set of mechanisms that allow individuals or groups to challenge discriminatory measures or procedures, a division of powers and a system that controls for corruption by private interests (Pettit 2012, 260). The operation of this system is then supposed to ensure that citizens pursue political debate in the form of an 'acceptability game' that seeks agreement by offering reasons that others should find compelling. This is contrasted with debate in the form of an 'acceptance game' that simply trades concessions. Because it requires people to argue in terms that are acceptable to all given the actual beliefs of the people concerned, rather than the beliefs they ought to have if they were sufficiently rational and reasonable, it is also contrasted with Rawlsian public reason. Political debate is subject to an overriding norm to the effect that 'participants should only offer considerations for or against a policy that all can regard as relevant' (2012, 254). To the extent that this norm operates in a given political community, so the argument goes, it should lead to the emergence of more specific norms regulating the kinds of considerations relevant to public policy.[4] And to the extent that such norms govern the process of policy formation, the outcomes will be in the public interest and properly acceptable to all.

Pettit refers to the historical example of the nineteenth-century transformation of British government to support the claim that, in the long run, democratic government can affect the direction of government in a manner that will be acceptable to all.[5] The transformation of government after the extension of the franchise in 1832 saw it assume responsibility for many aspects of social life that had previously gone unregulated, such as public health and employment conditions, the manufacture of food and drugs, and the operations of the civil service. This transformation is used to illustrate 'the depth at which policy-making norms can operate in a broadly democratic context to impose a slow, long-haul direction on government' (Pettit 2012, 271).

However, one example does not show that the existence of a democratically empowered acceptability game will always eliminate injustice and ensure legitimacy. One could equally point to countries established by colonisation, such as Australia, where more than a century of democratic government saw little change in the situation of a minority Indigenous population. When the Commonwealth of Australia was established in 1901, Indigenous people were not consulted either about the drafting or the adoption of the constitution. Section 51 (xxvi) of the Commonwealth of Australia Constitution Act, 9 July 1900, explicitly denied the Commonwealth power to make laws regarding 'the aboriginal race in any State', thereby leaving control over the lives of Indigenous people in the hands of provincial state governments (Commonwealth of Australia 1900). Section 127 excluded them from being counted in the population tables used to calculate states' entitlements to electorates and to portions of Commonwealth revenue. While these provisions were removed by referendum in 1967, others with the potential to allow discriminatory treatment remain. Indigenous Australians still live under a constitution that makes no mention of their distinct identity and prior occupation of the land. They continue to suffer injustice as a consequence of government policies adopted during the colonial period.

Pettit acknowledges that he presents an optimistic vision of the dual aspect of democracy in which, under the constraints of the acceptability game, the day-to-day struggles over public policy will generate norms that sustain the adoption of policies acceptable to all. This model will only work where popular influence over government is sufficiently individualised, unconditioned and efficacious, 'and where the rules of the acceptability game have a sufficient presence to ensure the deliberative regulation of public business' (Pettit 2012, 279). In many cases, these conditions will not be met and legitimate government will remain an aspiration rather than a feature of any actual government (2012, 180, 279).[6] The history of settler colonial countries offers little evidence to suggest that such a model would produce government that is legitimate from the perspective of Indigenous minority peoples.

RAWLS: LEGITIMACY, JUSTICE AND THE NON-IDEAL CASE
OF COLONIAL SOCIETY

In his later work, Rawls proposes a conception of legitimacy that is political rather than moral and that is compatible with deep and persistent
divergence between comprehensive moral views. As noted earlier, government is legitimate when it is exercised in accordance with a constitution,

> the essentials of which all citizens as free and equal may reason-
> ably be expected to endorse in the light of principles and ideals
> acceptable to their common human reason. This is the liberal
> principle of legitimacy. To this it adds that all questions arising
> in the legislature that concern or border on constitutional essen-
> tials, or basic questions of justice, should also be settled, so far
> as possible, by principles and ideals that can be similarly endorsed.
> (Rawls 2005, 137; see also 216, 393)

This statement of conditions under which the exercise of political
power is legitimate raises a number of questions. Here I will begin with
the question of what is meant by 'the essentials' of a political constitution,
returning below to the approach to legislation that concerns the matter
of basic justice. On one reading, 'essentials' might refer to key features of
a given constitution, including those that differentiate it from other constitutions devised in the light of the same principles of justice. I return
to this interpretation of the phrase below. On another reading, constitutional essentials might refer to the principles of justice that are the object
of an overlapping consensus and that inform the drafting of a constitution for a particular political regime. This reading would be consistent
with the idea that these essentials are such that it would be reasonable to
expect that all citizens might endorse them 'in the light of principles and
ideals acceptable to their common human reason' (Rawls 2005, 137).

Understood in this manner, political liberalism's principle ties legitimacy to justice, in contrast to Pettit's view that they are entirely separate

matters. Rawls acknowledges that legitimacy and justice are independent concepts. A democratic regime may be legitimate, yet neither its laws nor its policies may be just: 'laws passed by solid majorities are counted legitimate, even though many protest and correctly judge them unjust or otherwise wrong' (Rawls 2005, 427). The converse is also true insofar as a regime may be just but not legitimate. However, Rawls insists that even though neither procedures nor the laws that result from them need be acceptable 'by a strict standard of justice', the laws and policies of a democratic regime cannot be 'too gravely unjust'. At some point, the injustice of a political constitution or the outcomes of an otherwise legitimate democratic procedure will corrupt the legitimacy of the regime. Democratic regimes may not be just, but they must be 'sufficiently just in view of the circumstances and social conditions' (2005, 428).

This connection between legitimacy and justice, along with the overriding requirement of political liberalism that the principles of justice must be capable of being endorsed by all rational and reasonable citizens, raises a problem for government in societies established by colonisation. If, as in many cases, there is continuing injustice in their treatment of Indigenous peoples, to what degree does this undermine their claim to legitimacy? Given the injustices that accompanied colonisation and the subsequent treatment of Indigenous peoples, the legitimacy of government in such cases will depend upon the degree to which it has *become* sufficiently just. Further, the fact that the principles of justice must be the object of an overlapping consensus raises the prospect that legitimate government will only be achieved in colonial societies once the principles that inform their constitutions are acceptable to Indigenous as well as non-Indigenous citizens.

For these reasons, Rawls' liberal principle of legitimacy is more demanding than Pettit's neo-republican principle. In addition, I suggest, it has implications for the constitutional and legal conditions under which government in societies established by colonisation can become legitimate. To see why, we need to return to the details of Rawls' theory of justice.

THE CIRCUMSTANCES OF JUSTICE IN SOCIETIES ESTABLISHED BY COLONISATION

It might be objected that colonial society is a special, non-ideal case that Rawls' theory was not designed to address. The aim of his theory of justice was limited to determining the principles that should apply in an ideal situation. This assumes an ordered society, favourable circumstances and strict compliance with the principles of justice that would be chosen behind a veil of ignorance. Only after the fundamental principles of social justice are settled for the normal conditions of an idealised modern democratic society can we take up issues raised by departures from these normal conditions (Rawls 1999, 216). The methodological rationale for beginning with such an ideal case is familiar and compelling. As Rawls notes in *Political Liberalism*, ideal theory 'which defines a perfectly just basic structure, is a necessary complement to nonideal theory without which the desire for change lacks an aim' (Rawls 2005, 285). In these terms, the particular historical injustices involved in colonisation and its aftermath may be considered a matter for non-ideal theory. However, another way to approach the question of justice in settler colonial societies would be to modify the terms of Rawls' problem in order to ask what principles might be agreed to in an ideal postcolonial society. There are compelling reasons to modify the terms of the problem in this way. The question of justice for Indigenous peoples is a no less important and enduring problem within the political culture of liberal democracies established by colonisation than the ongoing disagreement over the appropriate balance of liberty and equality that Rawls' ideal theory initially sought to address.

Rawls' ideal case in *Theory of Justice* begins with the idea of society understood as 'a co-operative venture for mutual advantage' and described only in the most general terms under which 'circumstances of justice' could be said to obtain (Rawls 1999, 109). Two kinds of circumstance are relevant: first, objective conditions such as the coexistence of people 'at the same time on a definite geographical territory', where they are supposed to be roughly similar in physical and mental powers; second, subjective conditions such as roughly similar or at least complementary needs and interests such that 'mutually advantageous cooperation among them is possible' (1999, 110).

In the case of societies established by colonisation, geographical coexistence clearly applies. However, the peoples involved may have such culturally different mental and physical powers that there is no need for mutually advantageous cooperation: one group can simply dominate the other. In such cases, it is doubtful whether the relevant peoples ever participated in a cooperative venture for mutual advantage, especially where coexistence on the same territory was not established by negotiation or mutual consent. And if the relevant peoples might be said now to cooperate for mutual advantage, it is an open question at what point they came to form a single society.[7]

Leaving aside the historical facts about the manner in which coexistence came about, along with the cultural conditions that enabled the domination of Indigenous people, there is reason to ask how and in what ways the subjective circumstances of justice apply. While the needs and interests of Indigenous and settler peoples overlap in many respects, there are other ways in which they can be antithetical. For example, their different economic interests and forms of land use may come into conflict when the settler society takes no account of the ways in which land is also a spiritual and cultural dimension of Indigenous people's identity. Such differences imply that we cannot assume agreement about primary social goods. They point to the idea that, in societies established by colonisation, a political conception of justice should allow for differential rights available only to Indigenous people.

THE ORIGINAL POSITION

Besides the different circumstances of justice, another way in which the conditions of the non-ideal colonial case depart from the terms of Rawls' ideal case involves the kind of information that is relevant in determining the principles of justice. The political conception of justice that underpins judgements of legitimacy should be one that rational and reasonable individuals would agree to under the restrictions on information imposed by the original position. The 'original position' is Rawls' version of a social contract in which, to ensure fairness, parties are supposed to decide behind a veil of ignorance that prevents them from knowing details about their society or their own place within it. This information is excluded in order that the principles agreed upon do not reflect the interests of particular groups. Thus, in Rawls' initial formulation, parties to the original position are not only supposed to be ignorant of their own place in the society, they are also assumed not to know 'the particular circumstances of their own society', including its 'economic or political situation, or the level of civilization and culture it has been able to achieve' (Rawls 1999, 118). Their situation is one in which 'the course of history is closed to them' (1999, 175). Under these conditions, it seems clear that the parties should not be supposed to know that peoples with very different kinds of civilisation and culture coexist on the territory in question. The contingencies of colonisation are precisely the kinds of information expressly excluded by the veil of ignorance.

However, we should bear in mind that in the terms of Rawls' later formulations, the original position is only a device of representation designed to enable citizens to devise principles that accord with their considered intuitions. Moreover, it is a device that can be applied at any moment in the history of a given society. As such, 'it models what we regard – here and now – as acceptable restrictions on the reasons on the basis of which the parties ... may properly put forward certain principles of justice and reject others' (Rawls 2001, 80). In these terms, it is arguable that citizens or their representatives in the original position should be aware of the possibility that different peoples can coexist on the same territory. This might have consequences for the way in which the principles of justice take into account civilisational or cultural differences. If the device were applied in a society that was established by colonisation, then knowledge of this fact and its consequences might be necessary in order to arrive at principles of justice acceptable to all.[8]

CONSTITUTIONALISM AND THE FOUR-STAGE SEQUENCE

Whether or not we find compelling the case for modifying the information available behind the veil of ignorance in the original position, the situation is different with regard to decisions about constitutional principles. Rawls argues that constitutional and legal rights should be determined via successive iterations of the hypothetical original position. First, citizens' representatives must decide on basic principles of justice. Second, there will be a constitutional convention at which the parties should agree on a system for the constitutional powers of government and the basic rights of citizens (Rawls 1999, 172). The third stage involves legislation passed in accordance with the requirements of the constitution, while the fourth involves judicial review of legislation and acts of government. These stages correspond to the institutional structure of a liberal constitutional democracy. However, for Rawls, this sequence refers neither to an actual political process nor to a purely theoretical one. It is rather

> part of justice as fairness and constitutes part of a framework of thought that citizens in civil society who accept justice as fairness are to use in applying its concepts and principles ... This framework extends the idea of the original position, adapting it to different settings as the application of principles requires. (Rawls 2005, 397)

This framework makes it clear that the question of rights may be posed at different levels of the political order and that different information will be relevant at each level. Each stage represents a point of view from which certain kinds of questions about the bases of just government can be considered. The general principle governing the successive stages is that the veil of ignorance is supposed to be partially lifted so that progressively more information about the society is made available to the parties.

This framework provides a powerful lever with which to support the case for specifically Indigenous rights in societies established by colonisation. For even if there is good reason to exclude the historical contingencies of colonisation from the information available at the first stage, the same cannot be said in relation to the second stage. At the second stage, the principles of social justice agreed to in the first stage are supposed to be applied to the particular history and political culture of a given society to produce a just constitution, where this means a constitution that rational delegates subject to the relevant restrictions on information would adopt for their society (Rawls 1999, 176). The manner in which the conditions of the 'original position' are modified in the passage from fundamental principles of justice to constitutional principles offers a means to combine principles of justice applicable to all members of the society with specific rights available only to a particular minority. Whereas at the initial stage of the original position, parties were supposed to be ignorant of the particular circumstances of their own society, at the constitutional stage, the general facts about their society are supposed to be available to them. Rawls allows that, while the parties to the constitutional convention remain ignorant of their own social position, they now know

> the relevant general facts about their society, that is, its natural circumstances and resources, its level of economic advance and political culture, and so on. They are no longer limited to the information implicit in the circumstances of justice. Given their theoretical knowledge and the appropriate general facts about their society, they are to choose the most effective just constitution ... (Rawls 1999, 173)

In his 'Reply to Habermas', Rawls reiterates this condition in suggesting that the parties to the constitutional convention are bound not only by the principles of justice accepted in the first stage, but also by 'general information about our society, the kind framers of a constitution would want to know' (Rawls 2005, 398). It seems entirely reasonable to suppose that the relevant facts of colonisation and its aftermath should be available to the framers of a postcolonial constitution. They should know that the society includes among its members the descendants of Indigenous peoples who were in possession of the land at the time of European settlement and that many of these choose to live in accordance with the elements of Indigenous cultures that survived the process of colonisation.

Taking into account the differences between the original position and the constitutional convention suggests the alternative interpretation of the reference to the 'essentials' of a political constitution in Rawls' liberal principle of legitimacy mentioned above. On this reading, 'essentials' might refer to distinctive features of the constitution in question, including those that differentiate it from other constitutions devised in the light of the same or broadly similar principles of justice. So, for example, among the essentials of the United States' as opposed to the Australian constitution is the institution of a directly elected presidency. Understood in this manner, the principle of legitimacy imposes the stringent requirement that such features of the constitution be endorsed by all citizens.

Applied to the situation of a country established by colonisation in which there remains a significant minority of Indigenous peoples, this interpretation requires the drafting of a constitution that Indigenous as well as non-Indigenous citizens might reasonably be expected to endorse. In the case of colonisation where sovereignty over the territory was never ceded by the Indigenous peoples or their ancestors, and where a significant number of those people wish to live, as far as is possible under present conditions, in accordance with their distinctive traditions and cultural ways, could one reasonably expect Indigenous citizens to endorse a constitution that makes no mention of their prior occupation and ownership of the territory and that makes no allowance for their distinctive traditions, culture and way of life? Contemporary evidence suggests not. On the contrary, so long as there are citizens who wish to 'maintain and develop their distinct characteristics and identities', this interpretation of the liberal principle of legitimacy suggests that their right to live as Aboriginal people ought to be protected (Dodson 2000, 264).

Might not those Indigenous citizens, who are also the distinct and original peoples of the land in question, demand that the very principle of self-determination that informs the drafting of a constitution also be applied to them, subject to the constraints implied in their remaining citizens of the postcolonial polity? Consistent application of the principle of self-determination suggests that a constitution acceptable to them might require a right to self-determination in accordance with their distinctive traditions and political culture. Article 3 of the UNDRIP affirms the right of Indigenous peoples to self-determination, albeit qualified by Article 46 according to which the exercise of that right should be consistent with the territorial integrity and political unity of existing states (United Nations 2007). In effect, the UNDRIP reaffirms the compromise between the decolonising aspirations of Indigenous peoples and the sovereignty of UN member states reflected in the 1970 'Declaration on Principles of International Law concerning Friendly Relations and Cooperation among States', General Assembly Declaration 2625 (XXV) (United Nations 1970).[9] It is not clear, however, that this implies a different understanding of self-determination and a restricted sense of 'decolonisation' in the case of Indigenous peoples within settler colonial states. What matters is whether or not the constitutional arrangements under which Indigenous peoples exercise their right of self-determination are the outcome of negotiations between parties of equal status that truly reflect the collective will of the Indigenous peoples concerned (Anaya 2009).[10] The interpretation of the Rawlsian principle of legitimacy outlined above provides a framework consistent with constitutionally distinct rights and status for Indigenous peoples in settler colonial states that are exercised within a framework of national laws regulating the exercise of fundamental rights and freedoms available to all citizens.

CONCLUSION

Ultimately, whether or not government in a postcolonial state is legitimate will depend on the degree to which the limits on the capacity of some citizens to participate fully in the rights and benefits available to all under conditions of fair and equal opportunity have been removed, and on the degree to which the constitutional and administrative regime within the state has been transformed to allow for non-colonial relations between government and Indigenous peoples. For Rawls, no less than for Pettit, legitimacy remains an ideal of reason rather than an identifiable feature of government in societies established by colonisation. However, in Rawls' case, this requires substantive justice rather than simply the achievement of egalitarian norms of public policy-making or the establishment of mechanisms to address the problem of permanent minority in relation to policy outcomes. In addition, I suggest, some elements of his formulation of the principle of legitimacy and the requirements of a just constitution provide helpful guidance in relation to the conditions under which formerly colonial governments might decolonise and become legitimate.

Rawls notes that we always find ourselves governed in accordance with institutions that are the work of previous generations: 'we assess them when we come of age and act accordingly' (Rawls 2005, 399). He points out that there is no general answer to the question of how we should address the injustices of the political institutions that we inherit. The details of a given constitution, such as whether or not it should include provision for treaty rights or other forms of protection for rights of Indigenous peoples specified in legislation, should be decided in part as a function of the 'particular history and democratic culture of the society in question' (2005, 416). Acceptance of specific rights and a distinct constitutional status for Indigenous peoples may go some way towards removing the injustices associated with colonial non-recognition of Indigenous law and culture. In turn, removing those injustices goes some way towards ensuring the legitimacy of the postcolonial state.

NOTES

* An earlier version of this chapter was presented at a roundtable, 'Who are "we, the people"?: Constitutionalism, Recognition and Race,' held at Melbourne Law School in April 2017. I am grateful to the participants and especially to Nicole Roughan for her helpful comments. Subsequent versions were presented at Flinders University, Wuhan University, and the Johannesburg Institute for Advanced Study conference that produced this book, 'After the Prelude: Decolonisation, Revolution, and Evolution?', 9–11 July 2018. I am indebted to participants on these occasions for their questions and comments, and especially to Miguel Vatter for his comments on a written version.

1 See Rawls' discussion of the relationship between legitimacy and justice in 'Reply to Habermas' (Rawls 2005, 427–433).

2 Even Habermas is accused of 'going hypothetical' in *Between Facts and Norms* (Habermas 1995) by formulating his discourse principle of legitimacy in terms of what those affected 'could assent to as participants in rational discourse' (Pettit 2012, 145).

3 Given the imbalance of power between people and governments that dispose of overwhelming force as well as control of information, unconditioned control will in the final analysis rely on people's preparedness to resist or to rebel against an unresponsive government. For this reason, Pettit argues that the degree to which a people's control over its government is unconditional will be a matter of how 'resistive' a society is: how resistance-prone are the people and how resistance-averse is the government (Pettit 2012, 174).

4 Pettit relies on a further significant premise here, namely that the members of the society are all committed 'on a patriotic basis, to making their community work' (Pettit 2012, 261). Only this kind of patriotism will prevent entrenched divisions within the community from preventing the emergence of community-wide norms.

5 He draws on the historical research of MacDonagh (1958, 1961, 1977).

6 Like Rawls, Pettit uses this gap between the ideal and the real to argue for the realistically utopian and critical character of the ideal of legitimacy. Similarly, he acknowledges at one point that the republican conception is 'an ideal that democracy at its best, might be required to achieve or approximate' (Pettit 2012, 180). See Rawls, 'Reply to Habermas' in Rawls (2005, 372–433).

7 Charles Mills comments that acknowledging the origin of white settler states as established through invasion and conquest 'would explode the foundations of a conceptual framework predicated on treating society as "a cooperative venture for mutual advantage"' (Mills 2009, 171). He points out that Rawls' assumption indicates that his presumed audience is really the white settlers of North America and their descendants: 'only for this population could it not be ludicrously inapposite to represent the society as "a co-operative venture for mutual advantage" as Rawls suggests we do in *Theory*' (Mills 2009, 173).

8 I am indebted to Nicole Roughan and Miguel Vatter for drawing attention to the possibility that knowledge that more than one people may coexist on a given territory might be considered among the general characteristics of society and, as such, something to be considered even behind the veil of ignorance in the initial position.

9   This declaration affirms that 'all peoples have the right freely to determine, without external interference, their political status and to pursue their economic, social and cultural development', that all states are under a duty to respect this right, and that all states are under a duty to promote the realisation of the principle of equal rights and self-determination of peoples in order to 'bring a speedy end to colonialism'. At the same time, the declaration affirms that nothing it says should be construed as 'authorizing or encouraging any action that would dismember or impair, totally or in part, the territorial integrity and political unity of sovereign and independent States', where those states have a non-discriminatory legal structure and a government that represents 'the whole people belonging to the territory' (United Nations 1970).

10   See also the argument of Ludvig Beckman, Kirsty Gover and Ulf Mörkenstam from the perspective of the constituent power of Indigenous peoples that 'post-colonial settler-state legitimacy requires that Indigenous peoples are able to exercise constituent power commensurate with their right to self-determination, i.e. that they are able to participate as sovereign peoples in the design of the constitutional arrangements that facilitate their political participation' (Beckman et al. 2022, 12).

REFERENCES

Anaya, S. James. 2009. 'The Right of Indigenous People to Self-Determination in the Post-Declaration Era'. In *Making the Declaration Work: The Rights of Indigenous Peoples*, edited by Claire Charters and Rodolfo Stavenhagen, 184–198. Copenhagen: International Work Group for Indigenous Affairs.

Beckman, Ludvig, Kirsty Gover and Ulf Mörkenstam. 2022. 'The Popular Sovereignty of Indigenous Peoples: A Challenge in Multi-People States'. *Citizenship Studies* 26 (1): 1–20. https://doi.org/10.1080/13621025.2021.2011142.

Commonwealth of Australia. 1900. *An Act to Constitute the Commonwealth of Australia, 9 July 1900.* https://www.aph.gov.au/About_Parliament/Senate/Powers_practice_n_procedures/Constitution/preamble (accessed 7 February 2023).

Dodson, Patrick. 2000. 'Lingiari – Until the Chains are Broken'. 4th Annual Vincent Lingiari Memorial Lecture. In *Essays on Australian Reconciliation*, edited by Michelle Grattan, 264–274. Melbourne: Black Inc.

Habermas, Jürgen. 1995. *Between Facts and Norms: Contributions to a Discourse Theory of Law and Democracy.* Translated by William Rehg. Cambridge, MA: MIT Press.

Ivison, Duncan. 2017. 'Pluralising Political Legitimacy'. *Postcolonial Studies*, 20 (1): 118–130. https://doi.org/10.1080/13688790.2017.1334289.

Kymlicka, Will. 1989. *Liberalism, Community and Culture.* Oxford: Clarendon.

Lino, Dylan. 2018. *Constitutional Recognition: First Peoples and the Australian Settler State.* Sydney: Federation Press.

MacDonagh, Oliver. 1958. 'The Nineteenth-Century Revolution in Government: A Reappraisal'. *The Historical Journal* 1 (1): 52–67. https://doi.org/10.1017/S0018246X58000018.

MacDonagh, Oliver. 1961. *A Pattern of Government Growth.* London: MacGibbon and Kee.

MacDonagh, Oliver. 1977. *Early Victorian Government.* London: Weidenfeld and Nicolson.

Mills, Charles W. 2009. 'Rawls on Race / Race in Rawls'. *The Southern Journal of Philosophy* 47 (S1): 161–184. https://doi.org/10.1111/j.2041-6962.2009.tb00147.x.

Moore, Margaret. 2010. 'Indigenous Peoples and Political Legitimacy'. In *Between Consenting Peoples: Political Community and the Meaning of Consent*, edited by Jeremy Webber and Colin M. Macleod, 143–162. Vancouver: University of British Columbia Press.

Patton, Paul. 2009. 'Rawls and the Legitimacy of Australian Government'. *Australian Indigenous Law Review* 13 (2): 59–69. https://www.jstor.org/stable/26423137.

Patton, Paul. 2019. 'Philosophical Foundations for Indigenous Economic and Political Rights'. *International Journal of Social Economics* 46 (11): 1264–1276. https://doi.org/10.1108/IJSE-03-2019-0142.

Pearson, Noel. 2014. 'A Rightful Place: Race, Recognition and a More Complete Commonwealth'. *Quarterly Essay* 55: 1–72.

Pettit, Philip. 2012. *On the People's Terms: A Republican Theory and Model of Democracy.* Cambridge: Cambridge University Press.

Rawls, John. 1999. *A Theory of Justice.* Revised edition. Cambridge, MA: Harvard University Press.

Rawls, John. 2001. *Justice as Fairness: A Restatement.* Cambridge, MA: Harvard University Press.

Rawls, John. 2005. *Political Liberalism.* Expanded edition. New York: Columbia University Press.

Simmons, Alan John. 2001. *Justification and Legitimacy: Essays on Rights and Obligations.* Cambridge: Cambridge University Press.

United Nations. 1960. 'Declaration on the Granting of Independence to Colonial Countries and Peoples'. General Assembly Resolution 1514 (XV) of 14 December. https://www.ohchr.org/en/instruments-mechanisms/instruments/declaration-granting-independence-colonial-countries-and-peoples.

United Nations. 1970. 'Declaration on Principles of International Law concerning Friendly Relations and Cooperation among States in Accordance with the Charter of the United Nations'. General Assembly Resolution 2625 (XXV) of 24 October 1970. https://digitallibrary.un.org/record/202170?ln=en.

United Nations. 2007. 'United Nations Declaration on the Rights of Indigenous Peoples'. General Assembly Resolution 61/295 of 13 September 2007. http://www.un.org/esa/socdev/unpfii/documents/DRIPS_en.pdf.

8

Decolonisation – Real and Imagined

Steven Friedman

> … the popular modern antonyms are not always the true
> opposites … in every situation of organized oppression
> the true antonyms are always the exclusive part versus the inclusive
> whole … not the oppressor versus the oppressed but both of them
> versus the rationality which turns them into co-victims.
> — Ashis Nandy, *Exiled at Home*

Since the 'Rhodes Must Fall' protests which began at the University of Cape Town in March 2015, the decolonisation of knowledge and its dissemination have become central concerns – at least in theory – of South African universities. This has obvious implications beyond the academy, since it is hardly the only South African institution in which the values and assumptions of Europe have been normative in the three decades since the achievement of majority rule. Political commentator Aubrey Matshiqi observes that, in South Africa's democracy, the political majority remain a cultural minority (Matshiqi 2011). The demand for 'decolonisation' is, therefore, not restricted to universities – it speaks to all intellectual and cultural life.

The defeat of apartheid removed the legal impediments to citizenship for all, but left many of the hierarchies of the past in place: in effect, the cultural and intellectual underpinnings of Afrikaner Nationalism were discredited, only for those that had sustained an earlier British colonialism to take over (Friedman 2015). Given this, perhaps the only surprise about heightened demands for the decolonisation of thinking, writing and teaching is that they took so long to appear. There is clearly an urgent need for the intellectual equivalent of the negotiation process that produced the political settlement of 1994 – an exchange on how the society's thinkers, writers and teachers should begin to free themselves of colonial assumptions and to think about the society and its challenges in ways that do not reflect the view of the coloniser. That this discussion is overdue is underlined by the fact that a paper arguing for a broad negotiation on the nature of the university was written 30 years ago (Badat et al. 1993).

But, while calls for decolonisation have been very loud, they have not been very distinct: clear articulations of a decolonised intellectual framework have been largely drowned out by rhetorical flourishes. Equally important is that a frequent feature of the rhetoric is its essentialism. We are exhorted to adopt African modes of thinking in tones that assume both that the continent's many and varied cultures all see the world in the same way, and that the way in which they see it is so obvious to authentic Africans that it requires no explanation. It is assumed – or stated – that those who do not endorse these alternatives are colonial ideologues (Mangcu 2017). This is a manifestation of a deeper problem: 'it is not uncommon to hear testimonies of students positing that they do not feel black enough, given that a singular dominant narrative of what constitutes blackness is rigorously defended often at the cost of free expression' (Nymanjoh 2017, 264).

Those who take this view are no doubt used, to hearing from their targets angry protestations of their anticolonial credentials, and criticism from supporters of the dominant view denouncing their demands as excessively radical. They are not used to challenges to their own credentials – to being told that their militant opposition to the colonial world view is a product of precisely that order's way of thinking. This is, however, the view of one of India's most important intellectuals, the psychologist and social critic Ashis Nandy: his seminal study of colonial and anticolonial thinking, *The Intimate Enemy* (2005), makes precisely this argument. While aspects of Nandy's analysis are specific to Indian conditions, much of it speaks to the current South African debate: it provides a much-needed perspective that is yet to be heard in discussion here.

This chapter seeks to fill this gap. It will discuss those aspects of Nandy's diagnosis that are relevant to South African realities and seek to spell out their implications for our current condition. It will conclude by proposing an approach to decolonisation in this country that builds on Nandy's insights. Central to Nandy's critique of militant 'decolonisation' is a particular understanding of colonialism and its cultural underpinning. An obvious objection to the colonial world view that he analyses is that it is only one way of understanding colonialism, one which South Africans have experienced but which is not necessarily either the only or even the dominant understanding among colonisers past and present. This objection is important because it enables us to relate Nandy's critique directly to South African realities. But the chapter will argue that Nandy does indeed offer an adequate critique of the kind of intellectual and cultural colonisation that South Africans currently experience, and so points the way to an alternative.

THE ESSENTIAL COLONIAL

Nandy builds his critique on a discussion of two contrasting figures – the author Rudyard Kipling, who was perhaps the most articulate ideologue of the British Raj, and the Indian nationalist and spiritual leader Sri Aurobindo. His purpose is to contrast Kipling's cultural essentialism with Sri Aurobindo's syncretic and inclusive alternative.

Kipling serves Nandy's purpose well because, like many ideologues of racial or national power, he does not fully belong to the dominant group whose dominance he justifies and initially did not feel particularly at home in it. Nandy points out that Kipling was 'brought up in India by Indian servants in an Indian environment. He thought, felt and dreamt in Hindustani, mainly communicated with Indians, and even looked like an Indian boy' (Nandy 2005, 64). At a very young age, he was sent by his parents to England, where his 'idyllic' life in Bombay was replaced by a traumatic period in which he felt deserted by his parents and was reminded repeatedly of his Indianness and thus his strangeness. His response was a body of writing that aimed to prove that he belonged as an Englishman by offering an essentialist cultural defence of British colonialism. Besides his stress on the British right to rule India, Kipling 'absolutise[d] the relative difference between cultures' (Nandy 2005, 64).

Kipling's defence of colonialism is built on creating a strict and unbridgeable divide between 'British' and 'Indian' culture, which denies the possibility that either could be influenced by the other, let alone that they could blend: 'Kipling sought to redefine the Indian as the antonym of the Western man' (Nandy 2005, 79). He romanticised Indians who, in his view, made no attempt to become British and so, in his view, remained true to their identity. His scorn was reserved for the *babus*, the clerks and bureaucrats who adopted English ways in an attempt to become part of the dominant group. While Kipling and other British colonial ideologues who thought like him 'liked to see colonialism as a moral statement on the superiority of some cultures and the inferiority of others', they were so wedded to essentialism that they 'even accepted that some had the right to talk of Indian culture as superior to Western. Cultural relativism by itself is not incompatible with imperialism, as long as one culture's categories are backed by political, economic and technological power' (Nandy 2005, 100). It was not necessary to justify colonialism by claiming cultural superiority, as long as military superiority ensured that the culture of the coloniser dominated that of the colonised.

This implicitly recognised that colonisation rested on violence: 'Kipling correctly sensed that the glorification of the victor's violence was the basis of the doctrine of social evolution and ultimately colonialism, that one could not give up the violence without giving up the concept of colonialism as an instrument of progress' (Nandy 2005, 69). It was, therefore, perhaps inevitable that Kipling admired but greatly exaggerated the military strain in Indian culture. He thought that 'the ideology of Ksatriyahood' – the warrior caste – 'was true Indianness, apart from being consistent with the world view of colonialism'. He thus

> missed the limited role given to Ksatriyahood in traditional Indian cosmology and the vested interest his kind had in denying these limits in a colonial culture organized around violence and counter-violence, manhood and maximised potency, and a theory of history that saw all civilisations in terms of the high and the low and the justifiably powerful and the deservedly weak. (Nandy 2005, 78–79).

In this colonial ideology, then, essentialism is at the core. Judith Butler, in her attempt to develop a feminist alternative to essentialism, notes that it enables 'the regulation of attributes along culturally established lines of coherence' (Butler 1990, 33) – essentialisms are 'hostile to hybridity in that they promote policing the boundaries of identity and acts of exclusion and domination sanctioned by an appeal to an essential core of an individual' (Butler 1990, 8). Not only does essentialism ignore or suppress differences within identity groups and cultures – it denies the reality that all cultures are influenced by other cultures and that the loudest advocates of cultural authenticity are often promoting practices that are borrowed. To name but one example, the black frock coats and fur hats worn by Orthodox Jews as a badge of 'true' Jewishness are in reality the style of dress adopted by the eighteenth-century Polish gentry, who adopted it because they were trying to imitate the Iranians (Aust 2019). It is, in reality, a product of hybridity that cultural zealots have turned into a badge of supposed cultural distinctiveness.

It is this world view that underpins Kipling's colonial ideology. It is easy to understand why an essentialist response by Indian nationalists should be a vindication of that ideology rather than its antithesis. Violence is also at its core, and so it follows again that a violent response should be understood in the same way. The implicit critique of some 'militant' expressions of Indian 'decolonisation' becomes clear – they mimic the coloniser in their purported resistance. Nandy makes this critique explicit by contrasting to it, and to Kipling, Sri Aurobindo. He is chosen because he is, Nandy points out, almost the perfect counterpoint to Kipling.

Aurobindo was raised in precisely the sort of Anglophile Indian home that horrified Kipling – one of his given names was Ackroyd, although he later dropped it. He became a nationalist and a spiritual leader, abandoning the Brahmo Samaj, the Hindu reform movement whose monotheism attracted Indians seeking a more 'Western' identity because it was seen to be more compatible with Christianity, for a traditional form of Indian spirituality, which, in the context of his life, could also have been seen as an anticolonial choice. But, Nandy insists, Aurobindo did not fall into Kipling's essentialist trap. He searched for

> a more universal model of emancipation ... he never thought the West to be outside the reach of God's grace. Even when he spoke of race and evolution ... not once did he use the concepts to divide humankind ... While other Indian nationalists sought the help of Germany and Japan to remove the British, he always regarded Nazism as Satanic and abhorred Japanese militarism. (Nandy 2005, 85–86)

This response, for Nandy, meant more than an expression of intercultural tolerance and goodwill. It was also an acknowledgement that Aurobindo 'did not have to disown the West within him to become his version of an Indian' (Nandy 2005, 86).

> While the colonial system saw him as an object, he could not see the colonisers as mere objects ... As part of his struggle for survival, the West remained for Indian victims like Aurobindo an internal human reality, in love as well as in hate, in identification as well as in counter-identification (Nandy 2005, 87)

This required the acknowledgement of two realities. First, that contact with a dominant culture cannot simply be erased – it leaves indelible marks on the psyche of the colonised and to claim otherwise is to harbour a potentially dangerous pretence. Second, that, since all cultures are influenced by other cultures, a human shaped only by one culture is extremely rare: a poignant example of the power of cultural influence is offered by anthropologist Maurice Godelier's study of the Baruya of New Guinea, who were not subject to 'Western' influence until 1951 but, within a few years, had been catapulted into a Western-inspired modernity. They 'were transformed into citizens of a new state that was a member of the United Nations, furnishing one further proof of the West's advance in that part of the world' (Godelier 1991, 387). Being an authentic Indian (or African, European, or American) inevitably entails acknowledging the influence on your world view of other cultures – this does not in any way diminish the authenticity of a particular cultural identity.

These insights into Kipling and Aurobindo are the prism through which Nandy develops his diagnosis – that militant Indian nationalism, both before and after independence, is in reality an expression of colonial thought because it repeats its essentialism (and its violence). The real threat to colonisation and its world view, he argues, was not the Indian nationalist movements that colonialism 'bred and domesticated'. It was, rather, the India that refused essentialism: 'this other Orient, the Orient which was the Occident's double, did not fit the needs of colonialism; it carried intimations of an alternative, cosmopolitan, multicultural living which was … beyond the dreary middle-class horizons of Kipling and his English contemporaries' (Nandy 2005, 72). To construct an essentialised 'authentic indigenous identity' in opposition to an equally essentialised 'colonial identity' is not, in this view, to antagonise the coloniser – it is, rather, to endorse its world view. It is not to reject colonialism but to accept it.

Colonialism, Nandy argues, could not be complete unless it 'universalized and enriched its ethnic stereotypes by appropriating the language of defiance of its victims'. It both 'bred and domesticated' anticolonial movements and so 'the cry of the victims of colonialism was ultimately the cry to be heard in another language – unknown to the colonizer and to the anti-colonial movements' (Nandy 2005, 72–73). This 'other language' adopts an instrumental view of colonial culture – it takes that which is of use and discards that which is not. And, if this means, at times, pretending to admire the coloniser, that too is valid if it ensures survival – not only in the sense of continuing to live and breathe, but a psychic survival that enables the coloniser to better be who they really are.

To illustrate and expand on this point, Nandy recalls being told of a group of fifteenth-century Aztec priests who, on being forced by their conquerors to hear a Christian sermon that proclaimed that the Aztec gods were dead, declared that they would rather die. Their conquerors promptly obliged. Nandy responds: 'I suspect I know how a group of Brahman priests would have behaved under the same circumstances.' They would have embraced Christianity and some would have written eulogies in praise of it. In reality, they would have remained devout Hindus and, after a while, 'their Christianity would have looked … dangerously like a variation on Hinduism' (Nandy 2005, 107, 108). For Nandy, 'the response of the Aztec priests has seemed to the Westernized world the paragon of courage and cultural pride; the hypothetical response of the Brahman priests hypocritical and cowardly'.

All imperialist observers, he argues, have loved India's 'martial races' – who are seen as authentically Indian – and have felt threatened by Indians who are willing to compromise. Why do they valorise the priests and reject the Brahmans? The simple answer is that the Aztec priests oblige their conquerors by dying and leaving the scene – the 'cowardly' remain on the scene and may 'at an opportune moment' assert their presence. The more complicated one is that submission of this sort is itself deeply embedded in Indian culture (Nandy 2005, 207–211). It is derived not from some contemporary Western source but from 'non-modern' India 'which rejects most versions of Indian nationalism as bound irrevocably to the West'. 'Probably the uniqueness of Indian culture lies not so much in a unique ideology as in the society's traditional ability to live with cultural ambiguities and to use them to build psychological and even metaphysical defences against cultural invasions' (2005, 107). The 'cowardly' response threatens the coloniser because it expresses the autonomous understanding of the colonised rather than that which is imposed by the coloniser.

It would be easy to misinterpret the response of the hypothetical Brahman priests as a physical survival strategy in the face of power, an expression of what James Scott has called 'the weapons of the weak' (Scott 1985). Scott, who was criticising the notion of 'false consciousness', which holds that the dominated often endorse the legitimacy of their domination, argues that the powerless do not accept the morality of domination. They avoid fighting it head-on because they believe the power balance is stacked against them and that open resistance will lead to suffering and loss, not change. And so, they find ways of undermining power – by pilfering, or feigning ignorance or illness – while loudly endorsing its pretensions when the powerful are listening.

If this was all the Brahmans were doing they would hardly be a model of decolonisation – however much they might despise it, they would be complying with it. For Nandy, however, they are challenging colonialism – in a manner unavailable to the militant decolonisers – because they are refusing to buy into the myth of the 'noble savage', which insists that they are at their most authentic when they live out the cultural stereotypes of the coloniser. Indians who responded in this way were drawing on cultural wellsprings unknown to the British to relate to colonial power on their own terms, not those imposed by its anthropology. In that sense, they, and not those determined to live out an Indianness framed by the coloniser, are the authentic decolonisers: 'what looks like Westernization is often only a means of domesticating the West, sometimes by reducing the West to the comical and the trivial' (Nandy 2005, 108). Indians who adopt this strategy refuse 'to fight the victor according to the victor's values, within his model of dissent. Better to be a comical dissenter than to be a powerful, serious but acceptable opponent. Better to be a hated enemy, declared unworthy of any respect whatsoever, than to be a proper opponent, constantly making "primary adjustments" to the system' (2005, 111).

Colonialism, Nandy argues, 'tried to supplant the Indian consciousness to erect an Indian self-image which, in its opposition to the West, would remain in essence a Western construction'. The authentic rebellion against that was not to mimic the Kiplings by 'setting up the East and the West as permanent and natural antipodes'. This endorses and repeats 'the cultural arrogance of post-Enlightenment Europe which sought to define not only the "true" West but also the "true" East' (Nandy 2005, 73–74). The Indian

> has no reason to see himself as a counterplayer or an antithesis of the Western man. The imposed burden to be perfectly non-Western only constricts his … cultural self, just as the older burden of being perfectly Western once narrowed – and still sometimes narrows – his choices … The pressure to be the obverse of the West distorts the traditional priorities in the Indian's total view of man and universe and … binds him even more irrevocably to the West. (Nandy 2005, 73)

Two examples underline this point. The first concerns

> a sub-group of Kipling's Indian brain-children [who] have set up the martial India as the genuine India which would one day defeat the West at its own game … [they] are quite willing to alter the whole of Indian culture to bring that victory a little closer, like the American army officer in Vietnam who once destroyed a village to save it from its enemies. (Nandy 2005, 80)

The second is 'Hindutva' or 'Hinduness', the core principle of the currently dominant strand of nationalism in India and of its current governing party, which illustrates the point particularly well since 'Hinduness' was unknown in India until colonialism produced it to make sense of indigenous cultural and religious patterns. 'To use the term Hindu to self-define is to flout the traditional self-definition of the Hindu, and to assert aggressively one's Hinduism is to very nearly deny one's Hinduness' (Nandy 2005, 103). Nandy's point, that the loudest devotees of decolonisation are products of that which they decry, was poignantly captured by Rabindranath Tagore's early twentieth-century fictional masterpiece *Gora*, in which the eponymous character is a militant Hindu essentialist blissfully unaware that he is actually English and was adopted and brought up as Indian by his Indian foster-parents (Tagore 2002).

For Nandy, the alternative to colonialism is, therefore, not a cultural essentialism that seeks to replace colonial assumptions with an 'authentic Indianness' that claims to have no truck with other cultures. It is, rather a syncretism that draws both on 'pre-modern' Indian cultural understand-ings and those aspects of Western thought and practice that enhance it. This might entail using Western values to criticise Western practice. This, he believes, was Gandhi's project: 'instead of meeting the Western crite-rion of a true antagonist, he endorsed the non-modern Indian reading of the modern West as one of the many possible life styles which had, unfor-tunately for both the West and India, become cancerous by virtue of its disproportionate power and spread' (Nandy 2005, 102). He saw his task, therefore, as recovering and emphasising those aspects of the Western tradition that colonialism ignored. He therefore 'judged colonialism by Christian values and declared it an absolute evil' (2005, 200). In sum, 'one could perhaps say that in the chaos called India the opposite of thesis is not the antithesis because they exclude each other. The true "enemy" of the thesis is seen to be in the synthesis because it includes the thesis and ends the latter's reason for being' (2005, 99). Nor, in Nandy's view, does the synthesis necessarily need to be created by intellectuals – it is already there. Gandhi's attempt to remind the West of its own moral traditions was deeply embedded in Indian cultural understandings: 'Indian society has held in trusteeship aspects of the West which are lost to the West itself' (2005, 74).

Kipling and other colonisers' dismay at this response reflected 'the hostility which the liminal man always arouses as opposed to the proper alien' (Nandy 2005, 103, n.67). The colonised, for them, is guilty of the ultimate sin – trying to be the coloniser. This destabilisation of the boundaries between the two destroys the safety that the coloniser derives from keeping the colonised at a safe distance. A militant nationalist stressing her or his Indianness by adopting the outward trappings of indigenous culture is an ironic source of comfort, because it remains clearly alien. A cultural syncretist who uses Christian ethics to declare colonialism evil refuses to be alien and so erodes the barrier between coloniser and colonised. It is obvious which one breaks more firmly with cultural and mental colonisation.

SOUTH AFRICAN APPLICATIONS: FROM VERWOERD TO MILNER

If Nandy's understanding of colonial ideology is accepted, his critique of a resistance that mirrors that which it purports to reject is obviously of great relevance to current discussions of decolonisation in South Africa.

At its broadest level, it challenges the notion that decolonisation should be understood as the replacement of colonial assumptions by an 'authentic' African understanding free of 'Western' influence, since this would repeat precisely the essentialism that underpinned colonial thinking. It would argue even more obviously against attempts to distinguish between people who are 'African enough' and those who are not. It would insist that the antidote to colonial thought patterns is the 'hybridity' and syncretism which underpins Nandy's proposed antidote. But it could be argued, convincingly, that the strain of colonial thinking that he discusses is one that once dominated in South Africa but no longer does.

Kipling's cultural essentialism seems to fit far more closely the colonisation imposed by Afrikaner Nationalism through apartheid than the current version against which advocates of decolonisation are rebelling. Apartheid was founded on an essentialism that claimed, spuriously, that it was giving expression to the diversity of cultures.

This 'diffuse language of cultural essentialism' was pivotal to apartheid ideology because it enabled it to avoid the 'crude scientific racism drawn from the vocabulary of social Darwinism', while still justifying racial domination (Dubow 1992, 209). Races and ethnic groups were held to possess a distinctive culture that would be fatally diluted if mixed with others and this was said to be a rationale for strict racial separation. Apartheid ideologues also constructed a rigid and static notion of ethnic identity, extolling those among the colonised who, in their view, fitted the stereotype. According to De Wet Nel, then minister of Bantu administration and development, 'the Zulu is proud to be a Zulu, the Xhosa is proud to be a Xhosa and the Venda is proud to be a Venda, just as proud as they were a hundred years ago'. These ethnic groups, he added, derived the greatest 'fulfilment' from their identity (De Wet Nel, cited in Moodie 1980, 266) The obvious antidote to this form of colonisation was not to accept the stereotype. On the contrary, it was surely to embrace a cultural syncretism that apartheid was, its justifiers insisted, designed to prevent.

But apartheid is no longer the dominant form of South African colonialism – it was defeated in 1994. As this chapter suggested in passing earlier, it has been replaced, in large measure, by a cultural context that revives the pre-1948 form of cultural domination. Before the victory of Afrikaner Nationalism in 1948, South Africa was a British dominion – its prime minister, Jan Smuts, was a loyal servant of empire who served in the British War Cabinet in both the First and Second World Wars (Steyn 2017). The British colonial administration, originally at the behest of its early twentieth-century head, Alfred Milner, attempted to impose 'official' British culture on the entire country, including white Afrikaners. Since 1994, the dominance would perhaps more accurately be described as white and Western, rather than exclusively British, but the elements are much the same. The dominant framework in the academy, media and other sources of cultural influence is that of the liberalism described by Richard Turner more than four decades ago, whose adherents 'believe that "western civilisation" is adequate, and superior to other forms, but also that blacks can, through education, attain [its] level' (Turner 1972, 20). It is no accident that the student protests that became the catalyst for the current attempts to decolonise the academy were aimed at the statue not of an apartheid-era government figure, but of Cecil John Rhodes, the key figure in Britain's colonisation of Southern Africa. While Rhodes was certainly not a liberal, he did represent a different form of domination, one that took over in a modified guise when apartheid was ended.

This form of mental and cultural colonisation seems to be the polar opposite of Kipling's essentialism. It does not romanticise African culture to justify the domination of African people. Usually by omission rather than commission, it brands that culture inferior and assumes that black people attain 'civilised' status only by accepting 'Western' norms and assumptions. It assumes that political and social thought is the work of Westerners only and marginalises African societies and their ideas and values. In this view, the African equivalent of the 'Westernised' Indian *babus* whom Kipling despised are showing a desirable interest in thinking and acting out the assumptions of a superior culture. The antidote is then surely not Nandy's hybridity but a clean break with Western culture and the unconditional embrace of an African alternative.

The refutation of this conclusion lies in understanding what the current form of domination is seeking to do. In contrast to Kipling's essentialism and apartheid ideology, it operates not by imposing a template on society that overtly declares some ways of thinking permitted and demonises or outlaws others. It relies far more on excluding or erasing that which it decrees as contrary to its norms. Colonised education of this sort does not triumphantly declare the superiority of the 'West' and the inferiority of Africa. It simply excludes Africa, except for that version of it which is seen through Western eyes. Black political thinkers are not demonised as cowards or renegades to their 'true' cultural selves – they are ignored. Western frameworks are not exalted – there is no need, since they are the only ones that are taught. Much the same can be said, in myriad ways, of the South African media, which, while proudly proclaiming its cultural and political neutrality, assiduously presents the perspectives of a suburbia that mirrors the attitudes and perspectives of southern California (Friedman 2017). It is also pertinent that, while the dominant way of thinking is in theory open to all who accept its assumptions, the boundaries are very firmly set and there is very little room for pluralism or hybridity within the dominant culture. To cite one example, Mmusi Maimane, former leader of the official opposition the Democratic Alliance, whose white, suburban 'old guard' is one of the key enforcers of this form of domination, regularly ran afoul of the policers of colonial orthodoxy, most notably when he had the temerity to refer to 'white privilege' and 'black poverty' as he did at a Freedom Day rally (Van Onselen 2018). The vast majority of the colonised are never, in reality, integrated into the 'superior' culture, which they are by implication exhorted to join (given the intolerance of the culture's policers, it is open to doubt whether any of the colonised are ever fully accepted).

The dominant form of colonisation, then, dominates through exclusion and imposition. It assumes, rather than asserts, that a particular way of seeing is the only way and withholds acknowledgement of alternatives and those who adhere to them. It is as concerned as Kipling and apartheid to set boundaries – it chooses to use other methods. Its understanding of what is permitted and what is not is as rigid as apartheid's – it too has very little room for hybridity or syncretism. It does not profess or feign admiration for indigenous culture, but it is as committed to imposing a template upon it as the overt essentialists are.

Given this, an essentialised alternative, which seeks to replace the dominant Western culture with an essentialised African rival, meets the same objection as Kipling's essentialism. It liberates no one – it simply replaces one template with another. The term 'Western culture', used routinely by most participants in the debate, is itself an imposition because it assumes that, in Western Europe and North America, there is only one way of thinking and seeing when in reality there are many. Similar, there is no 'African culture' – there are African cultures, and to impose on Africans one cultural understanding as the only one is itself a form of colonisation.[1] In Africa, as in the 'West', culture is inevitably contested – claims by the powerful that particular practices are culturally embedded may be challenged by alternative understandings of what a particular culture expects (Nomboniso Gasa, cited in Breytenbach 2006).

India is, of course, no different. Nandy argues that an authentic anti-colonial position would need to recognise that 'culturally, it is a choice neither between the East and the West nor between the North and the South. It is a choice – and a battle – between the Apollonian and the Dionysian *within* India and *within* the West' (Nandy 2005, 74).[2] To be Indian – or African or European – is not to endorse a particular view of the world since, within each, no particular view can claim authentic indigeneity. Not only is ideological pluralism a constant feature of cultures – it is essential for their survival and growth: 'a plurality of ideologies can always be accommodated within a single lifestyle. Fittingly so; a living culture has to live and it has an obligation to itself, not to its analysts. Even less does it have any obligation to conform to a model' (2005, 82).

And so, opposing to the current dominant culture an essentialised 'African culture', which ignores alternatives or, worse, suppresses them by imposing on (African) doubters and dissenters a mandatory way of thinking, does not reject the dominant colonial culture – it replaces it with a home-grown culture every bit as inclined to imposition as the dominant variety. Hybridity and syncretism are equally impossible under both templates. Despite the differences between Kipling's essentialism and the colonial culture that currently dominates South Africa, Nandy's critique applies to both. The core features of both are not that they are Western and therefore the antidote to both is not to be as 'African' as possible. They are, rather, imposition and exclusion (which are arguably more severe in the current version because indigenous alternatives are not patronised, as they are by apartheid and Kipling – they are removed from consciousness). The alternative cannot be a new form of imposition and exclusion – it must, rather, be a view that is built on inclusion and on opening cultural and intellectual horizons to all influences in an attempt to build an authentic Africanness. It means recovering and validating those strains in indigenous understandings which, like those in India, validate hybrid, syncretic and inclusive ways of seeing, thinking and doing that, like Nandy's non-modern Indians, take from the dominant culture what is useful while rejecting that which is not.

DECOLONISATION, NOT RECOLONISATION

By now, the implications of Nandy's argument for current decolonisation debates should be apparent. But it is necessary to expand on them to avoid ambiguity.

To state the obvious (which, in the current intellectual climate, needs to be stated), this is not an argument against resisting intellectual and cultural decolonisation. On the contrary, it argues that colonisation's grip on our thinking may well be even more insidious than we imagined because many of the loudest current complaints against it may be deeply influenced by the colonial view of the world. It is, if anything, an argument for a more thorough form of decolonisation than those currently on offer. It insists that far more is needed than the adoption of 'African' ways of thinking and doing which may turn out to be as inauthentic as Kipling's or apartheid's fraudulent vision of the 'real' African, the cultural equivalents of the zealot's Polish frock coat mentioned earlier.

In essence, it argues that the core of intellectual or cultural colonisation is that it imposes and excludes. Its antidote cannot, therefore, be to reimpose and to re-exclude. The problem with the dominant form of South African colonisation is not that it sees value in 'the West'. It is, rather, that it values only the West and robs of legitimacy other ways of seeing and doing (including those within the 'West' that do not justify continued cultural colonisation). It rejects hybridity, syncretism and cultural pluralism because they import 'inferior' strands into the 'only and true' culture. Besides imposing mental and emotional burdens on the colonised, it silences their voices not because it is 'unAfrican' but because, beneath a veneer of tolerance, it insists that there is only one way of thinking about and seeing the world. To colonise is to close down and to suppress, whatever the identity of the coloniser and the colonised.

Many of the purported antidotes on offer would perpetuate this practice in the name of offering a radical alternative. A 'real African culture' that, as it inevitably must if it makes this claim, suppresses the diversity of actual African cultures, the differences of perspective included within them and the inevitable influence of Asian and European cultures on them, does not decolonise – it recolonises because it imposes and excludes. It is, therefore, hardly surprising that it prompts the phenomenon noted earlier, in which black voices can be silenced by the charge that they are not black enough. As Nandy shows, this 'decolonisation', and its claim that we can be 'truly African' only if we reject all Western thought and deny all difference between us, does not decolonise at all – it retains the barriers between the 'West' and the rest, while ostensibly choosing to be on the 'right' rather than the 'wrong' side of a ghetto, which remains firmly in the heart and mind of the rebel.

The really radical alternative insists on not being part of any ghetto at all. It rejects essentialism, imposition and exclusion. It seeks not to rid our minds of all that is 'Western' but to open them to all that is African (and Asian and European and Latin American). It seeks not to create a new essentialism but to open our minds to the full range of alternatives and so to allow the emergence of a plural, syncretic and hybrid understanding, which is the real antithesis of colonisation.

Fortunately, there are in the current South African debate voices that recognise this. Thus, one advocate of intellectual decolonisation observes that 'Western modes and forms of knowledge are important, but they are not the only valid or viable kinds; other forms of modern knowledge and thought, just as advanced and even ground-breaking, are available in cultures and civilisations the world over' (Omoyele 2017). This is clearly a non-essentialist understanding that seeks to broaden, not narrow, horizons and which opens the way to hybrid understandings.

A more systematic account of what may be possible is offered by this description of the Africanisation programme of the Johannesburg alternative education centre, Khanya College (Adriansen et al. 2017). The authors observe that in contrast to some proponents of Africanisation today, Khanya College did not disregard so-called Western knowledge. Instead, it drew the best from critical thinkers worldwide to develop students' own critical insights. Some students were political activists who were accepted on the basis of their community involvement rather than strictly academic results. At Khanya College, their political work was linked to more formal modes of critical analysis.

The college also 'taught students the curriculum they needed to know to succeed in a white, elite university. The students were introduced to the dominant discourses and practices within elite universities; they were taught to understand and evaluate these practices. Then they were supported in finding the tools to challenge such practices.' This, the authors add, 'shows how a curriculum can be Africanised without essentialising what it means to be African and what African knowledge is' (Adriansen et al. 2017).

It is significant that Khanya College sees its approach as one that explicitly 'Africanises' rather than decolonises. For it, intellectual pluralism and hybridity are essentially African and to maintain a curriculum that includes insights from all cultural traditions is a form of Africanisation. Just as Nandy suggests that hybridity is essentially Indian and offers a textured account of Indian cultural themes that demonstrate this, so Khanya College insists that it is entirely African. This invites the retrieval of those themes in African cultural understandings that seek to break down walls rather than to erect them. It is equally significant that Khanya College's approach highlights two reasons why cultural essentialism imposes new controls over the colonised rather than eliminating control.

The first is the perhaps trite but sometimes forgotten point that alternatives to dominant thinking are impossible without an engagement with that thinking. Anticolonial thinkers have, of course, developed their alternatives through a careful critical reading of colonial writing, a task they would have been unable to undertake had they been persuaded that a truly anticolonial mode of thinking requires no engagement with 'Western' thought. The second is that one of the many flaws in the essentialist understanding of decolonisation is that it ignores the power that is wielded within cultures. Khanya College's commitment to including political activists without the required formal qualifications indicates a desire to challenge the use of power to dominate, and to create educational models which allow that challenge. Thorough decolonisation is, as Khanya College shows, not only about rejecting imposition by engaging with all thought. It is also about engaging with power to ensure that new patterns of domination do not replace the old.

In these understandings lies a decolonisation that expands rather than narrows boundaries, and which recognises Nandy's warning against a purported alternative that merely mimics the imposition and the essentialism of that which it claims to replace. The task of fleshing out a detailed decolonisation strategy that recognises this is an urgent priority.

NOTES

*   A version of this chapter has been published as 'The Change Which Remains the Same: Towards a Decolonisation Which Does Not Recolonise' (Friedman 2021).
1   See, for example, the heated debate on whether consensus decision-making is inherent in African political culture (Wiredu 1997; see also Hountondji 2009).
2   For the distinction between Apollonian and Dionysian cultures, see Benedict (1932).

REFERENCES

Adriansen, Hanne, Kirstine Lene Møller Madsen and Rajani Naidoo. 2017. 'Khanya College: A South African Story of Decolonisation'. *The Conversation*, 10 October 2017. https://theconversation.com/khanya-college-a-south-african-story-of-decolonisation-85005.
Aust, Cornelia. 2019. 'From Noble Dress to Jewish Attire: Jewish Appearances in the Polish-Lithuanian Commonwealth and the Holy Roman Empire'. In *Dress and Cultural Difference in Early Modern Europe*, edited by Johannes Paulmann, Markus Friedrich and Nick Stargardt, 90–112. Berlin and Boston: De Gruyter.
Badat, Saleem, Zenariah Barends and Harold Wolpe. 1993. *The Post-Secondary Education System: Towards Policy Formulation for Equality and Development*. Bellville: Education Policy Unit, University of the Western Cape.

Benedict, Ruth. 1932. 'Configurations of Culture in North America'. *American Anthropologist* 34 (1): 1–27. https://www.jstor.org/stable/660926.

Breytenbach, Karen. 2006. 'Zuma Case "Highlights Misogynistic Culture"'. *Independent Online*, 20 April 2006. https://www.iol.co.za/news/south-africa/zuma-case-highlights-misogynistic-culture-274707.

Butler, Judith. 1990. *Gender Trouble: Feminism and the Subversion of Identity*. New York: Routledge.

Dubow, Saul. 1992. 'Afrikaner Nationalism, Apartheid and the Conceptualization of "Race"'. *Journal of African History* 33 (2): 209–237. https://doi.org/10.1017/S0021853700032217.

Friedman, Steven. 2015. 'The Janus Face of the Past: Preserving and Resisting South African Path Dependence'. In *The Colour of Our Future: Does Race Matter in Post-Apartheid South Africa?*, edited by Xolela Mangcu, 45–63. Johannesburg: Wits University Press.

Friedman, Steven. 2017. 'Speaking Power's Truth: South African Media in the Service of the Suburbs'. In *Media and Citizenship: Between Marginalisation and Participation*, edited by Anthea Garman and Herman Wasserman, 55–71. Cape Town: HSRC Press.

Friedman, Steven. 2021. 'The Change Which Remains the Same: Towards a Decolonisation Which Does Not Recolonise'. *The Thinker* 89: 8–18. https://journals.uj.ac.za/index.php/The_Thinker/article/view/685/391.

Godelier, Maurice. 1991. 'Is the West the Model for Humankind? The Baruya of New Guinea between Change and Decay'. *International Social Science Journal* 43 (2): 387–399.

Hountondji, Paulin. 2009. 'Knowledge of Africa, Knowledge by Africans: Two Perspectives on African Studies'. *RCCS Annual Review* 1 (1): 121–131. https://doi.org/10.4000/rccsar.174.

Mangcu, Xolela. 2017. 'Decolonisation That Assaults African Values Is Not Worth Its Salt'. *Sunday Independent*, 19 March 2017. https://www.iol.co.za/news/opinion/decolonisation-that-assaults-african-values-not-worth-its-salt-8256831.

Matshiqi, Aubrey. 2011. 'Why Manuel Is Right and Wrong about Manyi's "Racism"'. *Business Day*, 8 March 2011. http://www.businessday.co.za/articles/Content.aspx?id=136509.

Moodie, T. Dunbar. 1980. *The Rise of Afrikanerdom: Power, Apartheid and Afrikaner Civil Religion*. Berkeley: University of California Press.

Nandy, Ashis. 2005. *The Intimate Enemy: Loss and Recovery of Self under Colonialism*. In *Exiled at Home*. New Delhi: Oxford University Press.

Nymanjoh, Anye. 2017. 'The Phenomenology of *Rhodes Must Fall*: Student Activism and the Experience of Alienation at the University of Cape Town'. *Strategic Review for Southern Africa* 39 (1): 256–277. https://doi.org/10.35293/srsa.v39i1.330.

Omoyele, Idowu. 2017. 'Arrested Decolonisation'. *Mail & Guardian*, 14 July 2017. https://mg.co.za/article/2017-07-14-00-arrested-decolonisation-season-4/.

Scott, James C. 1985. *Weapons of the Weak: Everyday Forms of Peasant Resistance*. New Haven: Yale University Press.

Steyn, Richard. 2017. *Churchill and Smuts: The Friendship*. Johannesburg: Jonathan Ball.

Tagore, Rabindranath. 2002 [1910]. *Gora*. Translated by Suparna Ghosh. New Delhi: Rupa Publications.

Turner, Richard. 1972. 'Black Consciousness and White Liberals'. *Reality: A Journal of Liberal Opinion* 4 (3): 20–22. https://disa.ukzn.ac.za/rejul728.

Van Onselen, Gareth. 2018. 'Mmusi Maimane Presses the Self-Destruct Button'. *Business Day*, 9 May 2018. https://www.businesslive.co.za/bd/opinion/columnists/2018-05-09-gareth-van-onselen-mmusi-maimane-presses-the-self-destruct-button/.

Wiredu, Kwasi. 1997. 'Democracy and Consensus in African Traditional Politics: A Plea for a Non-Party Polity'. In *Postcolonial African Philosophy: A Critical Reader*, edited by Emmanuel Chukwudi Eze, 303–312. Oxford: Blackwell.

9

Decolonisation and the Crisis of African Literature in the Twenty-First Century

Sule Emmanuel Egya

I would like to begin with the question: how much of African literature in European languages is decolonised today, decades after flag independence?[1] Or, to put it in a more elaborate way, to what extent has African literature in European languages demonstrated its independence from the colonial hegemonies that enabled its existence, years after efforts to gain cultural, intellectual and epistemological self-determination and self-sufficiency? Rather than an answer, a yet more disturbing question follows: will African literature ever attain that status of decolonisation whereby its sources and resources (in terms of aesthetics, reception, ideological positionality, among others) are rooted in African indigenous epistemologies, from where the literature can reach the global literary markets?

These questions should bother us, given this age of cultural exploits, expansionism and transnationalism promoted by globalisation. They have in fact provoked the discussion that follows in this chapter about the fate of African literature in the twenty-first century. The impulse to frame this fate in the form of a crisis rests on the hypothetical contention that the production of literary works – including discourse on them – in Africa today appears to be overdetermined by Western factors, which have come to have a strong hold on the literature under the guise of universalism. Although these factors may not be new, since the literature itself is a product of Western colonialism, their greater control of the literature in the twenty-first century, accentuated by what has come to be known as the new African diaspora, strongly undermines efforts that have been made towards decolonising African cultural and literary production. These factors include the ways in which the West views and shapes the conception, production and reception of African literature within the frame of what I would like to see as the ontological rationality of migration. The condition of possibility for these Western factors having so much grip on African literature, which, in my view, should constitute greater worries, is made up of the following realities in many parts of Africa: the rather wilful neglect of educational and cultural institutions, the collapse of conventional publishing, declining readership as a result of increasing levels of poverty, and the sheer drive, especially among the younger generation of writers and artists, to emigrate to the West. This chapter, among other objectives, attempts to show how the aforementioned condition has subjected African literature in European languages to neocolonial pressures in two related ways: first, the lure of West-based publishing packages; second, the institutional suppression of indigenous knowledge and contents. While the issues presented here are common to most parts of Africa, and I shall attempt to refer to incidents from different regions of the continent, my references will be mostly to realities in Nigeria, whose situation I am quite conversant with. Also, while I am mainly concerned with the production of knowledge related to literature, the issues I raise here may be applicable to knowledge production in other fields in the arts and sciences. The case is made, by way of conclusion, that to achieve full decolonisation within the sphere of literary imagination and production as well as in other spheres of human endeavour in Africa there is a need for writers, literary scholars, publishers, government and non-governmental organisations to develop alternative instruments and take pragmatic steps in spite of the glaring difficulties being faced by the continent. Achieving genuine decolonisation requires courage and actions through sacrifice by all stakeholders.

POST-INDEPENDENCE DISILLUSIONMENT AND THE NEW DIASPORA

Perhaps the most resonant tragic story of most nations in Africa is the short-lived freedom, the rather aborted developmental stride, which followed declarations of independence from colonial authorities. Shortly after independence, conflicts, mainly in the form of civil wars and military takeovers of governments, came to stand against the nations' yearning for development (Decalo 1990, 1). One of the consequences of these conflicts, which became a common manifestation throughout Africa, was iron-grip despotism. It was marked by a landscape of self-perpetuating dictators, in military and civilian fashions, whose anti-enlightenment, anti-intellectual and anti-artistic activities dealt a severe blow to the literary and cultural exuberance showcased in some nations in the period immediately after independence. One of the striking accounts that instance this anti-intellectual stance of Africa's despots is Jack Mapanje's memoir entitled *And Crocodiles Are Hungry at Night* (2011).

This literary exuberance manifests the strong tradition of protest literature against colonialist cultural hierarchy. Foremost examples in this regard are, among others, the early writings of Athol Fugard, Dennis Brutus and Nadine Gordimer from South Africa; Mongo Beti from Cameroon; Chinua Achebe, Wole Soyinka and J.P. Clark from Nigeria; Léopold Sédar Senghor and David Diop from Senegal; Ngũgĩ wa Thiong'o from Kenya; Okot p'Bitek from Uganda; Naguib Mahfouz and Nawal El Saadawi from Egypt.

The robust literature produced by these writers would, in some nations, come under the heavily oppressive forces of colonial and home-grown dictators (Anyidoho 1997). Furthermore, some of the writers became the targets of their nations' dictatorships. Examples were Ngũgĩ wa Thiong'o and Micere Mugo of Kenya, Jack Mapanje of Malawi, Nuruddin Farah of Somalia, Nawal El Saadawi of Egypt and Wole Soyinka of Nigeria. These figures, because of their practice as writers as well as their ideological dispositions, faced diverse degrees of torture, detention, imprisonment and forced exile. The writers became antago-nists towards their home governments for failing to deliver the benefits of independence, to take appropriate steps to educationally, culturally, economically and politically decolonise their nations. They railed against the corruption and self-perpetuating bids of their governments, and cried out as their nations descended into the abyss of oppression. The role of the writers at this time is captured in the words of Mugo:

> As members of the intelligentsia, writers represent three main strands: conservatives, liberals, and revolutionaries. Given that under neo-colonialism members of the ruling elite (whether military or civilian) essentially represent the interests of imperial-ism at the expense of the economically deprived masses, the above ideological positions assume telling significance. (Mugo 1997, 84).

It became imperative for the writers to take on the role of social activists, to openly confront power, besides their literary writing. This echoes Soyinka's famous dictum that the man died in him who kept quiet in the face of oppression (Soyinka 1985). Rather than keep quiet, most pioneer African writers, especially in the period of post-independence dictatorial rule and mismanagement of resources, which was synchronous with violent apartheid in South Africa, preferred to speak truth to power.

As the nations of Africa gradually descended into intense despo-tism, the intelligentsia, as is the case with most societies, began to think of emigrating from their nations, in spite of the strong nationalism that had shaped their formative years in the 1960s and 1970s. In his introduction to the seminal book *The New African Diaspora*, the US-based Nigerian scholar Isidore Okpewho asks, 'how can anything be set right when a nation has lost its sense of mission in its blind pursuit of power and privilege':

> When writers, scholars and journalists are thrown into jail or relieved of their appointments simply because they dared to criticize political leaders and their misguided acts? When, indeed, a journalist could lose his life for exposing the abuses of leaders, and no efforts are made to apprehend or locate the culprits? So, what intellectual would want to remain in a country where the honest pursuit of truth is either derided or discouraged? (Okpewho 2009, 8–9)

With most nations turned into police states, governed by despots eager to kill real and imagined detractors, it was logical, as Okpewho implies here, that intellectuals, artists and writers found their way out of their homelands. This was a devastating period of brain-drain for Africa. In his introduction to *The Word Behind the Bars and the Paradox of Exile*, a collection of essays mostly written by writers living in exile, the Ghanaian poet-scholar Kofi Anyidoho laments the diminishing glory of the continent, saying 'this is Africa of the intellectual and creative writer's hope and despair, the Africa of the glory of vanished civilizations and of the pain of mass populations set adrift in a world falling apart and yet full of many possibilities' (Anyidoho 1997, 1). Regimes' clampdowns on writers, as the foregoing discussion has shown, would be the first assault on literature and the creative arts in the post-independence era.

However, a more devastating assault on literature and indeed on all kinds of knowledge production in Africa would come in the form of the gradual collapse of educational, intellectual and literary infrastructure. The sheer kleptocracy of most African leaders was compounded by the onset in the 1980s of the structural adjustment programmes (SAPs), and set most nations on the path of economic miseries, what Paul Zeleza calls 'the "lost decades" of structural adjustment programs' in Africa (Zeleza 2009, 36). The programmes consisted of loan packages from the Bretton Woods institutions (the International Monetary Fund and the World Bank) to countries in Africa to enable them to fight economic crises. But the conditionality clauses, some of which 'pressured African governments to disinvest in social services, devalue their currency, and shrink their provision of public services' (Iheka and Taylor 2018, 4), rendered the programmes counter-productive. SAP-induced miseries have had devastating consequences for all aspects of social and cultural life. The physical manifestation was not only in a decline in the provision of infrastructure, but also in the steady decay of existing social structures. Education was one of the worst hit, and has remained so today, in nearly all African countries. Evidence of the downturn in education consisted of the growing inadequacy of learning facilities for the growing populations, the inability to keep providing steady supplies of library and laboratory materials to the schools, and a steady decline in teacher numbers and teaching quality as a result of the inability of governments to pay teachers a living wage, as and when due.

One of the ways literary and cultural production has been negatively affected by this phenomenon is the misfortune experienced by conventional publishing of both literary works and educational textbooks. In the pre-SAP period, literary and knowledge production in Africa had been midwifed by institutionally powerful publishers such as Heinemann, Longman, Spectrum, Macmillan, Evans, Oxford University Press and so on. Emma Shercliff reports that these publishers 'established branch offices throughout the continent in the 1950s and 60s. The focus was firmly on educational publishing and even those works of fiction published by African authors were designed to appeal to that market' (Shercliff 2016, 10). Although these publishers had had colonial roots, as nearly all of them had their head offices in the colonial metropoles, their contributions, in terms of production outputs and editorial content, were robust, aimed at exporting African knowledge production to the world.

Under the weight of SAPs, the publishers, unable to sustain business on the continent, either closed their offices or turned down creative writing manuscripts. They could manage to continue with small reproductions of existing educational textbooks. They cashed in on the trendy business of publishing 'self-serving biographies of retired and serving army generals' (Adewale 2000, iii), but they could not sustain their series focused on creative writing, since these generally depended on the purchasing power of the public (libraries and individuals), which had considerably diminished. This condition, which reached a high point in the 1990s, constituted the worst assault on African literature, especially in the sub-Saharan region, precipitating the turn to what is today seen as the new migration of writers to the West. This migration, as Okpewho has described, is not specific to writers, and is not, in point of fact, what one may call a cultural migration; it is an economic migration. Faced with system collapse in their home nations, the new African migrants take desperate measures in order to get to the West, where they hope a life of Eldorado awaits them. Most of them are ready to bear what Valerie K. Orlando calls 'the horror of illegal crossings' and face the 'sociocultural and political face of Mediterranean illegal migration' (Orlando 2018, 19–20). But for the writers and the intellectuals (the intelligentsia), taking desperate measures involves manipulating conference and study visas, positioning oneself as an endangered species in need of asylum, and spousal engagement with someone in the hostland.

In most cases, it has not been difficult for successful African writers to migrate to the West. Nevertheless, an African writer's easy ticket to the West is often a deliberate form of self-projection in the direction of the West. Amatoritsero Ede has referred to this as identity politics that involves 'self-anthropologizing'. Identity politics may require a writer to take, in his words, 'the form of a cultivated eccentricity, idiosyncrasy, and conscious self-positioning, or an assumed political persona sometimes anchored on, and couched in, pre-exilic and life-threatening real-political terms' (Ede 2015, 112). Identity politics is a construction in which the writer is not only known by their creative work but also by their strategic activism, turning themself into a social victim in need of refuge in the West; by their extra-literary cultural self-presencing, West-facing lifestyle, which is usually either the cause or effect of literary lionisation. It could also be by their public utterances, often deliberately couched in polemics. Within this framework, many African writers have turned their backs on their continent, have been welcomed in the West, and have had to continue to stage themselves in such a way that they remain relevant in the literary and cultural circulations of the West.

AESTHETIC EXTROVERSION: WEST-POSITIONING AND CONTENT CONTROL

To live as an immigrant literary writer in a hostland is, no doubt, different from living as a writer in your homeland. The difference could be in degree or in kind, and is profoundly influenced by new realities and the capabilities of the writer as an individual to process and comprehend those realities. The import of this idea is usually trivialised, even denied by notions that are anchored in globalisation and its attendant freedom, especially for deterritorialised subjects. It is often remarked that a writer can live and write anywhere they choose. And indeed they can write just about anything that catches their fancy. What is more, a South African writer, say, can live and work in Paris and can perfectly embark on a political aesthetics that sees their writing historicising the political condition of their homeland; that is, if they want to be a concerned or engaged writer at all. The writer's freedom is such that they may choose not to be political at all, even though being apolitical is itself a political positioning. For the credo of postmodernism, which is fast influencing writers across the open, globalised world today, is based on the presumed collapse of national, racial and artistic boundaries. I shall, however, attempt here to argue that in spite of the rhetoric of neutralised boundaries, literary production and indeed any kind of knowledge production, as a consumable product, faces institutional control within national, racial and artistic boundaries – and this is the fate of African literature today in the West.

To live and write in the West, for an African, is to subject oneself to the publishing and editorial protocols of the West – this is, some may say, commonsensical enough, as intellectual and imaginative productions and formations may not be devoid of the exertions of their social environments. This, though, may hit an aporia if we consider the other side of the logic: for a Westerner to live and write in Africa is to subject themself to the publishing and editorial protocols of Africa. Questions of universal standards will inevitably arise whereby the African protocols are viewed with suspicion, obviously because of the 'substandard' and inadequate structures and facilities on the continent.

Let me at this point explain the idea of the West regarding African literary and knowledge production. Most African writers, intellectuals and thinkers who leave the continent, who settle outside their homelands, have preferred these destinations: the United States (US), the United Kingdom, Germany, France and the Netherlands. Each of these countries, no doubt, is endowed with a strong publishing tradition – a long-established publishing industry, a strong reading public (mostly in the form of reading clubs), a great tradition of public libraries, old and emerging grants and fellowships for writers, artists and intellectuals, established and emerging literary magazines, academic journals and other outlets, respected and prestigious literary awards, constant flows of literary events, and so on. The circulations of these, and their productive effects in making these countries powerful in terms of literature, arts and culture, make us regard them as literary capitals where writers are not only comfortable to settle and write, but also easily negotiate their ways to fame. This flux of institutions, events and modes of literary production is usually underlined by what one may call an aesthetic unconscious; that is, the overriding taste of literature that is institutionally acceptable, by which writers and their audiences are inducted into the mainstream of literary production and consumption. This usually determines what the publisher eventually publishes, what the editor and literary agent desire (in fact, require) of the writer, and what the writer eventually writes. The publisher, which commits its resources to the publishing of the work, may make the argument that from its survey a particular taste (thematic or stylistic) has become trendy with the reading public. It will insist on this taste being catered to since it will be committing its resources to the publication of the work, and since, after all, the main objective of producing a book is to sell it to readers. In other words, the production of literary works, like that of anything else in this time of capitalist commercialism, should be consumer-driven. In line with this, it is logical that writers understand the taste that drives their literary efforts. It follows that they ought to submit themselves to the aesthetic unconscious that rules the literary scene within which they have chosen to write.

It is, however, becoming a point of concern for writers and literary scholars, in both Africa and the West, that African writers living in the West, or literary works and knowledges produced in the West-based diaspora, face deliberate mechanisms that *other* them into a commodity to satisfy the aesthetic and cultural demands of the Western publics. And this is at the expense of the aesthetic independence of African literary and cultural production. One dubious way this is achieved is by posing questions to the effect that there is no need for Africa or nations of Africa to have anything 'authentic' or home-rooted in this twenty-first century, and asking whether this literature has, at all, ever been 'authentic' in any way. This, like migration or diasporisation itself, is not new: the West, since the inception of African literature in colonial languages, has, one may say, been controlling the taste and production of this literature in a way. Heinemann, perhaps the largest publishing player in the production of African literature in the post-independence period, might have had colonial editorial interventions that shaped its highly successful African Writers Series (AWS), although the series was edited by the iconic Nigerian writer Chinua Achebe. From manuscript acceptance, through in-house and external reviews, to copy editing, the works published under the AWS imprint would not have escaped being subjected to protocols that would enable them to appeal to the Western literary taste of the time.

And yet, like what is today referred to as the new diaspora, the present control of African literary and cultural production is, in my view, radically different from what it used to be in the past. Here, too, we can then say there is a new form of control, which, like the pitiable, self-surrendering new diaspora, may have had more devastating consequences for African literature – a literature that, in this twenty-first century, should have been gaining miles towards total decolonisation. Unlike the old diaspora when Africans were captured as slaves and sent across the Atlantic, the new diaspora is occasioned by Africans taking desperate measures to present themselves as economic and racial captives to the West. This is telling in that some parts of the West, in recent times, have pursued nationalist policies to reject the inflow of the new diaspora; a resounding example here is what has come to be known as Brexit, 'which called for the United Kingdom to leave the European Union in order to gain greater control over its borders' (Brown 2018, 39). In similar vein, we can talk of the new control of African literature, differentiated from the old control, in that in the past pioneer African writers had had no option other than to succumb to the publishing industry of the West, as African societies had not had adequate technological modernity to establish their own publishing industries. In the fashion of a civilising mission, or the order of things in the colonial time, the Western publishers came to Africa to not only discover literary talents (as exotica for the Western publics) but also, one may conveniently argue, to offer them a platform to recover their voices from the suppression of colonialism. As it turned out, pioneer writers who took advantage of these publishing opportunities ardently engaged in postcolonial counter-discourse in the bid to reverse colonial narratives.

The Western mechanism of literary and cultural production, marketing and readings that *others* and exotifies not only African literature but also literatures from other postcolonial locations is well captured in Graham Huggan's *The Postcolonial Exotic: Marketing the Margins*. This mechanism is based on, as Huggan says, 'global commodification of cultural difference' (2001, vii). Huggan puts this commodification down to 'the material conditions of production and consumption of postcolonial writings, and the influence of publishing houses and academic institutions on the selection, distribution and evaluation of these works [in the West]' (2001, vii). If the mechanism that Huggan points out, in the framework of the metropoles (the global North) commodifying literary and cultural productions from the margins (the global South) in the colonial and post-independence eras, has had a negative effect on African literature and knowledge, it has, in the present time, degenerated into a crisis that undercuts attempts at decolonising the literature. Like the new diaspora, the present crop of African writers aims to emigrate from their homelands to seek publishing fortunes in global literary capitals. To this effect, many African literary writers live in the West; while some of them are successful in entering the literary scene and consciousness of their hostlands, many of them are not, as they are faced with harsh existential conditions that denude them of their literary talent. For instance, the Nigerian poet Niyi Osundare has expressed concern that 'the free and open society [of the West; and by this he means the availability of infrastructure] may also deaden their creative imagination, as has been happening to many of the young writers who migrated from Nigeria in the past two decades' (Egya 2017, 268). However, the African writers who succeed in penetrating the literary consciousness of the West have had to subject themselves to the rules of its aesthetic unconscious. This is in order to write according to the code prescribed by the commodifying agents of the West, as their narratives, as well as their personal politics, must satisfy Western demands. These Western demands manifest themselves in the form of the kinds of stories to tell, the descriptions that are more appealing, the genre that is more acceptable, the mode of appearance and political correctness during literary events, and so on.

This Western gaze, made up of specific demands that should be met by any writer desirous of succeeding, is characterised by a disturbing parochialism – usually a function of what the Western media present as Africa. A critical view of this parochialism is presented by Eileen Julien in her sustained critique of how contemporary African narratives are *othered* and commodified in the West through what she calls the extroverted novel. One of her arguments is that

> some African stories effectively go unseen because of a steady diet in the North of clichéd fiction … the narrow novelistic diet to which the North had grown accustomed [offers] only a partial truth. It [robs] readers of the diversity of African narratives, thereby simplifying Africa, locking this massive, heterogeneous and dynamic continent into a supposedly imitative literary, intellectual, political and economic modus operandi. (Julien 2018, 374)

This narrowness is a product of the selective control of African aesthetics at the heart of what Huggan calls the commodification of cultural difference. The West – given African diasporic writers' desperation to excel in cultural capitals – dictates the kind of literature Africa in the diaspora has to produce. That in itself may not be a problem, since, as the old saying goes, he who pays the piper dictates the tunes.

However, the real problem, what I see as a crisis, is the acceptance of this parochial framing of African literature by Africans, even on the continent. Generalisations, such as that the best of African writers are living outside Africa, are simply accepted without a sustained comparative analysis of what is being produced in the West and on the continent. It is a disturbing form of reductionism, usually purchased and circulated by Africans themselves, to suggest that there is nothing good at all, in terms of literary production, being produced in the underdeveloped nations of Africa. African literary scholars working in Western knowledge capitals find themselves, in tune with the pressures of commodification, endorsing the Western gaze, thereby becoming complicit in the process of what Julien calls 'simplifying Africa' in line with the dominant aesthetic unconscious. Genre preference, as Julien mentions, needs stressing as a tool used in simplifying African literature. In their introduction to a special volume of *English in Africa* published in 2005, which they edited, Pius Adesanmi and Chris Dunton contend that the novel genre has 'become the face – especially in international circuits – of the third-generation of Nigerian writing' (Adesanmi and Dunton 2005, 11). This statement is elicited by, and in turn perpetuates, the Western projection – through its commodifying literary package – of immigrant Nigerian writers such as Chimamanda Ngozi Adichie, Sefi Atta and Helon Habila, who are famous in the global literary capitals for their novels. That Adesanmi (a Nigerian) and Dunton (a South African), writing in *English in Africa* (a South African journal), would reach such a conclusion, without considering the rich variety of literary offerings across genres (poetry, drama, other emerging genres) on the Nigerian literary scene, is a resonant testimony to the extent to which genre preference in the West has influenced African literary scholarship. The US has over the years become the epicentre of literary cultural capitalism attracting African writers, as some of those who initially migrated to European literary capitals have relocated to the US, with the thinking that the literary and intellectual scenes there are more liberal and less racist. This is, however, not usually the case (see Diala 2018).

The reason for this is, in part, the strong tradition of Master of Fine Arts (MFA) degrees in creative writing, an instrument that has proved viable for drawing to the US writers not only from Africa but from other parts of the global South as well. Furthermore, the growing establishment of African studies centres and departments in universities in the US solidifies the country as a base of African immigrant writers. Most immigrant African writers who fail as writers in the US take the second option of pursuing a PhD degree in order to secure teaching and research positions in US and Canadian universities.[2]

BEYOND THE CRISIS: STEPS TOWARDS THE DECOLONISATION OF AFRICAN LITERATURE

Let me reiterate that it would not have been quite as disturbing if what the West, or the global North, chose for itself as the 'best' face of African writing had remained in the West. It becomes quite disturbing that the canon-making machineries of the West powerfully influence intellectual conclusions about African literature even in Africa. This, in my view, is not much of the doing of Western institutional powers, of Western epistemology; it is much of the undoing of African institutions – it is, in point of fact, the failure of institutions in Africa to build a strong intellectual and literary base that will raise a counter-voice to what one would see as, at best, the half-truth with which the North continues to frame the South. It is disturbing that, in terms of form and content, African literature is still talking to the West, in the manner Achebe's *Things Fall Apart* published in 1958 did, in the manner the first-generation African writing had to explain sociological and anthropological issues. Those considered the best emerging voices of African writing today (Binyavanga Wainaina, Helon Habila, Chimamanda Ngozi Adichie, Leila Aboulela, NoViolet Bulawayo, Doreen Baingana and so on) are still speaking to the West by way of positioning their narratives to appeal to Western publics, with the aim of maintaining prominence in the Western literary capitals. For me, the crisis African literature faces today is its undue extroversion whereby its aesthetic mould, its protocols for production, its criticism are overdetermined by Western discourses and global capitalism.[3] This is worsened by lack of enduring publishing structures, good educational structures, any form of political will on the part of governments and other institutions in Africa. Shercliff shows us the bad picture in terms of the publishing industry:

> Thirteen of the eighteen publishers surveyed [in Africa] told us that their publishing houses employ less than a dozen people. Many of Africa's most well-known publishers of contemporary fiction publish fewer than ten books a year. Outlets for African writers remain limited, although there is a trend towards self-publishing operations, such as Kachifo's 'Prestige' and Parresia's 'Origami' imprints, which offer writers alternative routes to publication. (Shercliff 2016, 11)

The 'alternative routes to publication' are highly problematic. What the publishers mentioned above mostly do is to publish African editions of African novels published and celebrated in the West. Grabbing West-based writers, publishing an African edition of their works already celebrated in the West, promoting them as better than writing based at home, amounts to reinforcing the ideology of West-positioning. It will be hard for African literature to attain decolonisation with such a practice.

The task of decolonising African literature is as old as the literature itself. We recall that at the first conference on African literature held in Makerere, Uganda, in 1962, the Nigerian scholar Obiajunwa Wali, in his paper 'The Dead End of African Literature' (Wali 2007), argued that as long as a literature is written in a non-African language, it cannot or should not enjoy the status of being referred to as African literature. This engendered the great language debate in African literature. Ngũgĩ wa Thiong'o did not only make a powerful contribution to this debate in his *Decolonizing the Mind: The Politics of Language in African Literature* (1986), he opted to start writing in his native Gikuyu language. Also crucial is the publication in 1983 of *Towards the Decolonisation of African Literature* by Chinweizu Ibekwe, Onwuchekwa Jemie and Ihechukwu Madubuike, among other scholarly efforts that stress the need to decolonise African literature. What is disturbing, however, is that in the twenty-first century African literature appears to face stronger neocolonial forces than it did in the twentieth century. This is because, as has been shown earlier, the twenty-first century neutralises symbolic borders, opens the global space, and lures African writers into a global literary marketplace that dictates African aesthetics.

It is my firm contention that, despite the aesthetic dispersal of the twenty-first century, African literature needs to be fully decolonised, and I hereby give the following suggestions for doing so:

1. Although fiercely contested today, the notions of patriotism and nationalism, in my view, remain crucial to the political positioning of a writer. To this end, I think the spatial and temporal roots of a writer are crucial to their craft. While it does not matter where

a writer lives, it is important that they connect organically to their birthplace, their nation, and speak about them, to them. Every developing society needs the service of this kind of writer.

2. Institutions and scholars of African literature need to privilege literature written and published on the continent, no matter its imperfections. Indeed, such attention is necessary to improving the quality of African literature in terms of form and content. It is also by doing so that the canon-making machineries of African literature can return to the continent.

3. Governments, institutions and corporations or other organisations must take an interest in literary and cultural production in Africa by way of providing support for building enduring structures here in Africa for both emerging and established writers. Writers constantly need residencies, grants, fellowships, workshops, conferences, literary agencies and so on.

4. Perhaps the single most important factor in the process of decolonising African literature is the establishment of a solid publishing industry and culture on the continent. If there could be institutionalised support funds provided by governments in Africa directed towards building a strong publishing industry for literary writers, then we could be sure that African literature would escape the neocolonial forces of the West.

5. The cultural arm of the African Union should put in place an endowment that will consciously assist Africa to build its own literary capitals. Nations such as Nigeria, South Africa, Kenya, Senegal and others that have produced famous African writers should be places of literary pilgrimage for writers.

CONCLUSION

Given the issues raised in this chapter, the debate about and process of decolonisation started by earlier writers and scholars need to be pursued in the light of transnationalism and globalisation. It is crucial for writers themselves, as well as the knowledge industry in Africa, to realise that the forces of globalisation are not different from the forces of colonialism, and what we may end up achieving by allowing ourselves to be inducted into global literary capitalism is recolonisation instead of decolonisation. While Africa faces serious political and economic inadequacies, I do not think the situation is so hopeless that its writers, and its entire literary heritage, cannot be rescued from external protocols and made to serve humanity on the continent. Indeed, literary imagination should play a leading role in taking the continent out of misery, largely tied to imperial and capitalist forces; and it can only do so if it is considerably decolonised.

NOTES

1   It is important to point out that the literature I am concerned with here is modern literature written in European languages. Although colonialism and its epistemic violence may have had effects on literature written in indigenous languages, the condition I discuss in this chapter about literature in European languages may be different, in terms of degree and kind, from the one experienced by literature in indigenous languages.

2   One can safely contend that except for Chimamanda Ngozi Adichie, who has become something of a literary superstar, almost all African writers in the US have had to pursue a PhD to end up as university professors, or use their MFA qualifications to teach, in order to survive in the US.

3   Reducing the question of aesthetic extroversion of African literature to the reductionistic notion of 'authenticity' is one way to foreclose arguments about who controls the canon of African literature today. In places where I have presented papers on extroversion, most questions people ask are to the effect that arguments against extroversion are nativist, and an attempt to present an authentic African literature. Extroversion, as I see it, is beyond the notion of authenticity; it has to do with aesthetic, economic (in short, capitalist) control of African literary and cultural productions.

REFERENCES

Achebe, Chinua. 1958. *Things Fall Apart*. London: William Heinemann.

Adesanmi, Pius and Chris Dunton. 2005. 'Nigeria's Third Generation Writing: Historiography and Preliminary Theoretical Considerations'. *English in Africa* 32 (1): 7–19. https://www.jstor.org/stable/40239026.

Adewale, Toyin. 2000. 'Introduction'. In *25 New Nigerian Poets*, edited by Toyin Adewale, iii–v. Berkeley: Ishmael Reed.

Anyidoho, Kofi. 1997. 'Prison as Exile/Exile as Prison: Circumstances, Metaphor, and a Paradox of Modern African literature'. In *The Word Behind the Bars and the Paradox of Exile*, edited by Kofi Anyidoho, 1–17. Chicago: Northwestern University Press.

Brown, Matthew H. 2018. 'Nollywood Comedies and Visa Lotteries: Welfare States, Borders, and Migration as Random Invitation'. In *African Migration Narratives: Politics, Race, and Space*, edited by Cajetan Iheka and Jack Taylor, 39–54. Rochester: University of Rochester Press.

Decalo, Samuel. 1990. *Coups and Army Rule in Africa: Motivations and Constraints*. New Haven: Yale University Press.

Diala, Isidore. 2018. 'Esiaba Irobi: Poetry at the Margins'. In *African Migration Narratives: Politics, Race, and Space*, edited by Cajetan Iheka and Jack Taylor, 256–278. Rochester: University of Rochester Press.

Ede, Amatoritsero. 2015. 'Narrative Moment and Self-Anthropologizing Discourse'. *Research in African Literatures* 46 (3): 112–129. https://doi.org/10.2979/reseafrilite.46.3.112.

Egya, Sule. E. 2017. *Niyi Osundare: A Literary Biography*. Makurdi, Nigeria: SevHage.

Huggan, Graham. 2001. *The Postcolonial Exotic: Marketing the Margins*. New York: Routledge.

Ibekwe, Chinweizu, Onwuchekwa Jemie and Ihechukwu Madubuike. 1983. *Towards the Decolonisation of African Literature*. Washington, DC: Howard University Press.

Iheka, Cajetan and Jack Taylor. 2018. 'Introduction: The Migration Turn in African Cultural Productions'. *African Migration Narratives: Politics, Race, and Space*, edited by Cajetan Iheka and Jack Taylor, 1–18: Rochester: University of Rochester Press.

Julien, Eileen. 2018. 'The Extroverted African Novel, Revisited: African Novels at Home, in the World'. *Journal of African Cultural Studies* 30 (3): 371–381. https://doi.org/10.1080/13696815.2018.1468241.

Mapanje, Jack. 2011. *And Crocodiles Are Hungry at Night: A Memoir*. London: Ayebia Clarke.

Mugo, Micere Githae. 1997. 'Exile and Creativity: A Prolonged Writer's Block'. In *The Word Behind the Bar and the Paradox of Exile*, edited by Kofi Anyidoho, 84–97. Chicago: Northwestern University Press.

Ngũgĩ wa Thiong'o. 1986. *Decolonizing the Mind: The Politics of Language in African Literature*. Oxford: James Currey and Heinemann.

Okpewho, Isidore. (2009). 'Introduction: Can We Go Home Again?' In *The New African Diaspora*, edited by Isidore Okpewho and Nkiru Nzegwu, 3–30. Bloomington: Indiana University Press.

Orlando, Valerie K. 2018. 'Harragas, Global Subjects, and Failed Deterritorializations: The Tragedies of Illegal Mediterranean Crossings in Maghribi Cinema'. In *African Migration Narratives: Politics, Race, and Space*, edited by Cajetan Iheka and Jack Taylor: Rochester: University of Rochester Press.

Shercliff, Emma. 2016. 'African Publishing in the Twenty-First Century'. *Wasafiri* 31 (4): 10–12. https://doi.org/10.1080/02690055.2016.1216270.

Soyinka, Wole. 1985. *The Man Died: Prison Notes*. Ibadan: Spectrum.

Wali, Obiajunwa. 2007 [1962]. 'The Dead End of African Literature?' In *African Literature: An Anthology of Criticism and Theory*, edited by Ato Quayson and Tejumola Olaniyan, 281–284. Malden: Blackwell.

Zeleza, Paul. T. 2009. 'Diaspora Dialogues: Engagements between Africa and Its Diasporas'. In *The New African Diaspora*, edited by Isidore Okpewho and Nkiru Nzegwu, 31–60. Bloomington: Indiana University Press.

10

Pedagogical Disobedience in an Era of Unfinished Decolonisation

Amber Murrey

Through a critical synthesis of the teaching of political and rhetorical practices that are often considered in isolation (that is, neo-imperial political assassinations, the corporate appropriation of Indigenous knowledges and critical development geographies), I make the case in this chapter for what I call pedagogical disobedience: an anticipatory decolonial development curriculum and praxis that is attentive to the perpetual simultaneity of violence and misappropriation within the colonial matrix of power. The chapter contributes to debates within international development and development geographies about the future of the discipline, given its neocolonial and colonial constitutions, and functions with a grounded attention to how this opens up possibilities for teaching praxis and scholarship in action.

ABSENCES IN THE CURRICULUM

As educators, we often prepare for teaching by gathering course material around a related set of themes and concepts. We cull determinedly from the reference lists of insightful journal articles and pore over abstracts, print-outs, book reviews, library shelves, TED Talks and more in search of comprehensive teaching materials that fit the pedagogical, curricular, creative and logistical needs of students. For decolonial students and educators in pursuit of the transformation of Eurocentric knowledge through Freirian 'pedagogies of possibility' (Freire 1997) and decolonising of the university by 'teaching to transgress' (hooks 1994), these moments of curricular preparation and structuring have richer significance. The creation of a critical decolonial syllabus necessitates a determined flexibility, a willingness to foster spaces of challenge in the classroom and a level of aptitude to coax students through the discomforts of unlearning. It also requires a sensitivity to the reproduction of Eurocentric, colonial, patriarchal and 'whitestream' (Grande 2003, 329) epistemologies within even critical and radical works in the social sciences. Eurocentric ideas and works sometimes make their way onto the pages of syllabi in careless or unintentional ways; this might be because of disciplinary norms or 'disciplinary decadence' (Gordon 2006), or pressures to prioritise standardisation (Nyamnjoh 2019), or the academic search algorithms that reproduce white patriarchal hypervisibility (Noble 2018) and make internet searches for alternatives more difficult. Decolonial transformation requires systematic 'de-silencing' (Rutazibwa 2019) within an academy at the service of bureaucratic classes and 'benevolent empire' (Chatterjee and Maira 2014, 7). In my first years of university teaching, I often began each process of creating course syllabi by looking online for examples of readings, concepts and materials that had worked for students in other universities. However, not only can this be an unhelpful convention – it is also an avenue of syllabus creation that risks perpetuating the coloniality of knowledge.

In January 2019, for example, I performed a random sampling of 28 English-language syllabi for master's-level courses in international development. I conducted an online search for 'International Development Syllabus' – with a virtual private network engaged – through the search engine DuckDuckGo, a platform that does not personalise a user's search results. While this sampling was limited to syllabi in English and online availability, I was able to locate syllabi from universities in Canada, Germany, India, Namibia, South Africa, Sweden, Tanzania, the Netherlands, Uganda, the United Kingdom and the United States (US). I read and coded each syllabus using the qualitative analysis software ATLAS.ti.

My analysis revealed an inclination to examine impoverishment and well-being through particular frameworks. Capitalism appeared in four syllabi but the role of corporations was not addressed, as far as I could tell, in any. Colonialism appeared as a theme in eleven syllabi; neocolonialism was taught as a stated theme in two. Decolonisation was a theme for one course. Only in two syllabi did empire or imperialism feature; in each case these were topics addressed in course readings rather than as weekly or daily topics. Violence was a theme only via post-war settings, post-conflict societies and 'push' factors for migration. Forms of structural violence and political violence were not specified. Neither decoloniality, nor decolonial options, nor assassination, nor race appeared at all (for an analysis of the latter, see Kothari 2006; Pailey 2019). Capacity-building, sustainability, gender, resource availability, the environment and globalisation were the dominant framing devices.

This exercise was not designed to be exhaustive. Indeed, several arguments might be offered to justify the structural limitations of these syllabi. Perhaps the historical, political and economic dynamics informing and sustaining inequalities are addressed in other coursework as part of these master's programmes. As any educator will quickly tell you, an analysis of a syllabus cannot accurately capture or reflect the complete content of a course. At the same time, it is possible that the syllabi for more critical courses are not posted openly online, or are marginalised by search engine algorithms.

This cursory examination does, nonetheless, open up questions regarding the manner in which some conventional, international and postgraduate introductory courses in development studies are currently taught. While there is a need for further examination of the direction of the discipline (the way 'globalisation' stands in for capitalism and political economy, for example, or the preference for positivist examination), of interest to me here is the dearth of material on empire, imperialism and coloniality in directly stated form. In particular, in this chapter I am responding to a lack of attention in such pedagogical material to the functions and features of assassination and appropriation within imperialism or settler colonialism by international development studies instructors.

It is striking that at approximately the same time that I performed this syllabi analysis, reinvigorations of projects to 'decolonise development' and parallel movements to 'decolonise the university' maintained momentum and strength (Bhambra et al. 2018; Daley 2018; Murrey and Tesfahun 2019; Pailey 2019). Indeed, 'decolonisation' and 'decolonising' have emerged in the last three or four years as a standard organising theme for mainstream academic conferences in the social sciences, albeit not without considerable critique of the appropriative tendencies of the rhetorical moves – including 'moves to innocence' (Tuck and Yang 2012) – effected through such gatherings (Bhambra et al. 2018, 4; Esson et al. 2017; Noxolo 2017). In facing imperial collusions and seeking decolonised alternatives, Branwen Gruffydd Jones (2006) argues against wilful ignorance and other 'moves to innocence' (Tuck and Yang 2012) towards the kind of shame Edward Said identified for critical scholars working within hegemonic institutions: 'an acute and embarrassed awareness of the all-pervasive, unavoidable imperial setting' (Said 1995, 34). And perhaps some of these syllabi are already, as I write, being soundly decolonised and their 'disturbing complacencies' (Varadharajan 2019, 183) being rethought. Such moves are part of the collective project that Olivia U. Rutazibwa (2019, 173–174) calls 'de-silencing' the classroom, in particular an explicit 'de-naturalizing [of the] ideas of Western superiority' to shift the 'location of the solutions and the problems in International Development Studies'.

This chapter seeks to contribute to these collective decolonial projects to 'decolonise development' (De Jong et al. 2019; Rutazibwa 2019) by asserting *pedagogical disobedience* in our curricula and teaching. This means embracing decolonial pluriversals that service a *will-to-life* (Dussel 2013) rather than the colonial will-to-conquer or will-to-extract, what Julia Suárez-Krabbe (2016) refers to as coloniality's 'death project'. My pedagogical reflection centres on two useful pedagogical tools and concepts – assassination and appropriation – which I have drawn from in a teaching practice that refuses to foster the 'epistemological desire' of development thinking (Sabaratnam 2017), including its 'continued fantasies of superiority, homogeny and violent universality' (Rutazibwa 2019, 175).

OUTLINE OF ARGUMENTS

In this chapter, I offer reflections as an inadvertent educator within the shifting domains of 'international development' and critical development geographies. As an early career decolonial political geographer and scholar of pan-Africanism who works on resistance, imperialism and extraction, I have regularly been categorised as someone conversant enough in this beast we term 'international development' to structure courses around it.

I have organised my courses – among them 'Introduction to International Development' at Jimma University (Jimma, Ethiopia), 'Beyond Tokenism: Indigenizing, Feminizing, Queering Development' at Clark University (Worcester, MA, US), 'Development Theory' at the American University in Cairo (Cairo, Egypt) – around pan-African and decolonial critiques of the development paradigm. Some of these efforts parallel features of sister movements of 'decolonising development'. A commitment to decolonising how we teach development is a conversation to have broadly across the social sciences as we endeavour to move both beyond the critique of Eurocentrism (Amin 1972) and beyond Eurocentric frames.

Development studies curricula might also be valuably structured to address the real and present dangers of empire and imperialism. By this I do not merely mean the representations of Occidentalism, the Other and the colonial gaze (as per postcolonial thought); we must also attend to the simultaneous material violence that structures neocolonial state behaviour and structure: assassinations, economic 'hits' and the spectre of political eliminations. In this move to holistic and critical 'decolonisation', we embrace the potential of the interdisciplinarity of the sub-discipline. Suárez-Krabbe (2016, vii) importantly argues that decolonial work 'cannot fall into the trap of pretending that the dominant frameworks of thinking and the practices that they authorize have been overcome. A careful attentiveness to the conceptual frameworks of *other* knowledges needs to happen in equilibrium with the criticism of coloniality and the death project'.

By structuring sessions in the classroom around explicit attention to assassination and appropriation, students are enabled to attend to multi-layered global expressions of coloniality alongside the 'global tapestry of alternatives' (Kothari et al. 2019): decolonial modes of being and thinking that *seek* coexistence, well-being and dignity outside and beyond its bounds. I knowingly refer to this active process as *seeking*, drawing inspiration from the Gesturing Towards Decolonial Futures 'Gift Contract' (Andreotti et al. 2021), which emphasises the need to 'gesture towards decolonial futures' in a way that nonetheless acknowledges 'how immensely difficult (but not impossible) it is to interrupt these [systemic colonial] patterns and let go of the harmful attachments and co-dependence we have developed within the system'.[1] Working within the invitations posed by the decolonial 'Gift Contract', we see that the quick approach of 'identifying a problem' in order to offer a fix-it 'solution' frequently compounds (rather than challenges) colonial violence. This is because the proposal of the solution frames the resolver as expert or heroic protagonist (as we are encouraged to frame ourselves within the colonial university) and because such gestures can be performative moves for redemption and absolution (see also Esson and Last 2020; Tuck and Yang 2012).

In this chapter, I outline two contemporary instances of assassination and appropriation and their implications for teaching international development: the assassination of Thomas Sankara in 1987 within the patterned histories of neo-imperial assassinations; and the appropriation of certain Indigenous practices by social scientists contracted to work in southern Chad during the construction of the Chad–Cameroon Oil Pipeline. Teaching these histories highlights two mechanisms of postcolonial empire, which have significant implications for how students and future practitioners of development perceive 'development in Africa'. While my arguments have theoretical meaning, my focus here is on articulating their practical significance for radical pedagogy and taking seriously student-led demands to 'decolonise the university' (Bhambra et al. 2018; Chantiluke et al. 2018) as well as to conduct anti-racist work in the 'urgently racist times' of unfinished decolonisation (Esson and Last 2020; Kamunge et al. 2018, 2; Puttick and Murrey 2020). I sketch some of the curricula that I have drawn on in teaching critical development geographies. These are neither models to be replicated nor solutions to colonial logics or racialised capitalism. Rather, I offer something that is partly self-critique, partly reflection and tentative contribution to collective energies to move the discipline towards extinction, as to 'decolonise' development necessitates its abolition in pursuit of pluriversal will-to-life: 'The challenge is to de-link solidarity and global justice from the bathwater of the ideas, institutions and practices of development' (Rutazibwa 2019, 176). We might refer to this collective project as *pedagogical disobedience*.

PEDAGOGICAL DISOBEDIENCE AND CRITICAL DEVELOPMENT GEOGRAPHIES

Powerful critiques of development as Euro-normative have occurred alongside the rising international visibility of the limitations of Euro-hegemonic approaches to development (see, for example, De Jong et al. 2019; Hickel 2017; Kothari et al. 2019; Sabaratnam 2017), including direct protests by dissatisfied people against development projects in their communities. Other responses have included quiet or slow dissent (Murrey 2016) or begrudged acquiescence (Li 2014). While there is no singular story of development, what we know of as 'international development' writ large has been criticised as being ideologically and epistemologically informed by Eurocentric norms, priorities, 'expert knowledge', 'fantasy' and 'seductive logics' (Escobar 1995; Hickel 2017; Kothari et al. 2019). Development has, with some degree of regular frequency, been pursued through colonial logics – including colonial racial hierarchies, heteronormativity and patriarchal ideologies – rather than challenging them (Escobar 1995). Development agendas have often worked side-by-side with capitalist expansion, domination and coloniality (Ake 1996; Shivji 2006), although not without much ambiguity, friction and unexpected outcomes (Ferguson 1994; Li 2014; Tsing 2005).

Critical development and post-development scholars have worked hard to expose the varied complicities and complacencies of development logic (Escobar 1995; Shivji 2006). Sharad Chari (2018) explains that such moves require new forms of explanation. He writes that 'understanding historical geographies of racial capitalism today [is] inextricable from incomplete decolonization struggles of the twentieth century, including struggles to decolonize ... *our habits of explanation*' (Chari 2018, 22, author's emphasis). In this project, educators have sought to give particular attention to elucidating alternative imaginaries of 'progress', 'empowerment' and 'development' for meaningful, liveable futures that emphasise well-being, ecological balance, ubuntu, *buen vivir* and more. *Pluriverse: A Post-Development Dictionary*, published in 2019 by Ashish Kothari and colleagues, is a rich resource for dissenting and alternative outlooks for 'an ecologically wise and socially just world' (Kothari et al. 2019, xxi).

As a vocation-based area of study, 'decolonising' development entails a simultaneous critique of the practice and belief systems of development as constitutive of 'the colonial wound' in the present (Mignolo 2009, 161). This is a project that compels a decolonisation of our 'habits of explanation' (Chari 2018, 22) so that development is studied and considered as a possible *wound* rather than poultice. For which, pedagogical disobedience might be meaningful.

In my use of the term pedagogical disobedience, I draw from Walter Mignolo's 'epistemic disobedience', which calls for a delinking (*desprendimiento*) or 'spatial paradigmatic breaks of epistemic disobedience' from colonial logics and colonial epistemes (Mignolo 2011, 45). Pedagogical disobedience, like epistemic disobedience, entails a break or delinking. In this case, it entails working against the canon in our teaching and learning. In a 'colonial matrix of power', established canons function to border, enforce, police and contain knowledge. Ways of thinking and being are prioritised, ordered and catalogued; certain perspectives are privileged while others are suppressed or eliminated in what is known as 'epistemicide' or the killing of ideas (Nyamnjoh 2001), and authority is accumulated and guarded by 'experts' (Mitchell 2002).

Diane Gillespie (2000, 386) refers to pedagogical disobedience as a 'willingness to teach the wrong students at the wrong place', a usage of the term that further emphasises the importance of challenging authority and notions of expert knowledge within 'the Western university as a key site through which colonialism … is produced, consecrated, institutionalised and naturalised' (Bhambra et al. 2018, 5; see also Chatterjee and Maira 2014). Pedagogical disobedience demands a refusal of 'certain academic conventions [because such] disciplinary, geographical and other … rubrics are largely insufficient to the task of thinking anew and addressing the global attacks' on marginalised communities (Sharpe 2018, xvi).

Gurminder K. Bhambra, Delia Gebrial and Kerem Nisancioglu explain that decolonising

> involves a multitude of definitions, interpretations, aims and strategies … it is a way of thinking about the world which takes colonialism, empire and racism as its empirical and discursive objects of study; it re-situates these phenomena as key shaping forces of the contemporary world, in a context where their role has been systematically effaced from view. (2018, 2)

In a decolonial practice of pedagogical disobedience, development is looked at from its underside, its 'darker side' (Mignolo 2011). This is a transgressive act, much like teaching the 'wrong' students (people situated as workers or peasants in colonial capitalism) or teaching 'at the wrong place' (outside the colonial institution or university) might be seen as *unsettling*. Teaching development through a curriculum that firmly roots the students' awareness of the modern world in patterns of considerable environmental and structural violence and colonial power struggle is a *knowingly* transgressive undertaking. Christina Sharpe writes of the importance of beginning 'without illusion': 'we begin there, in the midst of brutality – quotidian, spectacular, cellular, organised and ongoing – against Black and Blackened people everywhere in the world' (Sharpe 2018, xv). To begin the discussion of development 'without illusion' of the 'the black pits that hide [capitalist and colonial] rhetoric' (Mignolo 2011, 46) is to refuse colonial 'moves to innocence' (Tuck and Yang 2012). Pedagogical disobedience builds upon important post-development and decolonial work, particularly in rooting students' understanding of global political economy and the *creation* of poverty. Such works include Walter Rodney's historicisation of uneven and combined development in *How Europe Underdeveloped Africa* (Rodney 1972); James Boyce and Léonce Ndikumana's analysis of the manifold impacts of capital flight alongside 'odious' or unjust debt in *Africa's Odious Debts: How Foreign Loans and Capital Flight Bled a Continent* (Boyce and Ndikumana 2011); and Jason Hickel's unmasking of post-independence 'development' as an imperial project originating in Harry Truman's 20 January 1949 inaugural presidential address, *The Divide: A Brief Guide to Global Inequality and Its Solutions* (Hickel 2017).

TEACHING ANTI-IMPERIAL ASSASSINATION WITHIN DEVELOPMENT STUDIES COURSES

'Dangerous ideas'

In my critical development studies courses, I have organised one week of readings and activities under the topic of 'dangerous' development. I first ask students to consider why I have used the adjective dangerous. What is helpful about seeing ideas as *dangerous*?

Our consideration of 'dangerous development' is used as a means to encourage students to confront the importance of language, concepts and categories within development. How might language be important in maintaining colonial knowledge regimes, including the ideological dismissals of reparations, redistribution, economic sovereignty, or socialism, for example? Our discussion centres on power, authority and situatedness: to whom is an anti-capitalist development idea, for example, *dangerous*? What ideas have been or continue to be neglected, dismissed, diminished, or 'killed' through colonial logics? What are the terms set by the logics of 'international development'? What is rendered impossible? How are the terms of development regulated, racialised and gendered? Students have sometimes been hesitant to engage with the concept of a 'dangerous' idea, given its contextual significance. During my teaching in Ethiopia, for example, students confronted the historically fraught role of Marxism in the country, including the overthrow of Haile Selassie in 1974 by the communist party (the Derg), and the party's subsequent economic mismanagement during a time of ecological crisis. In the US, my students connected 'dangerous' ideas to the capitalist backlash against communism and to the 'danger' of publicly acknowledging racism in the first months of Donald Trump's presidency. When I was teaching in Cairo after the 'January 25th Revolution', students were regularly wary of speaking of political transformation at any scale, either because they had internalised some of the dominant narrative that dismissed protesters as troublemakers or because of the painful memory of having had friends and family arrested, beaten and harassed for participating in the revolution.

In each classroom, our conversations would transition to a sustained consideration of the 'dangerous' development ideas of Thomas Sankara (a topic I have written on at greater length elsewhere; see Murrey [2018]). Through selected speeches, excerpts of a biography and screening of the 2009 documentary film *Thomas Sankara: The Upright Man* (Shuffield 2009) and Skype/videos calls with activists in Ouagadougou, students learned about Sankara, the former revolutionary leader and president of the West African country, Burkina Faso. While he was as remarkable as he was controversial, Sankara's political trajectory – from his ambitions to his ambiguities – offers important lessons for students of international development.

First, Sankara was unique for his adamant rejection of the logic of international development aid, which he deemed both neocolonial (famously saying, 'he who feeds you, imposes his will' [Sankara 1984, n.p.]) and detrimental in practice, for it fostered a certain form of complacency and discouraged collective, endogenous empowerment (for more on Sankara's critique of international development, see Biney [2018]). Second, Sankara and his revolutionary government accomplished nearly unthinkable successes in the promotion of well-being in nearly every sector of society: food, environmental and gender justice, health/well-being, the arts and anti-imperial justice were pursued holistically and relentlessly (for more on Sankara's notion of a 'political economy of happiness', see Murrey [2020]). Further, these accomplishments were made with remarkably little by way of material resources – in a landlocked country facing intermittent drought – and often in the face of economic and political obstacles from Western and regional elites who feared 'revolutionary contagion' (Murrey 2018). Sankara was impatient for change and convinced that the 'roots of the [development] problem were political, therefore the solution must be political' (Sankara 1984, n.p.). For Sankara, each and every Burkinabé needed to fight for their collective liberation for emancipation to be holistic and lasting. Well-being, happiness and justice could not come from external sources: *development* could not originate from outside Burkina and needed to be driven by and through the agencies, hopes and aspirations of the people.

Students are asked to consider Sankara's 'Political Orientation Speech', which he delivered on 2 October 1983 in a radio and television broadcast. In the speech, Sankara gave both a summary and an analysis of the 'immediate and medium-term revolutionary tasks' as well as a class analysis of Burkinabé society. He said:

> neo-colonial society and colonial society are not ... different. The colonial administration was replaced by a neo-colonial administration identical to its predecessor ... The colonial school system was replaced by a neo-colonial school, which set about the same object of alienating our children from our country and reproducing a society devoted to imperialist interests and to serving the footmen and local allies of imperialism. (Sankara 1985, 49)

In this way, Sankara's 1983 speech becomes a platform for students to address and analyse the persistence of colonialism following formal independence, particularly the ways in which the university generates, fosters and perpetuates dominant and imperial ideas and ideologies.

At the 39th Session of the United Nations (UN) General Assembly on 4 October 1984, Sankara denounced models and concepts imposed on African countries that perpetuated their economic subjugation to their former colonial masters. He said:

> there will be no salvation for our peoples unless we turn our backs completely on all the [Western development] models ... There can be no salvation for us unless we reject those models; there can be no development without that break ... we encourage aid that can help us to manage without aid, but in general the aid and assistance policies merely led us to become completely disorganized, to enslave ourselves, to shirk our responsibility in our economic, political and cultural areas (Sankara 1984, n.p.)

These and other excerpts from Sankara's speeches challenge students to return to the notion of 'dangerous' development ideas. While we do not shy away from considerations of frictions, contradictions and critiques of Sankara's politics, nor of the revolution – indeed, students are often the chief and most powerful opponents of university curricula and I have learned much from my students' provocations – Sankara's ultimate demise demands not only that students address the violence of empire and coloniality, but that we consider the role and function of killing and elimination in configuring and limiting possible political imaginaries, including how these relate to notions of well-being, community, knowledge and international development (see also Hickel [2017, 99–134] for an examination of the role of political coups and assassination in the underdevelopment of Africa).

Sankara's assassination

On 15 October 1987, Thomas Sankara and 12 of his comrades were gunned down during a meeting. Blaise Compaoré, Sankara's second-in-command and long-time friend, assumed the presidency that evening. Sankara's cause of death was declared to be 'natural causes' in the government's public statement the following day and in the belatedly released death certificate. From his autopsy report (only released to the public decades later), we know that he sustained 12 entry wounds, including one under the armpit. According to Alouna Traore, the only surviving witness of the assassination, Sankara walked out of the meeting room at the sound of gunfire, telling his comrades to remain in the room, as 'it is me they want' (for more on Sankara's assassination, see Jaffré [2018]). The weight and the significance of the tragic event are always painful to speak about and teach. Thomas Sankara probably walked peacefully to his death (Jaffré 2018).

Within the classroom, I circulate a timeline of some of the assassinations and suspicious deaths of African political dissidents, anti-imperialists and pan-African thinkers (see Figure 10.1).[2] I prompt students to consider: why might such a timeline be important for us, as people learning about, and possibly preparing for a vocation in, international development?

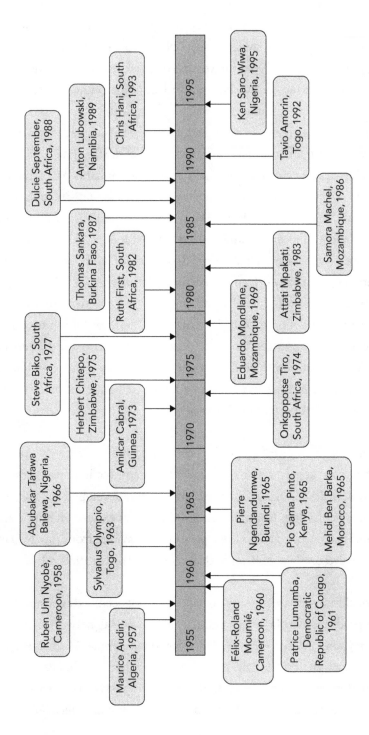

Figure 10.1: Assassinations in Africa

The scale of the timeline is often daunting, overwhelming and deeply meaningful. I have had students snap photos on their phones in the middle of our sessions. Given the volume of assassinations, students have been moved to anger, shame, or guilt. In Cairo, the outrage of students was equally split between anger at the historical injustices of imperial targeting and outrage that they had never had sessions on assassinations in other coursework. Ultimately, students acknowledge that the timeline is valuable for development students because it shows how Sankara's assassination fits within a larger landscape of the assassinations of anti-imperial and anti-capitalist leaders and activists. The assassination of political-economic dissidents and leaders during and beyond the post-independence and Cold War period in Africa occurred alongside the rise of 'Development' as an international, externally driven project for social change.

These assassinations curtailed radical projects for anticolonial sovereignty. I urge students to consider how the spectre of killing becomes a fog covering the political landscape, contributing to an atmosphere of instability and epistemic conformity. The frequency of assassinations created what Ali A. Mazrui (1968) refers to as a 'manifestation of instability'. He writes of postcolonial Africa:

> the risk of assassination was not only objectively there, but was keenly felt to be there by many leading participants in African politics. African leadership soon developed a conscious or subconscious fear of the assassin. This fear exerted an important influence not only on their personal behaviour from day to day, but also on their policies and ideologies. (Mazrui 1968, 42)

Targeted eliminations were not isolated events, but occurred as established sets of practices within wider colonial and political networks. In the classroom and in this chapter, I do not offer simple Machiavellian-style explanations that would presume to elucidate the details of each assassination as a singular plot. Rather, I emphasise that such violence is patterned and often fostered through colonial antecedents and imperial logics, and that the atmosphere of violence shapes and informs political possibilities, including the emergence of alternative, decolonial and Indigenous counter-epistemes. This includes the fostering of a 'fear of violent removal' (Shaw and Thomas 2017, 603) that constrains what is imaginable as development action.

Yet, development scholars have not paid much attention to the impacts of the assassinations of African anti-imperialist, anti-capitalist and pan-African figures, nor to the trauma, violence and limiting of possible alternatives effected through such killings. Indeed, domestically within Burkina Faso, sustained (albeit unsuccessful) efforts were made to efface Sankara's image, name and legacy from public memory. The decades-long erasure of postcolonial violence from global media and school education has been replicated in mainstream international development curricula.

Our discussions around assassination demythologise the ideology of a benevolent development project at the same time that they raise students' critical awareness of the importance of identifying silences in their 'development' curricula. This conversation creates the groundwork for our later readings that similarly expand the 'whitestream' syllabus of international development. For example, we look at Uma Kothari's pioneering article on the need to address the unspoken dominance of whiteness within international development (Kothari 2006) as well as Waibinte E. Wariboko's text tracing the historical longevity of whiteness and anti-blackness within colonial and later development ideologies (Wariboko 2011). Teaching students about Thomas Sankara emphasises that the will for anti-capitalist and anticolonialist projects of sovereignty, happiness and self-love has long existed, although these projects have been violently materially and ideologically supressed as *dangerous ideas*.

MISAPPROPRIATING PROJECTS TO CENTRE INDIGENOUS AGENCY AND DECOLONISE DEVELOPMENT

In my critical development courses, I organise one week of readings and activities to consider the appropriations of Indigenous, subversive, or alternative epistemes by corporate, financial, or hegemonic develop-ment entities and institutions. This session follows on a classroom dis-cussion of the rise of alternative, grassroots, participatory and sustainable approaches to development in the late 1980s (see, for example, Briggs and Sharp 2004; Cooke and Kothari 2001), while also setting the tone for a subsequent session with students on appropriations of decolonial thought and decolonising projects.

I begin by asking students to recall some of the techniques through which alternative epistemes in Africa have been trivialised or dimin-ished. These might include colonial language restructurings (Ngũgĩ wa Thiong'o 1986), imitation and mimicry (Bhabha 1990; Fanon 2008); colonial-missionary education (Nyamnjoh 2019; Wariboko 2011) and, later, austerity within higher education (Mamdani 2007; Ndlovu-Gatsheni 2014, 2017); structuring of knowledge around racist and Othering imag-inaries (Fanon 1963; Said 1978); segregation and objectification (Spivak 1988) or the threat of violence and reprisals (Césaire 2006). We think back to previous conversations on the importance of Indigenous and decolonial thought for the emergence of epistemological possibilities, including Seth Oppong's (2013, 36) assertion that 'endogenous or indig-enous knowledge refers to knowledge about the people, by the people and for the people' (see Harrison [1991]). Edward Shizha (2010, 116) similarly argues that 'Indigenous knowledge and voices should be inte-grated in the academic corridors in a manner that does not perpetuate their domination and recolonization. Through an antiracist and post-colonial approach, indigenous communities can contribute to the much needed voices in curriculum planning and knowledge dissemination'. In my courses, I have endeavoured to pursue a disobedient pedagogy that simultaneously seeks pluriversal alternatives while retaining a vig-ilance against the designs to erase and misappropriate *dangerous* ideas.

In this session, students are challenged to consider the ways in which Indigenous knowledges are often twice menaced – vulnerable to outright dismissal, effacement and epistemicide as well as misappropriation – and that these actions are undertaken, frequently, in the name of 'development'. By grounding our conversation in an awareness of ourselves within spaces of higher education, students are asked to consider the ways in which ideas in the social sciences can be weaponised. Nigerian political theorist Claude Ake called social science the 'most pernicious form of imperialism' (Ake 1982, 1) for its role in proliferating the imagined geographies and ideologies of the capitalist core (see also Cabral 1966; Poesche 2019). In such a milieu, what are the collective resources to resist or challenge appropriations, disciplining(s) and other efforts to render decolonial and Indigenous cosmologies and epistemologies not only manageable *but convenient* for the perpetuation of power (see, for example, Tuck and Yang 2012)?

The Chad–Cameroon Oil Pipeline

As part of this learning exercise, I introduce the Chad–Cameroon Oil Pipeline and I draw from my ethnographic research in two Cameroonian towns, Kribi and Nanga-Eboko, along the pipeline. The actors in this oil pipeline are ExxonMobil, the World Bank, a transnational advocacy network of various activists, intellectuals, non-governmental organisation (NGO) employees and others who have been publicly critical of the pipeline, the governments of Chad and Cameroon, and the people living in the 1 032 communities situated within 2 kilometres of the pipeline. The project was negotiated and engineered during the decade from 1990 to 2000, constructed between 2000 and 2003, and the first tanker with crude left the shores of Cameroon in late 2003.

Several things were unique about this pipeline. One of which was its scale: at 1 070 kilometres long, it appropriated enormous portions of land in Cameroon and Chad's most fertile regions. Another was the scale of the financial investment: it was the single largest private investment project on the African continent at the time, as well as being the World Bank's largest African investment. Another feature of this pipeline was its framing as a 'development' intervention in the context of a rising awareness of the so-called resource curse. This kind of intervention is often referred to through the offhand phrase 'oil-as-development', meaning the idea that petro-extraction will contribute to development in local communities or national governments (Murrey and Jackson 2020; Watts 2005).

In the classroom, students learn about some of the corporate attention to and investments in understanding and including local knowledge, local communities and local practices in the pipeline project. In one example, an American anthropologist was contracted by ExxonMobil in Chad. Ethnographic work in southern Chad revealed that she seems to have been involved in the deflection of NGO criticism of the project (Grovogui and Lori 2007). Her cultural and linguistic knowledge of the region helped in the domestication of potential tensions. In particular, we consider her role in curtailing community response to the destruction of spiritually meaningful places during the construction phase of the project. This anthropologist conducted a great number of chicken sacrifices during the construction period – so much so that people referred to her as 'Madame Sacrifice'.

In practice, many of the efforts to include Indigenous and alternative epistemes within large-scale development have not done much to alter existing political or economic structures, nor the power imbalances that they reproduce. Such forms of development are nonetheless bound up in a local-centric rhetoric that appropriates the language of critics – that is, a language of 'empowering the grassroots'. Proficiencies in 'local' knowledge are often redeployed against those very people for the purposes of containment and domestication (Cabral 1966). Suárez-Krabbe (2016, 1) explains that 'the force of colonial discourse lies in how it succeeds in concealing how it establishes and naturalizes ontological and epistemological perspectives and political practices that work to protect its power'.

Students are encouraged to think about the importance of distinguishing between different political projects carried out in the same name. As we see by comparing different development projects, there are a great many projects carried out in the name of Indigenous justice (Briggs and Sharp 2004), or environmental justice (Goldman 2001), or women's empowerment (Koffman and Gill 2013), yet they are not equivalent.

In the case of the Chad–Cameroon Oil Pipeline, the corporate appropriation of the practice of animal sacrifice (through the intermediary of the social scientist) assisted in the facilitation of dispossessing extraction. This was not a banal ideological misappropriation but an expression of colonial power in which people were deprived of land and livelihoods (Murrey 2015). Here, I circulate discussion questions that encourage students to make connections between the concepts of appropriation and assassination as a means, again, to demythologise the notion of development as benevolent, as innocent and as ahistorical. Students are asked to sit with and reflect upon the real, material violence of such 'development' practice. Finally, we bring the discussion back to considering the significance of appropriation for development as a *practice*. Students respond differently here, as some are committed to pursuing alternative (non-institutionalised) work for social and ecological justice, while others want to refashion 'development' by acknowledging these inaccuracies and wounds. We highlight the ways in which developing this critical capacity to identify such appropriations is an important part of the 'fight against further neo-colonial encroachments' (Shizha 2010, 121). These sessions are also important in guiding students to consider tendencies in their own work or writing to offer simplistic solutions or to presume development projects aimed at 'the local' or 'the grassroots' are decolonised. We see that efforts to 'incorporate' Indigenous knowledge and people begin with a (capitalist-colonial) logic and structure, and thus fundamentally limit the terms of participation. Ideas and epistemologies contrary to capitalist and colonial logics – and therefore *dangerous* – are contained through rhetorical appropriations.

CONCLUSION

What does it mean for students and potential pre-practitioners to engage with international development at the crossroads of the violent processes of appropriation and assassination?

If we are presently in a 'prelude to decolonisation', as suggested by the title of the conference at the University of Johannesburg's Institute for Advanced Studies from which this chapter emerged, how do we use it to anticipate frames and forms of coloniality in our pedagogies?[3] The call for papers for the Johannesburg conference urged contributors to 'retrieve the voices of indigenous opposition prior to the crescendo and irresistible force of decolonisation and postcolonialism'. A pedagogy of disobedience gestures to the colonial ontology eager to subsume and speak for the marginalised in the name of empowerment. This has long been the seductive logic of development-think. Should we be, for example, foretelling the World Bank's likely future workshop on 'Decolonising Lending' or the UN's potential new forum on 'Decolonising Bad Governance'? Can such an agenda be helpful for students in moving beyond critique or beyond that inclination to *react* rather than pre-emt and create in the will-to-life? In moments of critical and explicit exchanges in the classroom, I am fortunate to have participated in earnest and grounded conversations on precisely these matters.

In the context of coloniality and the neoliberal academy, the challenges to pedagogical disobedience are many. Oppong (2013, 47), Francis Nyamnjoh (2019) and many others have written at length on some of the logistical barriers and potential material dangers of radical scholarship, and their thinking can be expanded to include a disobedient pedagogy. Their critiques speak to the simultaneous violence of the coloniality of knowledge: the patterns, rhythms and potentialities of violence alongside pressures to conform, standardise and pursue efficiency. At the same time, collective projects to 'decolonise development' and to 'de-centre its white gaze' (Pailey 2019, 729) continue to grow in dynamism and collective intensity. The classroom is an ideal space to work towards what Robtel Neajai Pailey (2019, 14) calls 'an emancipatory kind of recruitment that values and elevates radical rabble rousers who challenge and dismantle the status quo'. Eve Tuck and Wayne Yang remind us of the importance of being humble and being real about the scale of coloniality in the present: 'the development of "critical consciousness" in the curriculum [is] a "stop gap" *en route* to decolonisation' (cited in Daley 2018, 84). A pedagogy of disobedience aims to foster tactical alertness to the practices of coloniality, including assassination and appropriation, while contributing to the already occurring meaningful engagements with decolonial possibilities for the will-to-life (Dussel 2013).

NOTES

1   The *Decolonial Futures* 'Gift Contract' demands that we recognise, for example, that time and labour are sacred; the invisible costs to un/learning; the importance of making serious commitments to deepen our learning; and much more.
2   The inspiration to use a timeline of assassinations in my teaching came from a discussion with the historian Carina Ray, who had put together a brilliant abridged sketch of the assassinations of pan-Africanists between 1961 and 2005, including those of Patrice Lumumba, Amílcar Cabral, Steve Biko, Maurice Bishop, Walter Rodney and Chris Hani.
3   'After the Prelude: Decolonisation, Revolution, and Evolution?', University of Johannesburg, 9–11 July 2018.

REFERENCES

Ake, Claude. 1982. *Social Science as Imperialism: The Theory of Political Development.* 2nd edition. Ibadan: Ibadan University Press.
Ake, Claude. 1996. *Democracy and Development in Africa.* Washington, DC: Brookings Institution Press.
Amin, Samir. 1972. *Neocolonialism in West Africa.* Harmondsworth: Penguin.
Andreotti, Vanessa, Elwood Jimmy and Bill Calhoun. 2021. 'Gift Contract'. *Gesturing Towards Decolonial Futures,* 24 February 2021. https://decolonialfutures.net/2021/02/15/gift-contract/.
Bhabha, Homi K. (ed.). 1990. *Nation and Narration.* London: Routledge.
Bhambra, Gurminder K., Delia Gebrial and Kerem Nisancioglu. 2018. 'Introduction: Decolonising the University?' In *Decolonising the University,* edited by Gurminder Bhambra, Delia Gebrial and Kerem Nisancioglu, 1–18. London: Pluto Press.
Biney, Ama. 2018. 'Madmen, Thomas Sankara and Decoloniality in Africa'. In *A Certain Amount of Madness: The Life, Politics and Legacy of Thomas Sankara,* edited by Amber Murrey, 127–146. London: Pluto Press.
Boyce, James and Léonce Ndikumana. 2011. *Africa's Odious Debts: How Foreign Loans and Capital Flight Bled a Continent.* London: Zed Books.
Briggs, John and Joanne Sharp. 2004. 'Indigenous Knowledges and Development: A Postcolonial Caution'. *Third World Quarterly* 25 (4): 661–676. https://doi.org/10.1080/01436590410001678915.
Cabral, Amílcar. 1966. 'The Weapon of Theory'. Address delivered to the first Tricontinental Conference of the Peoples of Asia, Africa and Latin America, Havana, January 1966. https://www.marxists.org/subject/africa/cabral/1966/weapon-theory.htm.

Césaire, Aimé. (2006 [1950]). *Discourse on Colonialism*. Translated by Joan Pinkham. New York: Monthly Review Press.

Chantiluke, Roseanne, Brian Kwoba and Athinangamso Nkopo. 2018. 'Introduction from the Editors'. In *Rhodes Must Fall: The Struggle to Decolonise the Racist Heart of Empire*, edited by Roseanne Chantiluke, Brian Kwoba and Athinangamso Nkopo, xv–xxii. London: Zed Books.

Chari, Sharad. 2018. 'Commentary on "From Exploitation to Expropriation: Geographies of Racialization in Historic Capitalism"'. *Economic Geography* 94 (1): 18–22. https://doi.org/10.1080/00130095.2017.1398044.

Chatterjee, Piya and Sunaina Maira. 2014. 'The Imperial University: Race, War, and the Nation-State'. In *The Imperial University: Academic Repression and Scholarly Dissent*, edited by Piya Chatterjee and Sunaina Maira, 1–52. Minneapolis: University of Minnesota Press.

Cooke, Bill and Uma Kothari (eds). 2001. *Participation: The New Tyranny?* 4th edition. London: Zed Books.

Daley, Patricia. 2018. 'Reparations in the Space of the University in the Wake of Rhodes Must Fall'. In *Rhodes Must Fall: The Struggle to Decolonise the Racist Heart of Empire*, edited by Roseanne Chantiluke, Brian Kwoba and Athinangamso Nkopo, 74–89. London: Zed Books.

De Jong, Sara, Rosalba Icaza and Olivia U. Rutazibwa (eds). 2019. *Decolonization and Feminisms in Global Teaching and Learning*. New York: Routledge.

Dussel, Enrique. 2013. *Ethics of Liberation in the Age of Globalization and Exclusion*. Edited by Alejandro A. Vallega. Translated by Nelson Maldonado-Torres, Eduardo Mendieta, Yolanda Angulo and Camilo Pérez Bustillo. Durham, NC: Duke University Press.

Escobar, Arturo. 1995. *Encountering Development: The Making and Unmaking of the Third World*. Princeton: Princeton University Press.

Esson, James and Angela Last. 2020. 'Anti-Racist Learning and Teaching in British Geography'. *Area* 52 (4): 668–677. https://doi.org/10.1111/area.12658.

Esson, James, Patricia Noxolo, Richard Baxter, Patricia Daley and Margaret Byron. 2017. 'The 2017 RGS-IBG Chair's Theme: Decolonising Geographical Knowledges, or Reproducing Coloniality?' *Area* 49 (3): 384–388. https://doi.org/10.1111/area.12371.

Fanon, Frantz. 2008 [1952]. *Black Skin, White Masks*. Translated by Richard Philcox. London: Pluto Press.

Fanon, F. 1963 [1961]. *The Wretched of the Earth*. Translated by Constance Farrington. New York: Grove Press.

Ferguson, James. 1994. *The Anti-Politics Machine: Development, Depoliticization, and Bureucratic Power in Lesotho*. Minneapolis: University of Minnesota Press.

Freire, Paulo. 1997. 'A Response'. In *Mentoring the Mentor: A Critical Dialogue with Paulo Freire*, edited by Paulo Freire, with James W. Fraser, Donaldo Macedo, Tanya McKinnon and William T. Stokes, 303–329. New York: Peter Lang.

Gillespie, Diane. 2000. 'Claiming Ourselves as Teachers'. In *Learning from Change: Landmarks in Teaching and Learning in Higher Education from Change Magazine, 1969–1999*, edited by Deborah DeZure, 384–386. Sterling, VA: Stylus.

Goldman, Michael. 2001. 'The Birth of a Discipline: Producing Authoritative Green Knowledge, World Bank-Style'. *Ethnography* 2 (2): 191–217. https://doi.org/10.1177/14661380122230894.

Gordon, Lewis R. 2006. *Disciplinary Decadence: Living Thought in Trying Times*. London: Routledge.

Grande, Sandy. 2003. 'Whitestream Feminism and the Colonialist Project: A Review of Contemporary Feminist Pedagogy and Praxis'. *Educational Theory* 53 (3): 329–346. https://doi.org/10.1111/j.1741-5446.2003.00329.x

Grovogui, Siba N. and Leonard Lori. 2007. 'Oiling Tyranny? Neoliberalism and Global Governance in Chad'. *Studies in Political Economy* 79 (1): 35–59. https://doi.org/ 10.1080/19187033.2007.11675091.

Gruffydd Jones, Branwen. 2006. 'Introduction: International Relations, Eurocentrism, and Imperialism'. In *Decolonizing International Relations*, edited by Branwen Gruffydd Jones, 1–22. London: Rowman and Littlefield.

Harrison, Faye V. 1991. *Decolonizing Anthropology: Moving Further Toward an Anthropology for Liberation*. Arlington: American Anthropological Association.

Hickel, Jason. 2017. *The Divide: A Brief Guide to Global Inequality and Its Solutions*. New York: Penguin Random House.

hooks, bell. 1994. *Teaching to Transgress: Education as the Practice of Freedom*. New York: Routledge.

Jaffré, Bruno. 2018. 'Who Killed Thomas Sankara?' In *A Certain Amount of Madness: The Life, Politics and Legacy of Thomas Sankara*, edited by Amber Murrey, 96–112. London: Pluto Press.

Kamunge, Beth, Remi Joseph-Salisbury and Azeezat Johnson. 2018. 'Changing Our Fate in *The Fire Now*'. In *The Fire Now: Anti-Racist Scholarship in Times of Explicit Racial Violence*, edited by Azeezat Johnson, Remi Joseph-Salisbury and Beth Kamunge, 1–12. London: Zed Books.

Koffman, Ofra and Rosalind Gill. 2013. 'The Revolution Will Be Led by a 12-Year-Old-Girl': Girl Power and Global Biopolitics'. *Feminist Review* 105 (1): 83–102. https://doi. org/10.1057/fr.2013.16.

Kothari, Ashish, Ariel Salleh, Arturo Escobar, Federico Demaria and Alberto Acosta. 2019. 'Introduction'. In *Pluriverse: A Post-Development Dictionary*, edited by Ashish Kothari, Ariel Salleh, Arturo Escobar, Federico Demaria and Alberto Acosta, xxi–xl. New Delhi: Tulika Books.

Kothari, Uma. 2006. 'An Agenda for Thinking about "Race" in Development'. *Progress in Development Studies* 6 (1): 9–23. https://doi.org/10.1191/1464993406ps124oa.

Li, Tania Murray. 2014. *Land's End: Capitalist Relations on an Indigenous Frontier*. Durham, NC: Duke University Press.

Mamdani, Mahmood. 2007. *Scholars in the Marketplace: The Dilemmas of Neoliberal Reform at Makerere University, 1989–2005*. Kampala: Fountain Publishers.

Mazrui, Ali A. 1968. 'Thoughts on Assassination in Africa'. *Political Science Quarterly* 83 (1): 40–58. https://www.jstor.org/stable/2147402.

Mignolo, Walter D. 2009. 'Epistemic Disobedience, Independent Thought and Decolonial Freedom'. *Theory, Culture & Society* 26 (7–8): 159–181. https://doi. org/10.1177/0263276409349275.

Mignolo, Walter D. 2011. 'Epistemic Disobedience and the Decolonial Option: A Manifesto'. *Transmodernity* 1 (2): 44–66. https://doi.org/10.5070/T412011807.

Mitchell, Timothy. 2002. *Rule of Experts: Egypt, Techno-Politics, Modernity*. Berkeley: University of California Press.

Murrey, Amber. 2015. 'Invisible Power, Visible Dispossession: The Witchcraft of a Subterranean Oil Pipeline'. *Political Geography* 47 (July): 64–76. https://doi.org/10.1016/j.polgeo.2015.04.004.

Murrey, Amber. 2016. 'Slow Dissent and the Emotional Geographies of Resistance'. *Singapore Journal of Tropical Geography* 37 (2): 224–248. https://doi.org/10.1111/sjtg.12147.

Murrey, Amber. 2018. 'Introduction'. In *A Certain Amount of Madness: The Life, Politics and Legacy of Thomas Sankara*, edited by Amber Murrey, 1–18. London: Pluto Press.

Murrey, Amber. 2020. 'A Political Thought "Rich with a Thousand Nuances": Thomas Sankara and a Political Economy of Happiness'. In *Palgrave Handbook of African Political Economy*, edited by Samuel Ojo Oloruntoba and Toyin Falola, 193–208. New York: Palgrave Macmillan.

Murrey, Amber and Nicholas A. Jackson. 2020. 'A Decolonial Critique of the Racialized "Localwashing" of Extraction in Central Africa'. *Annals of the American Association of Geographers* 110 (3): 917–940. https://doi.org/10.1080/24694452.2019.1638752.

Murrey, Amber and Antenah Tesfahun. 2019. 'Conversations from Jimma on the Geographies and Politics of Knowledge'. *Ufahamu: A Journal of African Studies* 40 (2): 27–45. https://doi.org/10.5070/F7402040941.

Ndlovu-Gatsheni, Sabelo J. 2014. 'Global Coloniality and the Challenges of Creating African Futures'. *Strategic Review for Southern Africa* 36 (2):181–202. https://go.gale.com/ps/i.do?id=GALE%7CA409069569&sid=sitemap&v=2.1&it=r&p=AONE&sw=w&userGroupName=anon%7E41df2ac0.

Ndlovu-Gatsheni, Sabelo J. 2017. 'The Emergence and Trajectories of Struggles for an "African University": The Case of Unfinished Business of African Epistemic Decolonisation'. *Kronos* 43 (1): 51–77. https://www.researchgate.net/publication/323853135_The_emergence_and_trajectories_of_struggles_for_an_'African_university'_The_case_of_unfinished_business_of_African_epistemic_decolonisation.

Ngũgĩ wa Thiong'o. 1986. *Decolonising the Mind: The Politics of Language in African Literature*. London: James Currey.

Noble, Safiya U. 2018. *Algorithms of Oppression: How Search Engines Reinforce Racism*. New York: New York University.

Noxolo, Patricia. 2017. 'Decolonial Theory in a Time of the Re-Colonisation of UK Research'. *Transactions of the Institute of British Geographers* 42 (3): 342–344. https://doi.org/10.1111/tran.12202.

Nyamnjoh, Francis. B. 2001. 'Delusions of Development and the Enrichment of Witchcraft Discourses in Cameroon'. In *Magical Interpretations, Material Realities: Modernity, Witchcraft and the Occult in Postcolonial Africa*, edited by Henrietta L. Moore and Todd Sanders, 28–49. London: Routledge.

Nyamnjoh, Francis B. 2019. 'Decolonizing the University in Africa'. In *Oxford Research Encyclopaedia of Politics*, edited by William R. Thompson. Oxford: Oxford University Press. https://oxfordre.com/politics/view/10.1093/acrefore/9780190228637.001.0001/acrefore-9780190228637-e-717 (accessed 25 January 2023).

Oppong, Seth. 2013. 'Indigenizing Knowledge for Development: Epistemological and Pedagogical Approaches'. *Africanus* 43 (2): 34–50. https://hdl.handle.net/10520/EJC142699.

Pailey, Robtel Neajai. 2019. 'De-centring the "White Gaze" of Development'. *Development and Change* 51 (3): 729–745. https://doi.org/10.1111/dech.12550.

Poesche, Jurgen. 2019. 'Coloniality in Sub-Saharan Africa and the Americas'. *Journal of Developing Societies* 35 (3): 367–390. https://doi.org/10.1177/0169796X19868317.

Puttick, Steve and Amber Murrey. 2020.'Confronting the Silence on Race in Geography Education in England: Learning from Anti-Racist, Decolonial and Black Geographies'. *Geography* 105 (1): 126–134. https://doi.org/10.1080/00167487. 2020.12106474.

Rodney, Walter. 1972. *How Europe Underdeveloped Africa*. London: Bogle-L'Ouverture Publications and Tanzanian Publishing House.

Rutazibwa, Olivia U. 2019. 'On Babies and Bathwater: Decolonizing International Development Studies'. In *Decolonization and Feminisms in Global Teaching and Learning*, edited by Sara de Jong, Rosalba Icaza and Olivia U. Rutazibwa, 158–180. New York: Routledge.

Sabaratnam, Meera. 2017. *Decolonising Intervention: International Statebuilding in Mozambique*. London: Rowman and Littlefield International.

Said, Edward. 1978. *Orientalism*. New York: Pantheon.

Said, Edward. 1995. 'Secular Interpretation, the Geographical Element and the Methodology of Imperialism'. In *After Colonialism: Imperial Histories and Postcolonial Displacements*, edited by Gyan Prakash, 21–39. Princeton: Princeton University Press.

Sankara, Thomas. 1984. 'Speech before the General Assembly of the United Nations'. UN General Assembly Official Records, 20th Plenary Meeting (A/39/PV.20), 4 October 1984, New York. https://www.marxists.org/archive/sankara/1984/october/04.htm.

Sankara, Thomas. 1985. 'The "Political Orientation" of Burkina Faso'. Speech republished in *Review of African Political Economy* 32: 48–55. https://www.jstor.org/stable/4005706.

Sankara, Thomas. 2007. *Thomas Sankara Speaks, The Burkina Faso Revolution 1983–87*. Atlanta: Pathfinder Press.

Sharpe, Christina. 2018. 'Foreword: The Heart and the Burdens of the Day'. In *The Fire Now: Anti-Racist Scholarship in Times of Explicit Racial Violence*, edited by Azeezat Johnson, Remi Joseph-Salisbury and Beth Kamunge, xv–xix. London: Zed Books.

Shaw, Mark and Kim Thomas. 2017. 'The Commercialization of Assassination: "Hits" and Contract Killing in South Africa, 2000–2015'. *African Affairs* 116 (465): 597–620. https://doi.org/10.1093/afraf/adw050.

Shivji, Issa. 2006. 'Silences in NGO Discourse: The Role and Future of NGOs in Africa'. *Africa Development* 31 (4): 22–51.

Shizha, Edward. 2010. 'Rethinking and Reconstituting Indigenous Knowledge and Voices in the Academy in Zimbabwe: A Decolonization Process'. In *Indigenous Knowledge and Learning in Asia/Pacific and Africa*, edited by Dip Kipoor and Edward Shizha, 115–130. New York: Palgrave Macmillan.

Shuffield, Robin (dir.). 2009. *Thomas Sankara: The Upright Man*. Lille: ZORN Production International.

Spivak, Gayatri. C. 1988. 'Can the Subaltern Speak?' In *Marxism and the Interpretation of Culture*, edited by Cary Nelson and Lawrence Grossberg, 271–313. Champaign: University of Illinois Press.

Suárez-Krabbe, Julia. 2016. *Race, Rights and Rebels: Alternatives to Human Rights and Development from the Global South*. London: Rowman and Littlefield International.

Tsing, Anna Lowenhaupt. 2005. *Friction: An Ethnography of Global Connection*. Durham, NC: Princeton University Press.

Tuck, Eve and K. Wayne Yang. 2012. 'Decolonization Is Not a Metaphor'. *Decolonization: Indigeneity, Education and Society* 1 (1): 1–40.

Varadharajan, Asha. 2019. ' "Straight from the Heart": A Pedagogy for the Vanquished of History'. In *Decolonization and Feminisms in Global Teaching and Learning*, edited by Sara de Jong, Rosalba Icaza and Olivia U. Rutazibwa, 181–197. New York: Routledge.

Wariboko, Waibinte E. 2011. *Race and the Civilizing Mission: Their Implications for the Framing of Blackness and African Personhood 1800–1960*. Trenton and Asmara: Africa World Press.

Watts, Michael J. 2005. 'Righteous Oil? Human Rights, the Oil Complex, and Corporate Social Responsibility'. *Annual Review of Environment and Resources* 30: 373–407. https://doi.org/10.1146/annurev.energy.30.050504.144456.

CONTRIBUTORS

Christopher Allsobrook is the Director of the Centre for Leadership Ethics in Africa at the University of Fort Hare, South Africa, where he leads research on democracy, heritage and citizenship. He is an associate editor of *Theoria* and the *South African Journal of Philosophy*. His research in African political theory, ethics, intellectual history and critical theory has examined contested concepts of critique, social rights, trusteeship, land reform and sovereignty.

Camilla Boisen is a historian of political thought and senior lecturer in the Writing Program at New York University, Abu Dhabi. Her main area of research is the intellectual history of empire and political theory in relation to the development of ideas of rights and trusteeship and their influence on contemporary problems such as postcolonial restitution and international relations. She is the author of numerous articles in journals such as *The History of European Ideas*, *Settler Colonial Studies*, *Journal of International Political Theory* and *Global Intellectual History*, and she co-edited the volume *Distributive Justice Debates in Political and Social Thought: Perspectives on Finding a Fair Share*.

David Boucher is Professor of Political Philosophy and International Relations, Cardiff University, and Distinguished Visiting Professor, University of Johannesburg. He has published on a wide variety of subjects, including colonialism and decolonisation, international relations, and the history of political thought. His recent publications include a special issue of the *International Journal of Social Economics* on colonialism (2018), *Appropriating Thomas Hobbes* (2019), *Bob Dylan and Leonard Cohen: Deaths and Entrances* (2021, with Lucy Boucher), and *Language, Culture and Decolonisation* (ed., 2022).

Ndumiso Dladla teaches jurisprudence in the Department of Jurisprudence, Faculty of Law, University of Pretoria. Prior to this, he taught African philosophy in the Department of Philosophy, Practical and Systematic Theology, University of South Africa. His research focuses on social, legal and political philosophy as well as South African historiography. He has written numerous scholarly articles and book chapters as well as a monograph, *Here is a Table: A Philosophical Essay on the History of Race/ism in South Africa*. He is a member of the Azanian Philosophical Society and the National Conference of Black Political Scientists.

Sule Emmanuel Egya is Professor of African Literature and Cultural Studies and the Director of the Centre for Arts and Indigenous Studies at Ibrahim Badamasi Babangida University, Lapai, Nigeria. His research interests include African literature, environmental humanities and the politics of knowledge production in Africa. He is also an award-winning writer. His latest publications include the novel *Makwala*, the monograph *Nature, Environment and Activism in Nigerian Literature*, and the co-edited book *Studies in Scientific and Cultural Ecology*.

Michael Elliott is a lecturer at King's College, London, and research associate of the NRF/British Academy Chair in Political Theory at the University of the Witwatersrand, Johannesburg. His research centres on questions of democracy and decolonisation, particularly as applied to settler colonial contexts. He has published numerous articles and book chapters, including in *Contemporary Political Theory*, the *Canadian Journal of Political Science* and *Constellations*. He is currently completing a monograph on the role of Western democratic inheritances in reproducing and potentially disrupting colonial power structures.

Steven Friedman is a Research Professor at the University of Johannesburg in the Humanities Faculty. He is a political scientist, specialising in the study of democracy. He has written widely on South Africa's transition to democracy and on the relationship between democracy, social inequality and economic growth. He is the author of *Building Tomorrow Today: A Study of the South African Trade Union Movement and Its Impact on Democracy*; *Race, Class and Power: Harold Wolpe and the Radical Critique of Apartheid*; *One Virus, Two Countries*; *Power in Action: Democracy, Citizenship and Social Justice*; and *Prisoners of the Past: South African Democracy and the Legacy of Minority Rule*.

Amber Murrey is a decolonial political geographer, ethnographer and educator, an Associate Professor of Political Geography at the University of Oxford and Tutorial Fellow at Mansfield College. Her research on resistance and social change in Africa integrates the political geographies of environmental and socio-political struggles with decolonial thought and resistance studies. She is the editor of *A Certain Amount of Madness: The Life, Politics and Legacies of Thomas Sankara* and co-author of *Learning Disobedience: Decolonizing Development Studies*. She has taught at the American University in Cairo, Clark University and Boston College in Massachusetts, and Jimma University in Ethiopia.

Ayesha Omar is a senior lecturer in political studies at the University of the Witwatersrand, Johannesburg, a research associate at SOAS, University of London, and a visiting scholar at the Centre for Political Thought, University of Cambridge. She is a Mellon Early Career Scholars Fellow. She works in the area of comparative political theory and South African black intellectual history. She is currently working on a monograph for Cambridge University Press, dealing with ethics and politics in the pre-modern and postcolonial Islamic State, and is a co-editor of the *Cambridge History of African Political Thought*.

Paul Patton is Hongyi Chair Professor of Philosophy at Wuhan University and editor of the *Journal of Social and Political Philosophy*. He is Emeritus Professor at the University of New South Wales and a Fellow of the Australian Academy of the Humanities. He co-edited *Political Theory and the Rights of Indigenous Peoples* and has published widely on issues related to the rights of Indigenous peoples. His recent publications include 'Indigenous Rights and Human Rights' in Vibe Ulfbeck, Yoshifumi Tanaka and Rachael Johnstone (eds), *The Routledge Handbook of Polar Law*.

Chris Saunders is Emeritus Professor at the University of Cape Town, where he taught in the Department of Historical Studies for many decades. He is now an Honorary Associate of the Institute for Democracy, Citizenship and Public Policy in Africa. After retirement, he worked as a research associate at the Centre for Conflict Resolution, Cape Town. He is the author and editor of numerous books, including *Historical Dictionary of South Africa* and *South Africa: A Modern History*, and he has published a number of articles on the Cold War in Southern Africa.

Ian S. Spears is Associate Professor of Political Science at the University of Guelph in Ontario, Canada. He is the author of *Believers, Skeptics and Failure in Conflict Resolution* and *Civil War in African States: The Search for Security*. He is a co-editor of *States within States: Incipient Political Entities in the Post-Cold War Era*. He has published numerous book chapters as well as articles in scholarly journals including *Global Change, Peace and Security, Journal of Democracy, Third World Quarterly, Review of African Political Economy, African Security Review, African Conflict and Peacebuilding Review, International Journal* and *Civil Wars*.

INDEX